RODNEY AND
THE BREAKING OF
THE LINE

Also by Peter Trew

The Boer War Generals, Sutton Publishing, 1999

RODNEY AND THE BREAKING OF THE LINE

by

Peter Trew

Pen & Sword
MILITARY

First published in Great Britain in 2006 by
Pen & Sword Military
an imprint of
Pen & Sword Books Ltd
47 Church Street
Barnsley
South Yorkshire
S70 2AS

Copyright © Peter Trew, 2006

ISBN 184415143 3

The right of Peter Trew to be identified as Author of this Work has
been asserted by him in accordance with the Copyright,
Designs and Patents Act 1988.

A CIP catalogue record for this book is
available from the British Library

Typeset in 11/13 Sabon by
Phoenix Typesetting, Auldgirth, Dumfriesshire

Printed and bound in England by
CPI UK

Pen & Sword Books Ltd incorporates the imprints of Pen & Sword Aviation,
Pen & Sword Maritime, Pen & Sword Military, Wharncliffe Local History, Pen
& Sword Select, Pen & Sword Military Classics
and Leo Cooper.

For a complete list of Pen & Sword titles please contact
PEN & SWORD BOOKS LIMITED
47 Church Street, Barnsley, South Yorkshire, S70 2AS, England
E-mail: enquiries@pen-and-sword.co.uk
Website: www.pen-and-sword.co.uk

IN MEMORY OF JOAN TREW
1936–2005

A life devoted to others

Contents

Maps and Diagrams

Acknowledgements

I am grateful to Conway Maritime for including my original article 'Rodney and the Breaking of the Line' in Volume 2 of *The Age of Sail* which was published in 2003.

In writing this book I have benefited greatly from the work of those who have gone before me, not only the distinguished authors who have written on and around the subject, but also those who have edited, published, collated or otherwise made more accessible the relevant parts of the great corpus of naval records. My thanks are due also to the staff of the London Library, the British Library, the National Archives (Public Record Office), the National Maritime Museum, the Admiralty Library and the Historical Manuscripts Commission. I am grateful to Lord Rodney for allowing me to reproduce in full Rodney's advice to his son, Captain John Rodney, on the duties of a captain (Appendix 8). Commander David Barraclough and my son, Martin Trew, read the manuscript between them and made valuable suggestions. Martin helped additionally with the Spanish account of the Moonlight Battle. My son-in-law Glen Miller continued my education in computer graphics and helped with the maps. Philip Ferris kindly helped me with research into Rodney's connections with Old Alresford. I am indebted to those who have allowed me to reproduce pictures in their possession and their contributions are acknowledged separately. It has been a pleasure to work with the team at Pen & Sword and in particular Bobby Gainher, my editor. Finally the book would not have been written without the support and forbearance of my wife, Jo, who died before she could see it in print and to whose memory it is dedicated.

Note on Money, Measurements and Terminology

MONEY

Any rule for arriving at the present-day value of the English Pound in the late eighteenth century has to be used with caution. It depends very much on what the money was spent on. With that proviso I have used the House of Commons Library Research Paper 02.44 11 Jul 2002 – *Inflation: The Value of the Pound 1750–2001*.

The French Livre was equal approximately to one English shilling, i.e. to one-twentieth of a Pound.[1]

MEASUREMENTS

Distances expressed in miles in the text have in some cases been converted from distances expressed in leagues in the relevant sources, on the basis of 3 nautical miles to the league. Confusingly, the French 'lieue' is translated as 'league', but it is a different unit of measurement, probably equivalent in the late eighteenth century to approximately 2.4 nautical miles, and I have used that conversion factor where appropriate.[2]

The cable, in Rodney's day, equalled 240 yards, i.e. 120 fathoms, the standard length of an anchor cable.

TERMINOLOGY

For greater clarity I have used 'port' and 'starboard' to define the two sides of a ship instead of 'larboard' and 'starboard', which would be more correct historically.

Chronology

1718,   13 February, Baptized St Giles-in-the-Field, London

1732,   July, Entered Navy as King's letter boy in Sunderland (60) Capt. Robert Man

1734,   January, Joined *Dreadnought* (60) Capt. Alexander Geddes (Capt. Henry Medley from Dec 1734)

1738,   May, Transferred to *Romney* (50) Capt. Henry Medley

1739,   July, Joined *Somerset* (80) flagship of Rear Adm. Nicholas Haddock

1739,   Joined *Dolphin*, frigate, Capt. Lord Aubrey Beauclerk (Rodney's uncle)

1741,   Lieutenant of the *Essex* under Sir John Norris

1742,   To Med with Adm. Mathews, rising to first lieutenant of *Namur* (90)

1742,   9 November, Promoted captain of *Plymouth* (60) then under orders for England

1743,   August, Captain of *Sheerness*, 24-gun frigate

1744,   September, *Ludlow Castle*, Employed during following year in North Sea under Adm. Edward Vernon

1746,   Captain of *Eagle* (60), Initially employed on trade protection in Western Approaches

1747,   With Commodore Fox in successful cruise to westward

1747,   14 October, Participates in defeat of French fleet under l'Etanduère

1749,   Captain of *Rainbow* (40) as Governor of Newfoundland

1751,   Elected MP for Saltash and thereafter successively MP for Okehampton and Penryn as nominee of the government or the Duke of Newcastle until 1768

1752,   Autumn, *Rainbow* paid off. In following years R. commanded *Kent, Fougueux, Prince George* and *Monarch*

1753,   Married Jane (d. 1757), daughter of Charles Compton, brother of the fifth Earl of Northampton

1756,   December, In London on leave. Excused sitting Byng's court martial on grounds of illness

1757,   February, Captain of the *Dublin*

1757,   Autumn, *Dublin* with Hawke's fleet in abortive expedition to Basque Roads

1758,   *Dublin* with Boscawen on coast of North America

1759,   19 May, Appointed rear admiral and appointed, with flag in *Achilles*, to command of squadron including several bomb-ketches

1759,   5 to 7 July, Bombarded Le Havre destroying stores and flat-bottomed boats intended for invasion of England. Off Le Havre for remainder of year and again in 1760

1761,   To West Indies as C-in-C of Leeward Islands station

1762,   February, Reduced Martinique and took possession of St Lucia, Grenada and St Vincent

1762,   21 October, Promoted vice admiral

1763,   August, Returned to England

1764,   21 January, Created baronet

1764,   Married Henrietta (d.1829), daughter of John Clies of
        Lisbon

1765,   16 December, Appointed Governor of Greenwich
        Hospital

1768,   Elected MP for Northampton on own resources and said
        to have incurred expenditure of £30,000

1771,   (early), Accepts command at Jamaica

1771,   August, Nominated Rear Admiral of Great Britain

1775,   (early), Takes up residence in Paris

1778,   May, Returns to England with financial assistance from
        the Maréchal de Biron

1778,   29 January, Promoted admiral

1779,   29 December, Sails from Plymouth Sound for the West
        Indies via Gibraltar having accepted command of the
        fleet on the Leeward Islands station

1780,   16 to 17 January, Defeats inferior Spanish force under
        Don Juan de Lángara south of Cape St Vincent and
        relieves Gibraltar. Nominated extra Knight of the Bath
        and presented with freedom of the City of London

1780,   17 March, Rodney reaches Barbados with four ships of
        the line

1780,   22 March, Comte de Guichen takes command of French
        fleet in Martinique

1780,   17 April, Rodney and de Guichen in inconclusive action
        west of Martinique

1780,   15 May, Rodney and de Guichen in inconclusive action
        east of Martinique

1780,   19 May, Rodney and de Guichen in inconclusive action
        east of Martinique

1780,   16 August, de Guichen returns to Europe, accompanied
        by de Grasse

1780,   15 September, Rodney arrives in New York with ten ships of the line

1780   Rodney elected MP for Westminster

1780,   16 November, Rodney leaves America

1780,   6 December, Rodney arrives in Barbados

1780,   20 December, Britain declares war on Holland

1781,   7 January, Rodney joined in the West Indies by Sir Samuel Hood with a large reinforcement

1781,   27 January, Rodney receives news of war with Holland and a recommendation to attack Dutch possessions in the West Indies

1781,   3 February, Rodney receives surrender of St Eustatius

1781,   22 March, de Grasse appointed *lieutenant général* and sails from Brest for the West Indies

1781,   29 April, de Grasse in skirmishes with Hood off Martinique

1781,   6 May, de Grasse enters Fort Royal, Martinique.

1781,   1 June, de Bouillé and de Grasse capture Tobago.

1781,   16 July, de Grasse arrives at Cap Français, St Domingo

1781,   1 August, Rodney sails for England having resigned command to Hood

1781,   5 August, de Grasse sails from Cap Français for North America

1781,   25 August, Hood arrives off the Chesapeake, with fourteen ships of the line, but finding no sign of de Grasse goes north

1781,   28 August, Hood arrives off Sandy Hook, New Jersey, with fourteen ships of the line

1781,   30 August, de Grasse arrives off the Chesapeake

1781,   5 September, Graves and Hood arrive off the Chesapeake and engage de Grasse indecisively

1781, 19 September, Rodney arrives in England

1781, 19 October, Cornwallis surrenders at Yorktown

1781, 6 November, Rodney appointed Vice Admiral of Great Britain

1781, 11 November, Hood leaves America for the West Indies

1781, 26 November, de Bouillé captures St Eustatius and subsequently restores it to the Dutch

1781, 4 December, Motion in House of Commons by Edmund Burke on Rodney's conduct at St Eustatius defeated

1781, 5 December, Hood arrives in Barbados

1782, 11 January, French land in St Kitts

1782, 14 January, Rodney sails from Torbay for West Indies

1782, 25 January, Hood lures de Grasse out to battle off Basseterre, St Kitts and steals his anchorage

1782, 14 February, Hood's fleet cuts its cables during the night and leaves St Kitts, evading de Grasse's fleet

1782, 19 February, Rodney arrives in Barbados

1782, 9 April, Partial engagement between Rodney's fleet and French fleet under de Grasse off Dominica

1782, 12 April, Rodney defeats Comte de Grasse in the Battle of the Saintes

1782, 22 May, Voted thanks of both houses of parliament

1782, 19 June, Created a peer with the title of Baron Rodney of Stoke-Rodney

1782, 27 June, Voted a pension by the House of Commons of £2,000 (which in 1793 was settled on the title for ever)

1782, 10 July, Rodney superseded by Admiral Hugh Pigot

1782, 2 August, de Grasse arrives in London

1792, 24 May, Rodney dies suddenly

Introduction

The Commander must know how to get his men their rations and every other kind of stores needed for war. He must have imagination to originate plans, practical sense and energy to carry them through. He must be observant, untiring, shrewd; kindly and cruel; simple and crafty; a watchman and a robber; lavish and miserly; generous and stingy; rash and conservative. All these and many other qualities natural and acquired, he must have. He should also, as a matter of course, know his tactics, for a disorderly mob is no more of a fighting force than a heap of building materials is a house.

Attributed to Socrates and quoted in
Your Ship – Notes and Advice to an Officer on Assuming His First Command, Admiralty, 1944, p. 22.

The esteem in which the Royal Navy held its former admirals at a particular time can be gleaned from the naming of new ships. In 1925 Rodney shared with Nelson the naming of a two-ship class of battleship. HMS *Rodney* and HMS *Nelson* both served with distinction in the Second World War and were scrapped in 1948. At the end of that war the new Battle Class destroyers included, inevitably, HMS *Trafalgar* but also HMS *Saintes*, commemorating Rodney's final and most famous battle. Whether the Navy's estimation of Rodney at those times was matched by the perception of the general public is uncertain, but his public standing at the end of the eighteenth century is confirmed by the use of 'Rodney' as a first name, which survives to this day, although it is doubtful whether many of the men so called, or their parents who

1

chose the name, are aware that they have been named after the admiral.[1] While Nelson remains high in public awareness, Rodney is largely forgotten by the public at large, which is reflected in the vast and growing number of books about Nelson compared with the comparative handful that have been written about Rodney. There are four full biographies, the last of which, *Rodney* by David Spinney, was published in 1969 and remains the standard. There are also several short biographies in biographical collections, the most recent of which is Kenneth Breen's contribution in *Precursors of Nelson* edited by Peter Le Fevre and Richard Harding and published in 2000.* Breen has also published papers on various Rodney-related subjects and has contributed the entry on Rodney in the new *Oxford Dictionary of National Biography*. The Navy Records Society is publishing *The Rodney Papers* in three volumes the first of which, edited by David Syrett, is now in print.[2] It is greatly to be regretted that Professor Syrett died in October 2004.

Rodney has been described as a lucky admiral[3] and in one sense he was. Despite much experience of fighting he was never wounded and when he fought circumstances were often to his advantage, notably when on the way to relieve Gibraltar at the beginning of 1780 he encountered, within eight days of one another, an under-defended Spanish convoy and an inferior Spanish squadron.[4] His luck was to some extent the fortune that favours the bold. A French writer described him as, 'un amiral anglais qui fut l'homme des coups d'audace et des coups de bonheur'.[5] Perhaps his most celebrated piece of good luck was during the Battle of the Saintes, when a sudden change in wind direction led to his breaking the French line, but there are good grounds for believing that if that had not happened and if Rodney had remained to leeward, instead of passing through the French line to windward, his victory would have been more complete and he would not have been reproached with failure to pursue the escaping enemy fleet. With that proviso, it is true to say that Rodney had more than his fair share of circum-

* See Bibliography.

stantial luck, but in another sense, and particularly in the timing of his career, he was less fortunate.

Much is revealed about the course of Rodney's career by two portraits of him by Sir Joshua Reynolds painted over a quarter of a century apart (Plates 1 & 2). The first, painted in 1759 after his successful bombardment of Le Havre, is of a recently promoted rear admiral, young, good-looking and self-confident. The second, painted in Rodney's retirement five years after the Battle if the Saintes, is of a man unmistakably old, careworn, grim and battered but defiant. At the end of the Seven Years' War in 1763 Rodney, with the Le Havre bombardment and the capture of Martinique, St Lucia and Grenada behind him, was in much the same position as Nelson after the Battle of St Vincent a generation later. He had established himself as one of England's most promising young fighting admirals, poised on the threshold of great achievement. Nelson went on to the Nile, Copenhagen and Trafalgar, but it was sixteen years before Rodney hoisted his flag again in wartime, years during which, through nobody's fault but his own, he got himself horrendously into debt through high living and political ambition and had to seek refuge from his creditors by going into exile in Paris. There he got further into debt and it was only through the chivalrous intervention of a French aristocrat that he was able to return to England to offer his services in the American War of Independence. The change in Rodney during the long period of peace is described by Sir John Knox Laughton:

> The man destined by the fortune of war to be his (de Guichen's) opponent was Sir George Brydges Rodney, admiral of the white squadron, and at this time just sixty-one, but effectively perhaps the older of the two. He suffered horribly from gout, gravel, and their kindred complications; so that, at times, for days together, he was quite incapable. In his youth he had been a fine, dashing officer; and even now, when but the wreck of his old self, gave forth marks of genius and energy which have raised his name to a lofty pinnacle of glory; but these seem to have been intermittent, and there were long periods when he had neither the power to decide himself

nor the temper to permit others to decide for him. Well or ill, he was determined to be commander-in-chief; and his juniors, who sometimes thought that they were better qualified to do the work, did not always like it.[6]

What is remarkable about Rodney is that despite this diminution of his powers he was able to achieve so much. Of twenty-one enemy ships (French, Spanish and Dutch) captured or destroyed by the Royal Navy during the American War of Independence from 1778 to 1783, fifteen were credited to Rodney, all of them in the period 1780 to 1782.[7] Furthermore on two occasions he captured the enemy admiral. However, it was during that period that he encountered what was possibly his greatest misfortune in terms of his reputation, namely to have been ordered to capture the fabulously wealthy Dutch Island of St Eustatius in February 1781. It put him in an unenviable position of conflict of interest. With his known history of financial problems and his talent for making enemies, it was inevitable that many of his contemporaries would maintain that his professional judgment was impaired by the dazzling prospect of enrichment through prize money, and many historians have come to the same conclusion.

All human beings have their faults and gifted naval commanders are no exception, but Rodney's have attracted a great deal of attention. There are three main allegations against him: firstly that he he had an inordinate desire for money and was hopeless at managing it; secondly, that he abused the powers of patronage available to him as an admiral; and thirdly, that he was difficult to get on with and that, in particular, his autocratic style of command alienated his subordinates. There is truth in all those allegations but they are not the whole truth. One has to look at Rodney in the round. This book is primarily a study of him as a fighting admiral and in that capacity even his critics would concede that he was formidably effective on a good day. Tempting as it would be to consider his ability as a commander in isolation, one has to ask to what extent his perceived personal failings impacted on his duty. Thus, did his desire for prize money impair his professional

4

judgment? Did his exercise of patronage harm the Navy? Did his style of command contribute to the misunderstanding which ruined his well-conceived plan in the Battle of Martinique on 17 April 1780? Those questions are addressed in the appropriate places, but some general comments on his character might be appropriate here.

Sir Nathaniel William Wraxall, a Member of Parliament, some thirty years younger than Rodney, spent much time with him in 1779 between Rodney's return from France and his taking up his appointment as Commander-in-Chief in the Leeward Islands. Many years later, Wraxall left this recollection of him:

> His person was more elegant than seemed to become his rough profession. There was even something that approached to delicacy and effeminacy in his figure: but no man manifested a more temperate and steady courage in action. I had the honour to live in great personal intimacy with him, and have often heard him declare, that superiority to fear was not in him the physical effect of constitution; on the contrary, no man being more sensible by nature to that passion than himself: but that he surmounted it from the considerations of honour and public duty. Like the famous Marshal Villars, he justly incurred the reputation of being '*glorieux et bavard*'; making himself frequently the theme of his own discourse. He talked much and freely upon every subject; concealed nothing in the course of conversation, regardless who were present; and dealt his censures, as well as his praises, with imprudent liberality; qualities which necessarily procured him many enemies, particularly in his own profession. Throughout his whole life, two passions, both highly injurious to his repose, women and play, carried him into many excesses . . . Rodney possessed no superior parts; but, unlike Keppel, his enterprising spirit always impelled him rather to risk, than to act with caution, when in presence of the enemy. The ardour of his character supplied, in some degree, the physical defects of his health and constitution, already impaired by various causes: while his happy audacity, directed by the nautical skill of others, controlled by science, and propelled by favourable

circumstances, at length enabled him to dissipate the gloom that had so long overhung our naval annals, at the same time that he covered himself with great personal glory.[8]

Of Rodney and money his first biographer, Major General Godfrey Mundy, said with the delicacy one would expect of a son-in-law:

> It is to be lamented, that natures the most generous and ingenuous, from an honest zeal which flows through all their conduct, can seldom bring themselves to bear the dry methodical labour of arithmetical calculation, nor to bestow that attention to their financial concerns, which is, to a certain degree, indispensable in every condition of life. Sir George, it is to be apprehended, was one of this class. Possessing a pleasing and handsome exterior, with the courteous manners and address of the accomplished gentleman [qualities not particularly valued by the navy in those days], he had, at all times, when on shore, been received into the highest circles of fashion, where he took in the draught of pleasure, as others did; and his heart being warm and generous, he not unfrequently found himself involved in pecuniary difficulties.[9]

Apart from his temperament and tastes his attitude to and use of money may have been conditioned by the circumstances of his birth and childhood. Born of poor but well-connected parents he was brought up by wealthy relatives, an arrangement which gave him a taste for a mode of life which he lacked the means to sustain. It may also have imbued him, as suggested by N.A.M. Rodger, with 'the insecurity typical of the *parvenu*'.[10] Initially he prospered financially. As a young captain in the War of Austrian Succession he earned between 1744 and 1748 over £15,000 in prize money, a sum equivalent in modern purchasing power* to approximately £1.9M.[11] This enabled him to build a substantial mansion in Old Alresford, Hampshire and to buy farms in the area. Although he distinguished himself as a junior flag officer at the end of the Seven Years' War, it was not as productive of prize money as the previous war and it is possible that he ended the war out of pocket.[12]

6

Following his successful reduction of Martinique and other islands his hopes of wider responsibility and success in the West Indies had come to nothing when he was superseded by Admiral Sir George Pocock, much his senior, who was sent out with Lieutenant General the Earl of Albemarle to capture Havana, an operation which was both successful and immensely lucrative for both of them.

During Rodney's long spell of unemployment following that war his enjoyment of life in society, and the gambling that went with it, depleted such wealth as he had acquired previously, but his financial ruin was assured by his contesting the parliamentary seat of Northampton in the general election of 1768. Under the patronage of the Duke of Newcastle Rodney had been a Member of Parliament since 1751. Although strongly conservative by conviction there is no evidence that he had a marked interest in politics per se, or any particular skill in the political arts, but like many officers of his day, naval and military, he saw a seat in Parliament as an indispensable means of furthering his professional career. With Newcastle's political demise Rodney lost his patronage, but in his determination to remain an MP he decided to contest Northampton on his own account, taking advantage of the fact that the nomination was partly in the gift of his brother-in-law and former ward, the Earl of Northampton. Rodney was successful, but the election was notoriously corrupt, even by the standards of the time, and his share of the expenses was said to be £30,000[13] (approximately £2.8M at 2001 prices).* Early in 1771, before taking up his appointment as Commander-in-Chief in Jamaica he entered into a usurious arrangement, in order to consolidate his debts, with Sir James Lowther, a wealthy MP, and 'Bob' Mackreth, a former waiter at White's Club. Under the arrangement they advanced him £6,000 in return for which he paid them an 'annuity' of £800 for an unspecified number of years.[14] His absence in Jamaica gave him some respite from his financial problems but on his return to England in August 1774 he was dismayed to learn that the early dissolution of Parliament had deprived him of an expected

* House of Commons Library Research Paper 02/44, 11 Jul 2002 – Inflation: The Value of the Pound 1750–2001.

nine-month period of immunity from his creditors. There followed his four-year exile in Paris and his rescue by the Maréchal de Biron which allowed him to return to England in 1778. An accommodation with his creditors and the release of money owed to him by the Navy Board cleared the way for his appointment as Commander-in-Chief in the Leeward Islands in October 1779. Thereafter his financial position was eased by the grant of a pension of £2,000 per annum in recognition of his success in the Moonlight Battle, but any hopes of restoring his fortune by his share of prize money from St Eustatius were dashed when the convoy taking the booty to England was captured by the French. Subsequently a large number of successful claims against him by British merchants, arising out of his actions in St Eustatius, ensured that he ended his days in genteel poverty.

In his study of Rodney's use of patronage during his command in the West Indies from 1780 to 1782 David Syrett concluded:

> To further his own political and social ends, as well as to maintain his own self image, his style of life, and his position within society and the Royal Navy, Rodney, whenever possible, employed patronage to promote relations, friends and political and professional allies.

To some extent that is a statement about the times in which he lived as much as it is about Rodney himself. The granting of reciprocal favours was an indispensable adjunct to conducting business and getting on in the world. Patronage underpinned the appointments system in the Royal Navy[15] and Rodney was importuned by politicians, naval officers and members of the landed aristocracy, amongst others, to favour their nominees. Syrett estimated that some 30 per cent of the appointments and promotions made by Rodney from 1780 to 1782 were in some way tied to patronage.[16] There was a tacit assumption that those promoted thereby were properly qualified to do the job, a requirement which Rodney sometimes disregarded notoriously, but not exclusively, in the case of his own family. In 1774 when Rodney was Commander-in-Chief in Jamaica, Sandwich, as First Lord of the Admiralty, refused to

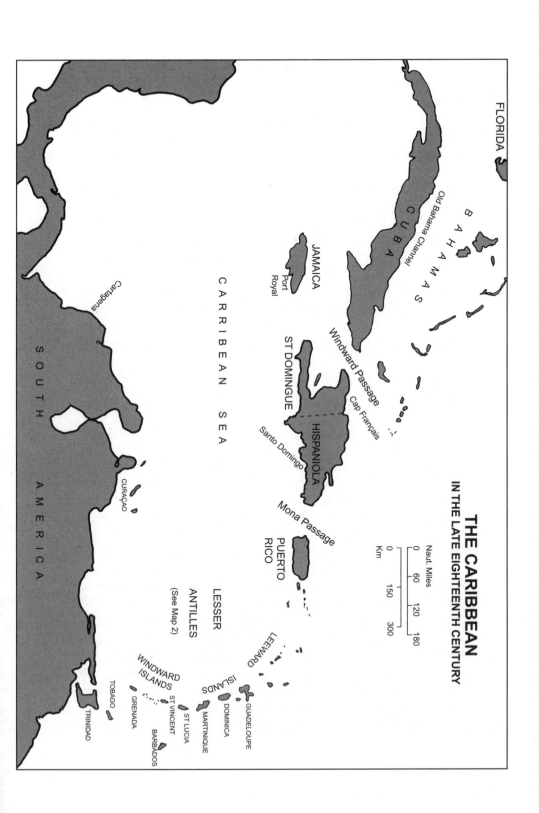

THE CARIBBEAN
IN THE LATE EIGHTEENTH CENTURY

FLORIDA

B A H A M A S

Old Bahama Channel

C U B A

JAMAICA
Port
Royal

Windward Passage

ST DOMINGUE

Cap Français

HISPANIOLA

Santo Domingo

Mona Passage

PUERTO
RICO

CARRIBEAN SEA

Cartagena

SOUTH

AMERICA

CURAÇAO

LESSER
ANTILLES
(See Map 2)

LEEWARD
ISLANDS

GUADELOUPE

DOMINICA

MARTINIQUE

ST LUCIA

ST VINCENT

WINDWARD
ISLANDS

GRENADA

BARBADOS

TOBAGO

TRINIDAD

Naut. Miles
0   60   120   180

0   150   300
Km

confirm the promotion of Rodney's twenty-year-old son, James, from Lieutenant to Post-Captain. When Rodney took up his appointment as Commander-in-Chief in the Leeward Islands in 1779 the Admiralty effectively waived its veto on irregular appointments when Sandwich assured him that confirmation of his appointments would be automatic. In October 1780 in his most flagrant abuse of patronage Rodney appointed his fifteen-year-old son John as a Post-Captain little more than a year after he had left school.[17] Another highly irregular appointment, in February 1780, was that of his thirty-year-old private physician, Gilbert Blane, as Physician to the Fleet, a new role invented by Rodney.[18] At that time Blane had negligible experience of naval medicine. However the appointment proved to be inspired for Blane had administrative and analytical gifts which enabled him to introduce, with Rodney's full backing, measures which recognized the link between diet, cleanliness and ventilation, and the health of sailors to the great benefit not only of Rodney's West Indies fleet, but of the Navy in general.

If Nelson was the great exemplar of the empathetic and inspirational style of leadership, Rodney has been stereotyped as the autocrat, intolerant of initiative on the part of his subordinates. To some degree that reputation rests on his withering and much-quoted riposte after the Battle of Martinique to the unfortunate Rear Admiral Joshua Rowley, who had taken ships in his rear division out of the line to pursue escaping French ships. When Rowley sought to justify his action Rodney replied that he required only obedience from inferior officers, adding 'the painful task of thinking belongs to me.'[19] That remark has to be seen in context. What had incensed Rodney was not so much Rowley's use of initiative per se, but that he had left Rodney (in the *Sandwich*) fighting off three French ships without any support. On the voyage home, when Rodney had finally left the West Indies in August 1782, he wrote out for his son, Captain John Rodney, some 'maxims' on the duties of a captain (see Appendix 8).[20] These include his thoughts about the place of initiative: 'Never attempt to deviate from the orders you may receive, unless on very particular occasions, and where you can answer, as an officer, for the deviation.' That seems to be unexceptionable advice and it is unlikely that Nelson would have disagreed with it.

Rodney's comments on obedience applied, of course, to situations in which the fleet was directly under the admiral's control, notably when the signal for line of battle was flying. When that was not the case as, for instance, in the Moonlight Battle and in the closing stages of the Battle of the Saintes, there is no evidence that officers under Rodney's command felt discouraged in any way from using their initiative; indeed, there is much evidence to the contrary. Rodney regarded fleet discipline as the bedrock of fighting efficiency. More than once in his private correspondence he harked back to 'the good old discipline' of the Western Squadron in which he had served as a captain under Hawke and Anson.[21] He expected not only obedience to the admiral's orders, but alacrity in responding to them: 'When a signal is made for a line of battle, you are not to execute it slowly and deliberately, but to set every sail you can crowd till you get into the station allotted you.'[22] When it came to ship's discipline as opposed to fleet discipline, Rodney was no tyrant: 'Keep your ship's Company in strict and good discipline, a good natured, not an ill natured discipline.' There is evidence that sailors liked serving under him when he was a captain.[23] On one occasion some of his former sailors deserted from another ship in order to be with him and he had to intercede with the Admiralty on their behalf to save them from draconian punishment.[24] Whether his officers felt the same way about serving under him is less certain – he did not cultivate their friendship but he considered that he owed them the duty of 'good manners, politeness and civility'.[25] There is no reason to doubt that he discharged that obligation but it is likely that in the case of those he disapproved of, the good manners were coupled with icy disdain. On this theme he wrote in November 1780 to George Jackson, Second Secretary of the Admiralty:

> I am resolved to do my duty, and no rank whatsoever shall screen any officer, who does not do his duty; the good, the worthy, the truly brave officer, will love and honour me,

11

others are unworthy of my notice, all shall be treated as gentlemen, and none under my command shall ever have reason to tax me with disrespect to them – *but I will be the Admiral* [author's italics].[26]

One cannot write about Rodney's command in the Leeward Islands from 1780 to 1782 without writing about Hood* who was his second-in-command from January 1781 onwards and who was acting Commander-in-Chief during Rodney's absence on sick leave from August 1781 until February 1782. Hood is one of the most perplexing of our great admirals. A man of estimable moral stature and great professional ability he earned the ultimate accolade from his protégé, Nelson, who described him as 'the greatest Sea-officer I ever knew'.[27] Yet he was never in supreme command in a great sea battle. He gave a brilliant display of tactical virtuosity at St Kitts in December 1781 when he stole the anchorage of his opponent de Grasse, but in strategic terms it achieved nothing – St Kitts was captured by the French and de Grasse's fleet remained intact. It must, however, have been a great morale booster to the British West Indies fleet after the dismal outcome of the Battle of the Chesapeake, and probably contributed thereby to Rodney's victory at the Saintes just over three months later. If Hood's performance at the Chesapeake, where he served as second-in-command to Rear Admiral Thomas Graves, was controversial, he was an outstanding second-in-command to Rodney at the Saintes. His least attractive characteristic was his constant criticism of others, and Rodney in particular, behind their backs.

There are many worthy and pious definitions of leadership, but some may prefer the more down-to-earth description of the commander, attributed to Socrates, which heads this chapter. It seems to be particularly apt in the case of Rodney.

---

* Rear Admiral Sir Samuel Hood, later the 1st Viscount Hood 1724–1816.

Chapter 1

Early Life

George Brydges[1] Rodney was baptized in St Giles-in-the-Fields in the County of Middlesex on 13 February 1718 and was probably born in January of that year or late in 1717. The family was one of great antiquity which up to the death in 1657 of his great-grand-father, Sir Edward Rodeney, had owned properties in and around Rodney Stoke in Somerset for four centuries. Sir Edward's only son, George, having predeceased him, the estate passed to his daughter, Anne, and thence by marriage to Sir Thomas Bridges of Keynsham in Somerset, a kinsman of the Barons Chandos, the ninth of whom, James, became the First Duke of Chandos in 1719. The Rodeney or Rodney family had never attained any particular fame or distinc-tion but several of Rodney's ancestors had been military men, including his father, Henry, who served in a regiment of marines in the War of the Spanish Succession (1702–13). He retired as a captain, settled in Walton-on-Thames in Surrey and was reduced to poverty by a late investment, in 1720, in the South Sea Company. The story that he had commanded the Royal Yacht and that, as a consequence, King George I had been one of Rodney's godfathers is thought to be without foundation. Rodney's mother, Mary, was the daughter of Sir Henry Newton, a distinguished diplomat and a judge of the High Court of Admiralty. A brother-in-law by her sister Catherine's second marriage was Lord Aubrey Beauclerk, son of the Duke of St Albans, a grandson of King Charles II and a serving naval officer. Thus Henry Rodney, although impoverished,

13

did not lack for aristocratic or wealthy relations some of whom rallied round to help him with the upbringing of his four surviving children, of whom George, the future admiral, was the second youngest. He was taken under the protection of his godfather George Bridges, the MP for Winchester, in whose home at Avington Park he spent part of his childhood.[2]

Rodney was educated at Harrow, probably not for long, and on 7 May 1732, at the age of fourteen and a half, joined the Navy as a volunteer per order or 'king's letter boy', one of the last such entries before the system was abolished. Eleven years later he was a post-captain. The speed of his advance owed much to the exercise of influence, mainly on the part of the Duke of Chandos, but there is no reason to doubt Rodney's fitness for command. He served first in the *Sunderland* (60), possibly on paper only, but he then served for nearly four years, from January 1734 to September 1737, in the *Dreadnought* (60), commanded for most of that time by Captain Henry Medley, who made him a midshipman near the end of 1734 and took an interest in his progress. While he was in the *Dreadnought* she spent a total of fourteen months, between 1735 and 1737, at Lisbon, a city which he was to visit several times in the future and where he probably met the families of both his future wives. After serving briefly in the *Berwick*, possibly another paper appointment, Rodney transferred in May 1738 to the *Romney* (50), commanded by his former mentor, Captain Henry Medley. She spent the summer of that year on fishery protection work in Newfoundland, where Rodney was later to serve as governor.

In 1739, after serving briefly in the *Somerset* (80), flagship of Rear Admiral Nicholas Haddock, he joined in the Mediterranean the *Dolphin* (20), commanded by his uncle (by marriage) Lord Aubrey Beauclerk. The ship returned home shortly after Rodney joined her and his uncle was replaced by Captain Francis Holburne in February 1740, at about the same time as Rodney was commissioned as a lieutenant at the age of twenty-two. Later that year, between 1 and 3 November he experienced one of the worst storms of the century on the east coast of England. Many merchant vessels sank and the *Dolphin* survived only by jettisoning some of her guns. Rodney transferred briefly to the *Essex* (70) before

14

returning to the Mediterranean to join the *Namur* (90), flagship of Admiral Sir Thomas Mathews, the Commander-in-Chief.* Through a series of fortuitous promotions of those above him, Rodney moved up from fifth to first lieutenant of the *Namur* in five months. He was indebted to Mathews for two significant events in his career. He gave him not only his first experience of warfare, but also his promotion to the rank of Captain. In August 1742 Mathews ordered Rodney, by then first lieutenant of the flagship, to take a 28-oar rowing boat to destroy stores and supplies stock-piled at Ventimiglia for use by Spanish forces threatening to invade the Republic of Genoa. He accomplished this successfully and was mentioned in Mathews's despatch. Two months later when the *Plymouth* (60) had to be sent home for repair, Mathews appointed Rodney as her captain. After calling at Lisbon where he collected a convoy of nine merchant ships, he arrived at Spithead at the end of March 1743, having lost contact with most of the merchant ships in heavy weather. At Lisbon he had taken on board for passage home one Lewis Ledger, reputedly Anson's missing cook, who had been captured ashore during the ill-fated round-the-world cruise.

Rodney's commission as a post-captain was confirmed soon after his return to England, making him, at twenty-five, one of the youngest captains in the Navy. After taking his first command around to Plymouth for decommissioning he was appointed in August 1743 to command the new frigate, *Sheerness* (24), still awaiting launching at Rotherhithe. Manning difficulties meant that she was not fully ready for service until December. For the next nine months, before moving to a new command, Rodney gained useful experience of convoy and escort work around the British Isles and in the North Sea. His time in the *Sheerness* was notable for the fact that Samuel Hood served under him as a midshipman. At the end of September 1744 he moved to the *Ludlow Castle* (40), another new ship and still being fitted out at Deptford. She was one

---

* Best remembered for his role in the Battle of Toulon on 11 February 1744 and the subsequent courts martial of himself and his second-in-command Vice Admiral Richard Lestock.

of a new class of heavily armed two-decked ships, a design which proved to be unsatisfactory, mainly because the ships were over-crowded and wet. They were also top-heavy and it was difficult to open the lower deck gun ports even in a moderate sea. Under Rodney's command the *Ludlow Castle*'s work, mainly in the North Sea, included blockading the east coast of Scotland to contain the Jacobite rebellion and convoy work on the east coast of England and to Lisbon. His knowledge of seamanship was extended by the experience of going aground in the *Ludlow Castle* on two occasions, in November 1744 on the Standford shoal near Yarmouth and in December 1745 on the Whiting Sand near Harwich. The second episode was the more serious, but what-ever her other faults the *Ludlow Castle* was stoutly built and she survived despite damage to her hull and the loss of her rudder. Rodney took her to Sheerness for repair and did not go to sea in her again. Hood had moved with him from the *Sheerness* to the *Ludlow Castle* but had gone on to the *Exeter* after four months. Rodney's brother, James, had been with him throughout his command, as a midshipman and a master's mate, but decided that the Navy was not for him.[3]

On 8 January 1746 Rodney took command of the recently launched ship *Eagle* (60). She was fitted out, manned and ready for sea by the end of February and for several weeks was part of a squadron blockading Ostend, a continuing source of supplies and reinforcements for the rebels in Scotland. She left the squadron on 24 April and after escorting a convoy to Plymouth was refitted there. From 21 May she was sent on a series of cruises in the Western Approaches to the English Channel, sometimes as one of a small group of ships, and sometimes alone. The *Eagle* proved to be a fast sailer which, coupled with Rodney's enterprise and skill, made this one of his most successful commands. He took his first of many prizes in her, a 16-gun Spanish privateer, on 24 May.

At the end of July 1746 the *Eagle* joined the newly formed Western Squadron, an amalgamation of the main squadrons in home waters into a single fleet, so-called because it was intended to operate in the Western Approaches. Two factors made this a better place from which to defend the Channel than the Channel itself. Firstly the prevailing wind was from the south-west, and secondly neither France nor Spain had a naval base in the Channel. In theory an invasion of England could be launched from one of France's Channel ports, but the naval escort to cover it would have to come up from the west. The Western Squadron would be well placed to intercept it, as it would be to prevent an invasion of Ireland and to cover British merchant ships entering and leaving the Channel. It was the implementation of an old idea by a new Board of Admiralty in which George Anson played an important part and who, as a Vice Admiral, was its first Commander-in-Chief. He was succeeded in the spring of 1747 by Vice Admiral Sir Peter Warren, but when he was incapacitated by illness Rear Admiral Edward Hawke was appointed his second-in-command and effectively commanded the Western Squadron from the beginning of August 1747.[4]

After joining the Western Squadron the *Eagle* continued to take prizes. Between May 1746, when she was sent on her first cruise, and June 1747 Rodney was directly involved, either independently or in company with other ships, in the capture of sixteen enemy ships, half of which were armed.[5] Of the operations which led to these captures two are of particular interest. On 3 February 1747, in company with HM ships *Nottingham* and *Edinburgh*, Rodney in the *Eagle* took the French privateer *Bellona* (36 guns and 310 men). From the evidence of two prisoners in the *Bellona* and the subsequent confession of some of her crew, it appeared that the privateer's captain, M. Claude Lory, had committed what we would today call a war crime. A distressed English merchant ship, the *Elenor*, bound for Barbados, had surrendered to the *Bellona,* then cruising with another privateer, in the hope of saving the lives of those on board before she sank. However, the *Bellona*'s captain, probably incensed when he found that the *Elenor*'s cargo was worthless, consisting chiefly of mules and horses, and that she was in danger of sinking, refused her plea for succour and left her crew and passengers to perish after plundering them. The other privateer had behaved rather better and had taken some of the *Elenor*'s crew on board but had then been reprimanded by the *Bellona*'s captain for doing so. In their joint report to the Admiralty, Rodney and Philip de Saumarez, captain of the *Nottingham*, concluded:

> As there appears to us strong presumption that this unnatural treatment of His Majesty's subjects will on proper examination be fully proved, we have taken the liberty to lay it before their Lordships, whom we are persuaded will punish such a flagrant violation of the laws of nations and arms as the heinousness of (the) crime deserves.[6]

After his capture on 1 May 1747 of a French privateer, which he took into Kinsale in the south of Ireland, Rodney put to sea again. He fell in with and joined a small squadron under the command of Commodore Thomas Fox, which was on its way to join the Western Squadron as a reinforcement. It was too late to take part in the First Battle of Finisterre on 3 May in which Anson defeated an inferior French squadron under M. de la Jonquière north of Cape Ortegal, and in the process captured many merchant ships. However, fate provided Fox's ships with their own opportunity when they sighted early on 20 June a French convoy of more than a hundred ships on its way from St Domingo to the Biscay ports. With the wind north-north-easterly the convoy was 10 to 15 miles to windward on a more or less easterly course on the port tack. Fox's ships were on the starboard tack but at 8.00 am he ordered them onto the same tack as the convoy, a manoeuvre which put Rodney's *Eagle* in the rear half of the squadron. Throughout the day the British gained slowly on the convoy and by the next morning it was much closer. Furthermore there was no sign of its escort of four warships. At 5.00 am Rodney, on his own initiative, tacked and set off towards that part of the convoy lying to the north-west, ignoring two signals from Fox to return. Over the next five days he captured six of the French merchant ships and with his prizes sailed independently to the Downs.* Fox had arrived in

---

* An anchorage, much used in the age of sail, lying between the Goodwin Sands and the Kent coast.

Spithead with sixteen prizes two days earlier. Including Rodney's prizes his squadron had taken forty-eight French merchant ships.[7] Rodney's decision to act on his own initiative and to ignore attempts to recall him is interesting in the light of his reputation later as an admiral who demanded unthinking obedience from his subordinates. While he was in the Downs, one of the St Domingo prizes, not Rodney's, was stranded on the Goodwin Sands and attracted the attention of shore-based looters. Rodney apprehended forty of them and pressed them into His Majesty's service. Presumably because others were thought to need them more than he did, he was instructed to send them to Spithead.[8]

On 14 October 1747 twelve ships of the line of the Western Squadron, accompanied by three smaller ships, were cruising 140 miles west of Ushant and approximately 200 miles north of Cape Finisterre steering slightly south of west with a moderate wind from SSE. At about 7 am a large number of French ships, both merchant and warships, were sighted to the south-west, the number of the latter being estimated initially at seven. Hawke gave the signal to chase and the British fleet gradually got closer. At 10.00 am he made the signal for line of battle on the port tack and by now it was apparent that the enemy's fighting strength was eight ships of the line compared to his twelve. However, the French ships were more heavily armed, averaging 70 guns per ship compared with 60 guns in Hawke's squadron, but the averages understate the relative strengths since five of the French ships had 74 guns or more including the 80-gun *Tonnant*, the flagship of the Marquis de L'Etanduère. The British were mostly of 60 guns, with six of 64 guns or more including Hawke's flagship, the *Devonshire* (66). Furthermore the French ships were more strongly built and had larger ship's companies.

As the British fleet closed the gap de L'Etanduère ordered the large convoy to flee to the north-west under the protection of a 64-gun Indiaman which had been sailing in company with his warships. Like the British, the French were in line ahead on the port tack and were somewhat to windward. To gain on the enemy more quickly Hawke again signalled his fleet to chase and gave the signal to engage at 11.30 am when his leading ships were nearly within gunshot. At this time Rodney in the *Eagle* was almost the rearmost British ship with Fox in the *Kent* on his port quarter.

The French ships, normally the faster sailers, were not under full sail in order to remain in position to protect the escaping convoy, and Hawke's ships were therefore able to pass down the French line. For the most part the British attack was from to leeward, but one ship the *Monmouth* passed down the line to windward thus ensuring that a number of French ships were fired on from both sides. Later in the action the *Edinburgh* went through the line to windward and engaged the *Tonnant*.

Rodney was among the last group of ships to come into action (*Nottingham*, *Defiance*, *Eagle* and *Kent*). He engaged some time after 12.20 pm and was in difficulty when he found himself under fire from two French ships, the *Neptune* (70) to port and the disabled *Fougueux* (64) to starboard. The latter soon dropped astern where she was engaged by and struck to the *Hector* (40). Rodney continued his engagement with the *Neptune* until 2.00 pm when an unlucky shot carried away his steering wheel. As his masts and sails were also much damaged the ship became ungovernable and collided twice with the *Devonshire* as she came up on his lee quarter to assist. Rodney was incensed that Fox in the *Kent* had not come to his assistance when he was in action with the *Neptune* and the *Fougueux*. Before the engagement Fox, who by then had moved up and was before Rodney's weather beam, had backed the *Kent*'s mizzen topsail to allow Rodney to overtake him on the *Neptune*'s lee side. Whatever idea Fox might have had of coming into action was frustrated by an upper-deck gun's crew who dismantled some rigging that was in their way, which resulted in the mizzen topsail remaining aback for longer than Fox intended. The impression that he had been reluctant to engage the enemy was seen as consistent with his conduct later in the action, particularly his engagement with the French flagship, the *Tonnant*, which was regarded by his fellow captains as overcautious. Rodney gave evidence at the subsequent court martial.

The action ended after dark with all but two of the eight French ships having surrendered. The two which escaped were the

Tonnant and the *Intrépide*. At about 6.00 pm Rodney bore away to engage these ships and was joined by Philip de Saumarez in the *Nottingham* (60) and Charles Saunders in the *Yarmouth* (64). They caught up with and engaged the two ships from 7.00 pm for about an hour and a half. De Saumarez was killed early in the action. So ended what came to be known as the Second Battle of Finisterre, Rodney's first experience of a major fleet action.[9] Fox's court martial was held in Portsmouth at the end of 1747, when he was found guilty of misconduct and dismissed his ship. The court acquitted him of any imputation of cowardice, but thought that he had been too much under the influence of his First Lieutenant and Master.[10]

The *Eagle* was back at sea again in the new year and, as part of a small squadron under Commodore Cotes in the *Edinburgh*, took part in February in the capture of five stragglers from a well-defended convoy out of Cadiz. After calling at Lisbon, she returned to Plymouth, where she was decommissioned on 13 August 1748. Rodney's share of the prize money from these latest captures brought the total accumulated by him during his command of the *Eagle* to over £15,000, equivalent in modern purchasing power* to approximately £1.9M.[11] He was now not only financially secure (for the time being, at least), but had established a professional reputation. Moreover, his service under Anson and Hawke in the elite Western Squadron, with its high standards of fleet discipline and profiency, was one of the most important formative influences in his career.

On 1 March 1749 Rodney took command of the *Rainbow* (50). To have been given a command at all in a Navy much reduced in size after the ending of the Austrian war was evidence that he had made his mark, and for a 31-year-old Captain it was a prestigious command, carrying with it the governorship of Newfoundland. Furthermore, since in addition to the *Rainbow* he had two ships under his command, he was able to wear a commodore's broad pennant. These were the *Mercury* (20) and the sloop *Saltash*. The

* House of Commons Research Paper 02/44, 11 Jul 2002, *Inflation: The Value of the Pound 1750–2002.*

title of Governor was rather a grand one for what was essentially a fishery protection role requiring a British naval presence during the summer only, but that is not to say that there was no governing to be done. Rodney was required to maintain order among the fishermen and to ensure that none remained behind at the end of the fishing season, since the fisheries had an important secondary purpose in providing a reservoir of trained seamen to man the Navy in wartime. He also had secret orders to support the colony against the encroachment of the French in Nova Scotia. In a private letter on this subject Lord Sandwich,* the First Lord of the Admiralty, expressed his confidence in Rodney's discretion:

> It is judged improper, as yet, to send any public order upon a business of so delicate a nature, which is the reason of my writing to you in this manner, and I am satisfied that your prudence is such as will not suffer you to make any injudicious use of the information you now receive. There are some people that cannot be trusted with any but public orders; but I have too good an opinion of you to rank you among them, and shall think this important affair entirely safe under your management and secrecy.[12]

Apart from Rodney's professional activities during his command of the *Rainbow* (1749–52), he succeeded in entering Parliament. Having in 1750, with the support of the Duke of Bedford, contested unsuccessfully a by-election in the Borough of Launceston in Cornwall, he was elected to the House of Commons in May 1751 to represent Saltash, a safe Admiralty seat adjoining Plymouth dockyard, again with Bedford's support. At the end of his third annual visit to Newfoundland, Rodney left for the last time on 20 September 1751 and sailed with the trade bound for the Iberian Peninsula as he had done before. After visiting Lisbon and Cadiz, the *Rainbow* reached Spithead on 18 March 1752. As Rodney was taken ill after arrival there, he

---

* John Montagu, 4th Earl of Sandwich, 1718–92, First Lord of the Admiralty 1748–51, 1763 and 1771–82.

22

requested and was granted permission to allow the *Rainbow* to be taken round to Woolwich by his First Lieutenant to be paid off.[13]

For the next ten months Rodney was unemployed, a break which enabled him to attend to his private life, including his property in Old Alresford in Hampshire, which he had acquired out of his prize money and where he had begun to build a substantial mansion before his first season in Newfoundland.[14] He also turned to the question of marriage, and was torn for a while between Kitty and Jane (Jenny), daughters of the Hon Charles Compton, whom he had probably come to know during his several visits to Lisbon. Compton, whose father was the 4th Earl of Northampton, had been the British consul there, and then envoy extraordinary to the Portuguese court. He decided in favour of Jenny, whom he married on 31 January 1753. It was a happy but short-lived marriage: she died four years later, having borne him three children, George, born in 1753, James (1754) and a daughter (1756), who died in infancy. Such were the joys of early domesticity that they prevailed for a while over Rodney's professional zeal. From 16 January 1753 he commanded a succession of Portsmouth guard ships – *Kent, Fougueux,** *Prince George and Monarch* – contriving to move to a new command whenever there seemed to be a serious prospect of having to go to sea. The *Prince George* did go to sea in Hawke's squadron from July to September in 1755, and the *Monarch*, to which he was appointed on 5 May 1756, joined the Channel Fleet under Boscawen for a brief cruise in July and August of that year, but was ordered back to Portsmouth when found to be in urgent need of repair.[15] Rodney did not go to sea in her again and towards the end of 1756 both he and his wife became seriously ill. He recovered but she died on 29 January 1757. After Rodney had left her, the *Monarch* earned her place in history when Admiral Byng was executed on her quarterdeck on 14 March 1757. Rodney had managed to be excused serving as a member of Byng's court martial on the grounds of illness. While he deplored Byng's conduct he

---

* The *Fougueux* was captured from the French and the *Kent* was commanded by Captain Thomas Fox in the Second Battle of Finisterre on 14 October 1747.

thought the sentence excessive and, with Captain Augustus Hervey, worked unsuccessfully for his reprieve.[16]

There had been a setback in Rodney's political career in 1754 when, after the dissolution of Parliament, his Saltash seat was wanted for a more important candidate and he was not offered another. Determined to return to Parliament, he stood against the government in the Bedford interest at Camelford in Cornwall, but lost the contest at a cost to himself and his backer of £3,000.[17] Rodney's father-in-law, Charles Compton, died on 20 November 1755, leaving Rodney as his executor and the ward of his sons Charles and Spencer Compton.

In February 1757 Rodney was appointed to the *Dublin*, the first of the 74-gun ships, which were to become the workhorse of the British Navy in the classic age of sail. It was his first and only active command as a captain in the Seven Years' War (1756–1763), but he saw little in the way of direct action. The *Dublin* was one of Hawke's squadron which took part in the abortive raid on Rochefort in the last week of September 1757, commanded jointly by Hawke and Lieutenant General Sir John Mordaunt. Rodney took part in the Councils of War requested by the Army, but other- wise was not much involved. If the operation was a failure it was noteworthy for the fact that of the sixteen captains of the ships of the line present, eleven, including Rodney, eventually reached the rank of Vice Admiral or higher.[18] During this expedition the *Dublin* became badly infected with typhus caught from soldiers embarked for passage. She was also found to have a serious problem with her rudder. On 2 March 1758, Rodney was ordered to take Major General Amherst across the Atlantic for the attack on Louisbourg on Cape Breton Island, a voyage which occasioned the first serious accusation against Rodney of allowing his interest in prize money to interfere with his duty. On 19 March he captured a French East Indiaman with a valuable cargo off Ushant and took her into Vigo, because he considered that the scurvy and sickness which he found raging among the prisoners threatened the health of his own ship's company. According to one eminent historian he spent nearly two weeks in Vigo despite the fact that 'he was engaged in the special duty of carrying to the seat of war the belated commander-in-chief of the main operation of the campaign.'[19] The charge was unfounded, since Rodney appears to have spent not more than four days in Vigo.[20] There was a fresh outbreak of fever in the ship while in Halifax, Nova Scotia, and probably for that reason the *Dublin* did not take part in the reduction of Louisbourg on 25 July 1758. Rodney sailed for England on 15 August as senior officer of five ships of the line which, together with the ten transports they were escorting, were taking to England the late garrison of Louisbourg and the crews of captured French warships. On the voyage home there was a serious outbreak of scurvy to which Rodney himself succumbed. The *Dublin* anchored at Spithead on 17 July. Rodney was granted extended sick leave and did not rejoin her. When he next went to sea it was as a Rear Admiral.

Chapter 2

Flag Rank

Rodney became a Rear Admiral of the Blue on 19 May 1759 and for a few weeks stood in as Commander-in-Chief at Portsmouth for his former captain in the *Dolphin*, Vice Admiral Francis Holburne. However, on 5 June he was put in charge of a small squadron, whose task was to blockade and bombard Le Havre, at the mouth of the Seine, then also known as Havre de Grace. This project, which was thought to be the brainchild of Anson as First Lord of the Admiralty,[1] was in response to intelligence reports that the French were assembling a fleet of barges there for the invasion of Britain. Anson briefed Rodney personally, emphasizing the need for secrecy, and with that in mind arranged for the issue of false orders to make it appear that Rodney's squadron was bound for Gibraltar.[2] It was difficult to maintain the deception because Rodney had to recruit pilots for that part of the Normandy Coast, having no personal experience of it, and by 18 June he was reporting that his true destination was being referred to in the newspapers.[3] His genuine and secret orders were not issued until 26 June, the day on which he reported that his squadron was ready to proceed. These referred to 130 flat-bottomed boats under construction at Le Havre and enjoined him 'to endeavour as well as by a bombardment as by all other means in your power, to destroy the boats building upon the beach, and also any naval or warlike materials that may be there, or any boats, magazines, stores, provisions, and materials that may be in the basin, harbour and town of Le Havre'.[4]

For the next few days Rodney was delayed at Spithead by winds which blew 'very fresh' from WSW or NW, which in both cases he was advised would cause heavy seas off Le Havre, presenting him with a particularly dangerous lee shore because of the shoals outside the harbour entrance. However, the weather moderated and he was able to report on 4 July that he had anchored the ships under his command off Le Havre. Apart from the *Achilles* (60) in which he flew his flag, his squadron included four 50-gun ships, the *Chatham*, *Deptford*, *Isis* and *Norwich*, six frigates, two sloops and six bomb-vessels or 'bombs' as they were known. The latter were small ships designed primarily for high-trajectory shore bombardment. At that time they were ketch rigged and were equipped with two mortars, one of 10-inch calibre and one of 13-inch, placed on the centre line of the ship, one forward of the mainmast and one between the masts. In two respects they were years ahead of their time: the mortars were on revolving beds, enabling them to fire on either beam of the vessel, and they fired explosive shells, the only ships in the Navy to do so. The spherical shells weighed up to 200lb each and consequently relatively few could be carried, fresh supplies being provided by tenders. Strict firing discipline was necessary to prevent accidental explosions. The gun crews were provided by the Army and joined the naval crews when required.[5] One of Rodney's problems was that the gun crews assigned to him in the bomb-vessels, apart from one officer, had no previous experience of this work, but this was remedied to some extent by the appointment of two artillery officers, Colonel Desaguliers and Captain Smith, who divided their attention among the bomb-vessels as necessary.[6]

Among the frigates was the *Vestal* (32), commanded by Captain Samuel Hood, and this helped to overcome another of Rodney's problems, namely that the pilots proved to be 'totally ignorant of the place' when it came to anchoring the bomb-vessels in their firing positions as close as possible to Le Havre. Hood, together with the captains of the *Deptford* and the frigate *Juno* and the latter's first lieutenant, came to the rescue.[7] Rodney shifted his flag to the *Vestal* to get a better view of the proceedings. The 'bombs' were anchored bow to stern, heading approximately north-west and just over a mile offshore, with the leading vessel close to the shoal known as the Banc de la Jambe.[8] All six were in position by the early morning of 5 July, and 'continued to bombard for fifty-two hours without intermission, with such success, that the town was several times in flames and their magazine of stores for the flat bottom boats burnt with very great fury for upwards of six hours, notwithstanding the continual efforts of several hundreds of men to extinguish it, many of the boats were overturned and damaged by the explosion of the shells'.[9] According to a French intelligence report, 500 shells fell in the space of twenty-four hours, causing consternation among the populace and the exodus of women, children and the elderly.[10] The bombardment ceased when the bomb-vessels were rendered unserviceable by the continuous shock of firing their heavy ordnance. Rodney took his squadron to Spithead, leaving behind enough ships to prevent materials for completing the boat-building from reaching Le Havre.

On 17 August Rodney was ordered back to Le Havre to renew operations,[11] and arrived there with his squadron twelve days later, but this time circumstances were against him. During the brief interval before the arrival of fast-running spring tides, the weather was mostly bad, so that it was not possible to position the bomb-vessels. Furthermore the French had taken steps to improve their defences and in particular, by 30 August had brought down the river two floating batteries with heavy cannon, later augmented by a third, in a position calculated to 'annoy the bombs in the most effectual manner'. The batteries were protected by small armed vessels. Notwithstanding these difficulties, Rodney was 'determined to try the force of my small squadron when I have a favourable opportunity to make the attempt, provided I find it can be done without bringing disgrace to His Majesty's arms'. That opportunity did not present itself and on 11 September he wrote to the Admiralty: 'Their Lordships I am sure are convinced that the captains of the squadron I have the honour to command, are men of gallantry and spirit, and would exert themselves to the utmost upon all occasions for His Majesty's service. I think it my duty to acquaint their Lordships that they are unanimously of opinion that

28

nothing further can be done by bombardment, without risking the whole squadron against the enemy's bombs and batteries. And even then the event would be very doubtful.'[12] The Admiralty accepted that judgment, but Rodney was recommended to keep Le Havre as closely blockaded as possible. His successful bombardment in early July does not appear materially to have interrupted the building of invasion barges, but it was an important demonstration of the Royal Navy's command of the English Channel. Any hope that the French might have had of disputing that command for long enough to mount a successful invasion was removed by Hawke's victory in Quiberon Bay on 20–21 November 1759.

The remainder of Rodney's Channel command which continued with interruptions until February 1761 was devoted to the blockade of Le Havre and the Bay of the Seine. On 24 November 1759, following the death of the incumbent, Rodney was elected unopposed as the Member of Parliament for Okehampton in Devon under the patronage of the Duke of Newcastle. In the 1761 election, which followed the death in October 1760 of King George II, Rodney was dismayed to learn that he would not again be the government candidate at Okehampton. His letter to the Duke of Newcastle's political manager illustrates both the value attached by Rodney to being in Parliament and the importance of patronage:

A letter I received by last night's post has given me inexpressible concern . . . For God's sake Sir what have I done to gain his Grace's displeasure. You know full well Sir that it was to serve him that I came into Parliament, and was desirous to continue on no other foundation.

I must entreat you Sir, to represent my case in the humblest manner to his Grace not to let me suffer in the eye of the public, as a person obnoxious to him, and unworthy [of] his protection, which I shall infallibly do, unless his Grace vouchsafes to let me have a seat in Parliament, by his influence.[13]

Rodney had not fallen into disfavour, but the seat was required for someone else, as had happened to him at Saltash in 1754. Arrangements were made for him to contest the election at Penryn in Cornwall in which he was successful and where he remained the Member of Parliament until 1768.

During the summer of 1761, the British Government decided to launch an invasion attempt against Martinique, France's prize possession in the Leeward Islands and a centre of privateering activity which was a menace to British trade. It was not only one of the richest of the sugar islands but also one of the best placed strategically, with an excellent harbour at Fort Royal (now Fort de France) on the west coast. Rodney's performance in his Channel command had created a good impression in the right quarters. In particular he had shown the ability to master an out-of-the-ordinary operation in his successful bombardment of Le Havre. He was now chosen by Anson, over the heads of more senior officers,[14] to command the naval element in the proposed combined operation against Martinique. It is probable that he learnt of this some time in advance of his formal appointment and began work on his detailed instructions for the landing and re-embarking of troops.[15] On 5 October 1761 he was notified of his appointment as Commander-in-Chief in the Leeward Islands and his formal and detailed instructions followed two days later.[16] He hoisted his flag in the *Marlborough* (68) at Spithead on 9 October.

The naval force under his command off Martinique was eventually to number seventeen ships of the line, four 50-gun ships and a large number of smaller warships.[17] Of the ships of the line, seven were already in the West Indies under the command of Commodore Sir James Douglas,[18] who had been ordered to blockade Martinique to prevent help of any kind reaching it. The main army contingent consisted of ten battalions from America with engineers and artillery. They had been put on notice as early as December 1760 and had received their orders in July, but no major military operation could take place in the West Indies until the end of the hurricane season. The troops from America were to be supplemented by as many troops as could be spared from local garrisons and militia in the West Indies, and four regiments of foot were to be sent from Belle Isle on the coast of Brittany, bringing the total army strength to just under 14,000 troops, commanded by Major General the Hon Robert Monckton, who had been Wolfe's second-in-command at Quebec.

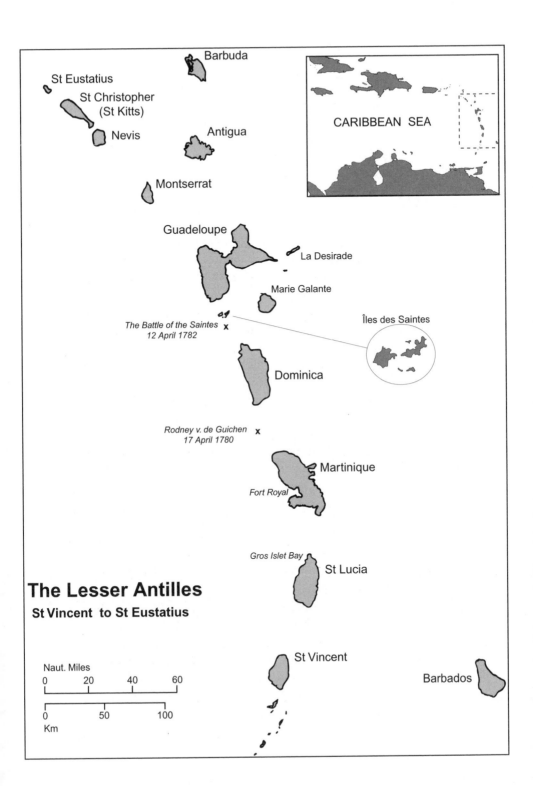

Barbuda

St Eustatius

St Christopher
(St Kitts)

Nevis

Antigua

Montserrat

CARIBBEAN SEA

Guadeloupe

La Desirade

Marie Galante

Îles des Saintes

The Battle of the Saintes **x**
12 April 1782

Dominica

Rodney v. de Guichen **x**
17 April 1780

Martinique

Fort Royal

Gros Islet Bay

St Lucia

The Lesser Antilles

St Vincent to St Eustatius

Naut. Miles

| 0 | 20 | 40 | 60 |

| 0 | 50 | 100 |

Km

St Vincent

Barbados

The combined land and sea force was to set out from Carlisle Bay, Barbados, an ideal place from which to mount the operation since of all the islands in the West Indies Barbados lay furthest to windward, but assembling the force there did not go smoothly. Rodney's departure from Portsmouth with six ships of the line and two bomb-vessels[19] was delayed by adverse winds so that by 20 October he had only got as far as Plymouth. Then, having cleared the Channel, his squadron was scattered by a gale. The *Marlborough*, accompanied only by a bomb-vessel tender, made the crossing to Barbados alone and arrived there on 22 November. The rest of Rodney's squadron arrived over the next two and a half weeks, and the transports carrying the four regiments from Belle Isle arrived on 14 December. The large convoy carrying Monckton and the troops from New York did not arrive until 24 December. In compliance with his orders Rodney took Douglas and his ships under his command and his fighting strength was augmented by another four ships of the line which had escorted the troop convoys.[20] Apart from some of Douglas's ships which were already off Martinique, the entire combined force with its transports and auxiliaries, 175 ships in all,[21] sailed from Barbados for Martinique on 5 January 1762 and arrived two days later.

The island of Martinique is approximately 40 land miles in length by 20 miles wide with its long axis lying south-east to north-west. It is mountainous with many ravines, which in 1762 made the overland transport of troops and artillery difficult if not impossible. The main objective of Rodney's and Monckton's expedition was Fort Royal, the administrative centre, which lay on the north shore of Fort Royal Bay, but a frontal attack was ruled out by the guns on Pigeon Island on the south shore at the entrance to the bay. It was therefore necessary to land troops as close as possible to the town and hope to overcome the difficulties of crossing the terrain. On 8 January the invasion fleet anchored in St Ann's Bay on the south-western extremity of the island where Douglas's ships had silenced the guns in advance of the fleet's arrival. In doing so the *Raisonable* (Captain Shuldham) had gone aground on a small reef, but her crew and her stores had been saved. From here Rodney sent northwards Commodore Swanton with a small squadron and two brigades of troops, and Captain Augustus Hervey in the *Dragon* to take possession respectively of the small adjoining bays of Petite Anse d'Arlet and Grand Anse d'Arlet, a few miles south of Pigeon Island. The troops, with Swanton and Hervey's marines and sailors, made successful landings but found that there was no realistic prospect of attacking Pigeon Island or getting around to Fort Royal. Rodney and Monckton now transferred their attention to Case Navires Bay, 2 miles north of Pointe des Nègres at the northern entrance to Fort Royal Bay and about 3 miles from the town. Three years earlier there had been an unsuccessful British landing but it was decided to try again. The new attack took place on 16 January and three days later Rodney reported to the Admiralty:

> I landed General Monckton with the greatest part of his force by sunset; and the whole army was on shore a little after day light next morning, without the loss of a man (the boats being commanded by Commodore Swanton in the centre, Captain Shuldham on the right wing, and Captain Hervey on the left) with such necessaries as they were most in want of, and had all the ships and transports anchored as much in safety, as this coast will admit.
>
> I also landed two battalions of marines, consisting of 450 men each.
>
> The army are now carrying on their approaches to the heights of Mount Grenie and Mount Tortenson, which the enemy have made as art can do, and from whence the General proposes to lay siege to Fort Royal.
>
> I have the happiness to add, that the army and navy continue in perfect health; and carry on the service with the greatest spirit and harmony.[22]

The artillery was in place by 25 January and the British troops attacked the next day. The mountains referred to by Rodney were Morne Garnier and Morne Tortensen, which the French abandoned after two days of heavy fighting and retired inside the citadel of Fort Royal. The town surrendered on 3 February.[23] Reporting to the Admiralty a week later, Rodney praised the contribution of naval officers and seamen in 'transporting numbers of the heaviest mortars and ship's cannon, up the steepest mountains at a very considerable distance from the sea, and across the enemy's line of fire'. An army officer's account of them at work confirms the high state of morale in Rodney's fleet:

> As soon as we were all safely disembarked, our engineers were immediately set to work in raising batteries, as well to estab-lish our footing in the island as to cover us in our approaches to dislodge the enemy from their posts. For this purpose all the cannon and other warlike stores were landed as soon as possible, and dragged by the Jacks to any point thought proper. You may fancy you know the spirit of these fellows; but to see them in action exceeds any idea that can be formed of them. A hundred or two of them, with ropes and pullies, will do more than all your dray-horses in London. Let but their tackle hold, and they will draw you a cannon or mortar on its proper carriage up to any height, though the weight be never so great. It is droll enough to see them tugging along, with a good twenty-four pounder at their heels: on they go, huzzaing and hallooing, sometimes up hill, sometimes down hill; now sticking fast in the brakes, presently floundering in the mud and mire; swearing, blasting, d-m-ing, sinking, and as careless of everything but the matter committed to their charge as if death or danger had nothing to do with them. We had a thousand of these brave fellows sent to our assistance by the admiral; and the service they did us, both on shore and on the water, is incredible.[24]

All organized resistance in Martinique had ceased by 16 February. The capture of the island led to the collapse of the French position in the Leeward Islands generally and to the successive surrender of other islands. St Lucia surrendered to a squadron commanded by Captain Hervey on 26 February and Grenada to Commodore Swanton and Brigadier Walch on 5 March. On 10 April Rodney was able to report that the surrender of St Vincent completed the capture of all the French Caribbean islands, leaving St Domingo and Louisiana as the only French possessions on the far side of the Atlantic.[25]

Rodney did not have long to enjoy the euphoria of victory. On 5 March, the day that Grenada surrendered, he received a letter from the Admiralty dated 26 December informing him that Britain was at war with Spain and instructing him to commence hostilities (he had learnt that they had started sometime before this). On the same day he received intelligence to the effect that a French squadron, consisting of seven ships of the line and five frigates with 2,000 troops on board, had escaped from Brest on 23 January. On the assumption that it was heading for the West Indies, Rodney repeated his orders to all the frigates stationed to windward along the whole chain of Caribbean islands to be very vigilant, and made dispositions of his ships of the line which would give him two squadrons sufficiently strong to engage the approaching enemy squadron, whether it appeared to the north or the south of Martinique. On 9 March thirteen enemy ships, of which eight were ships of the line, were sighted 15 miles east of Martinique on a southerly course. Rodney immediately set off round the island in pursuit, but was unable to catch up with them and he learnt subsequently that, having discovered that Martinique was in British hands, they had headed for St Domingo. On the basis of credible intelligence in letters from Lyttleton, the Governor of Jamaica and Commodore Forrest, the senior naval officer there,[26] Rodney judged that island to be under imminent threat of a combined French and Spanish attack and took steps to support it. He was unable to persuade Monckton to send troops as the General did not 'think himself sufficiently authorised to detach a body of troops without orders from England'. Rodney took a different view of his own instructions and made arrangements to send to Jamaica 'without a moment's loss of time' ten ships of the line, four frigates and three bomb-vessels. Reporting to the Admiralty on 24 March he expressed the hope that 'their Lordships will not be displeased with me, if I take the liberty to construe my instructions in such a manner as to think myself authorised and obliged to succour any of His Majesty's colonies that may be in danger.'[27] Julian Corbett described Rodney's decision as 'a fine resolve, and should live as a classical example of a seamanlike interpretation of orders, and of the true spirit of command'.[28]

Two days later everything had changed. Having put to sea with the squadron for Jamaica, Rodney received from the Admiralty, when off St Kitts, his new orders sent on 5 February informing him that, following the entry of Spain into the war, an expedition of combined sea and land forces was to be mounted against Spanish colonies in the West Indies. The naval force was to be commanded by Admiral Sir George Pocock, who had distinguished himself in the East Indies and who was much senior to Rodney. The Admiralty assured him that this was not because of 'having conceived the least diffidence' of his abilities, 'but the largeness of the force destined on this important expedition, and the urgency of the present crisis requiring an officer of high rank, and one, who by being on the spot to receive the necessary instructions, could be fully apprised of the present views and intentions'.[29] The land forces were to be commanded by Lieutenant General the Earl of Albemarle and Monckton received corresponding orders from the Earl of Egremont, Secretary of State, Southern Department. These revealed that the object of the expedition was Havana in Cuba, and Monckton was required to hold all his troops in readiness for embarkation, apart from the Belle Isle contingent which was to remain behind as a garrison.[30] Rodney, by his orders, was required to provide the necessary transports and have ten ships of the line together with three or four frigates and the bomb-vessels ready to proceed on further service by the middle of April. There was now no question of Rodney himself going to Jamaica, but he took upon himself the decision that its safety must take precedence over the Havana operation and accordingly ordered Sir James Douglas to continue to Jamaica with what he described in a subsequent despatch as 'ten sail of the line . . . the number commanded by their Lordships' orders to be ready [for Pocock]'.[31] Corbett, who had praised Rodney's earlier decision to reinforce Jamaica, thought that his persistence with that plan in the changed circumstances was, at best, stretching the latitude of interpretation to its extreme limit, although he conceded that Rodney was aware, as the Home government was not, that the French squadron which had escaped from Brest was now at Cap Français in St Domingo.[32] As it happened, Douglas, having reached Jamaica, decided that the invasion threat had receded and, on his own initiative, decided to blockade Cap Français, thus protecting Pocock's approach to Cuba.[33]

When Pocock arrived at Case Navires Bay in Martinique on 26 April, Rodney was ill ashore further up the coast at St Pierre and they did not meet. If Pocock was angered by Rodney's despatch of ships to Jamaica, there is no evidence of his displeasure, but it may have motivated his decision to requisition Rodney's flagship, the *Marlborough*, thus leaving Rodney no immediate option but to move to the much smaller and unsuitable *Rochester* (50). The Havana operation was successful (the city capitulated on 13 August) and immensely lucrative for Pocock and Albemarle, but victory was won at a terrible cost in human life. The combined losses of both services, mostly from disease, ran into thousands and were worst in the Army. Of the 16,000 troops involved 5,366 men were lost between 7 June and 18 October, of whom 4,708 died of disease.[34]

When Pocock had departed for Havana, Rodney was left with a small squadron with nominal responsibility for all the Leeward Islands. His main activity was attempting to counter the activities of enemy privateers, which he described as lurking in every creek among the conquered islands and 'too much assisted by the inhabitants thereof'. For this purpose he hired a number of small armed vessels.[35] In June he was involved in an acrimonious dispute with the Army when it was found that an intermediary appointed by Monckton was creaming off a 1 per cent commission on prize money[36] and he fell out with the veteran Captain Robert Duff when he decided to shift his flag to Duff's ship, the 80-gun *Foudroyant*, the most powerful ship on the station. Rodney could have done this when he first arrived in the West Indies but had decided not to because of Duff's declared aversion to being an Admiral's captain. Rodney now changed his mind, but in deference to Duff's views decided to take Shuldham with him as his captain and to offer Duff the 64-gun *Modeste*. Duff declined the exchange as inappropriate and decided to stay in the *Foudroyant* as Rodney's captain after all. Rodney decided that this was unrealistic in view of his previously declared views and Duff went home to England as a passenger feeling much aggrieved.[37] Rodney was promoted Vice Admiral in October 1762 and the definitive treaty of peace was signed in Paris on 10 February 1763. Britain gained Canada and Florida, but returned Martinique and Guadeloupe to France and Cuba to Spain. Ill once again, Rodney left the Leeward Islands in the *Foudroyant* on 4 July and arrived in Spithead on 12 August 1763.

In the professional sense Rodney had had 'a good war', but he was bitterly disappointed with the financial rewards.[38] The good fortune of those who took part in the Havana Expedition, including his friends Keppel and Hervey, can only have aggravated his feeling of having lost out. Apart from prize money, he had failed to get a grant of land in St Vincent because Lord Egremont died before he could deal with his application. Monckton was luckier and got his grant before the Earl's death. Consolations came Rodney's way in the shape of a baronetcy granted on 21 January 1764 and the governorship of Greenwich Hospital, to which Rodney was appointed on 16 December 1765. During 1764 Rodney married again. His new bride was Henrietta (Henny) Clies, twenty years younger than him, whose mother had taken charge of Rodney's household when his first wife Jenny (née Compton) had become ill at the end of 1756. The Compton and Clies families had been acquainted in Lisbon, where Henny's father had been a merchant.

The governorship of Greenwich Hospital was a prestigious appointment, carrying with it an annual income of £1,000 and splendid living accommodation. The hospital was in fact a retirement home for old sailors of whom there were nearly 2,000 in residence.[39] The governorship was almost a sinecure. Rodney delegated the day-to-day administration to his Lieutenant Governor, Captain William Boys, and presided infrequently over the weekly meetings of the Council. However there is no doubting Rodney's concern for the welfare of ordinary sailors and on one of the rare occasions when he did preside he castigated Boys, who had risen from the lower deck, for resisting his proposal for greater generosity in the issue of greatcoats to pensioners:

Many of the poor men at the door have been your shipmates, and once your companions. Never hurt a brother sailor; and let me warn you against two things more: The first is, in future not to interfere between me and my duty as Governor, and the second is, not to object to these brave men having great coats, whilst you are so fond of one as to wear it by the side of as good a fire as you are sitting by at present. There are very few young sailors that come to London without paying Greenwich Hospital a visit, and it shall be the rule of my conduct, as far as my authority extends, to render the old men's lives so comfortable, that the younger shall say, when he goes away, 'Who would not be a sailor, to live as happy as a prince in his old age!'[40]

His less than onerous duties at Greenwich left Rodney the leisure to indulge in other activities, including gambling at White's, of which he had been a member for many years. By early 1767 it is probable that he was having money problems, but his financial ruin was assured by his decision to contest Northampton at his own expense in the 1768 election.* The estimate which put Rodney's share of the expenses at £30,000[41] is uncorroborated and may be excessive, but whatever the figure he was certainly in considerable financial difficulty thereafter. At the beginning of 1770 an attack by Spain on the small British outpost at Port Egmont in the Falklands Islands provided him, indirectly, with the opportunity both to leave the country and to enhance his earnings. This attempt to resolve by force a difference about the sovereignty of the islands raised the possibility of war with Spain, one of the consequences of which was a decision to reinforce the West Indies squadron and to send a more senior officer to relieve the commodore in charge in Jamaica. In January 1771 Lord Sandwich returned to the Admiralty and offered the appointment to Rodney, who was eager to accept but wanted to retain the governorship of Greenwich. He argued that this was a reward for past services and that others had been allowed to retain it in similar circumstances. He failed to

* See Introduction p. 7.

persuade Sandwich, but accepted the appointment as Commander-in-Chief at Jamaica none the less. The squadron to reinforce the station was ready at Spithead in May and consisted of four ships of the line and two frigates. Rodney hoisted his flag in the *Princess Amelia* (80) on 13 May, but because of contrary winds the squadron did not clear the Channel until 3 June. Most of his family accompanied him to Jamaica, but his eldest son George remained at home to pursue his career in the Army. The squadron arrived at Port Royal, Jamaica on 24 July.

Rodney had not been in Jamaica long when the schooner *Sir Edward Hawke*, commanded by Lieutenant Anthony Gibbs, returned from a cruise to report that she had been detained by two Spanish coastguard vessels and taken into Cartagena on the Caribbean coast of what is now Colombia. After two days she had been released with a warning, but it transpired that Gibbs had submitted to this treatment without even a token show of resistance. He was court-martialled and dismissed the service. Rodney sent the *Achilles* (60) and the *Guadeloupe* (28) to Cartagena to demand an apology. On his return to England, Gibbs put it about that Rodney was trying to provoke a war with Spain, and his story gained sufficient currency to alarm Sandwich at a time when the government was hopeful of negotiating a peaceful settlement to the Falklands dispute. He wrote to Rodney on 27 November expressing his concern:

I am sorry to say that the last dispatches we have received from you are not only full of interesting but very disagreeable business; I hope the accounts we shall receive concerning the reception of the *Achilles* will not bring any fresh matter to add to our apprehensions. But be that as it may, I cannot help cautioning you as a friend to be upon your guard, and to avoid by every justifiable measure the drawing this country into a war which, if it comes on too speedily, I fear we shall have cause to lament.

I cannot conceal from you that many people have industriously spread stories here that, among the foreign ministers and others, you have expressed your wishes for a Spanish war.

He ended the letter with a strong hint that if war did break out it would be necessary to send out to most stations in foreign parts larger squadrons and 'very probably senior officers'.[42] He wrote again a month later expressing his relief at the news that nothing untoward had happened when the *Achilles* and the *Guadeloupe* went to Cartagena, but regretted that Rodney had thought it appropriate to send the *Guadeloupe* back to demand an explanation of insulting remarks by a subordinate Spanish officer.[43] His fears proved again to be groundless as the Spanish blamed the apparent insult on an interpreter[44] and he was in placatory mood when he replied to a letter from Rodney expressing his unease at the tone of his correspondence:

> I take the earliest opportunity to do all in my power to remove any such impression by assuring you that everything you have done is thoroughly approved at home; and you will observe that what I wrote before was only meant to guard you against what might happen hereafter by the indiscretion of the officers under you.[45]

Despite these soothing words it is probable that this incident weakened Sandwich's previously expressed confidence* in Rodney's reliability.[46]

There was no war with Spain. Both sides found it convenient to regard the attack on Port Egmont as an unauthorized act by the Spanish governor of Buenos Aires. The settlement of the sovereignty issue was deferred indefinitely and in the meanwhile the parties agreed in secret to evacuate the Falklands to avoid any immediate reopening of the dispute.[47] The duties of a peacetime Commander-in-Chief of Jamaica were not unduly onerous. Rodney busied himself improving the water supply for ships by building an aqueduct (and in the process breaking the monopoly which controlled the supply), surveying the harbour and improving the dockyard, preventing smuggling and gathering intelligence on French and Spanish naval bases. Some of the expenditure he

* See p. 22.

incurred on these projects was subsequently challenged by the Navy Board as being inadequately accounted for, and retention of money due to him delayed his attempts to resolve his financial difficulties.

The threat of war having receded, the squadron under his command was gradually reduced so that by the time he was relieved by Rear Admiral Gayton when his three-year appointment ended in 1774, he had only a 50-gun ship, the *Portland*, together with frigates and smaller craft. His hopes of staying on in Jamaica as Governor were not fulfilled, but Sandwich, aware of Rodney's financial difficulties, gave him leave to remain there until his affairs were settled. Rodney thanked him but felt that remaining there in 'a private station' was unthinkable 'after commanding in chief with the approbation of the whole island'.[48] He returned to England with his family in the *Portland* and arrived at Spithead on 31 August 1774. His son James stayed behind as Master and Commander of the sloop *Ferret* and was lost at sea when the ship disappeared after a hurricane in the autumn of 1775.[49]

Rodney's decision to return to England was based on the fatal miscalculation that, as a Member of Parliament, he would have a nine-month period of legal immunity from his creditors. To his dismay, he learnt on arrival that Parliament had been dissolved early, depriving him of the hope of an orderly settlement of his affairs. Having tried unsuccessfully to find a government-sponsored seat in the new Parliament, and seeing no way of resolving his financial difficulties at home, he went to live in Paris in October 1774, planning to be there for only six months. He stayed for four years, his financial problems aggravated initially by the refusal of the Navy Board to release money due to him until satisfied about his expenditure in Jamaica and then, when they were released, by the fact that his creditors had a prior claim on his half-pay as a Vice Admiral and on his salary as Rear Admiral of Great Britain.*

There is little information about Rodney's life in Paris, where he was joined after a while by his wife and younger children. Through

---

* An honorary appointment procured for him by Sandwich at the time that he took up the Jamaica command.

force of circumstances they lived modestly, but Rodney appears to have been received into Paris society. His main preoccupations were the resolution of his financial affairs and the obtaining of a new appointment in the Navy. The two were interlinked since he was not eligible for re-employment while in dispute with the Navy Board. The most satisfactory development in his financial affairs was his decision to allow his son George, now in his early twenties, to take over the task of resolving them. In such matters he was level-headed and methodical in a way which his father was not. Rodney continued to keep contact with people who were or might be influential, notably (though with diminishing hope) with Sandwich. After the outbreak of war with the American colonists, he wrote to Lord George Germain, an old acquaintance, to congratulate him on his appointment as Secretary of State for the Colonies, the ministerial post which carried with it the principal responsibility for the land war in America.[50] Some time between 1776 and 1777 Rodney wrote at length to Lord Shelburne, alerting him to the dangers of a French invasion of England. His letter seems to have been prompted more by his knowledge of the weakness of the Royal Navy in home waters, much of its strength having been deployed across the Atlantic, than by any intelligence that had come his way in Paris. He also drew on his own experience during his Channel command from 1759 to 1761.[51]

In the autumn of 1776 he sent his wife on a hopeless mission to England to alert Sandwich and others to his plight. Sandwich's sympathetic reply to her letter contained a sentence which said it all:

> I am sure that if Sir George will consider the thing impartially he will see that though his merit as a sea officer is undeniable, there are reasons which make it impossible for me to prevail on His Majesty to appoint him to the command of a foreign station.

He ended:

> If it would give your ladyship any satisfaction I will certainly wait on you before you leave London, but I think such an

interview can have no other effect than giving much pain to us both, for as a man in office your husband has deprived me of the power of being useful to him, and as a private man, though I have the warmest inclination to serve him to the utmost of my ability, unless his friends can point out to me some mode in which I may be useful to him, my offer of service is, I am sensible, little more than general professions of friendship.[52]

In early 1778, at about the time that France entered into a Treaty of Amity and Commerce with the American rebels, Rodney reported to Germain through an intermediary that La Motte Piquet, commanding a French squadron, had returned the salute of two American ships, one of them commanded by John Paul Jones, thus effectively recognizing American independence.[53] By this time Rodney's position was becoming desperate. As a British admiral he was in the invidious position of living in what was potentially an enemy's country and, having run up debts in France, he was in serious difficulty with his creditors there. Help came from an unexpected quarter. The elderly Maréchal de Biron, the premier nobleman of France and the Constable of Paris, was appalled that Britain had apparently abandoned one of her senior admirals and offered him a loan to settle his French debts. After first refusing the loan Rodney accepted it on 6 May.[54] He returned to England that month able, through de Biron's extraordinary act of chivalry, to offer his services to his own country in the renewed hostilities with France.

Chapter 3

The Moonlight Battle

Rodney returned to England in May 1778 at the same time as General Burgoyne, whose defeat at Saratoga on 17 October 1777 had encouraged France to support the American rebellion, prompted not so much by sympathy for the colonists as by recognition of an opportunity to redress the humiliations of the Seven Years' War. A Treaty of Amity and Commerce between France and the American colonies had been signed on 6 February 1778, and the British Government had been made aware of it on 13 March. Its effect was to transform a domestic dispute in America into a European war in which Britain was to find herself severely overstretched, particularly when in due course Spain and then Holland joined the war against her. In these circumstances, dealing with the American rebellion became secondary to the global struggle, a struggle in which the West Indies were to assume considerable importance. 'The Sugar Islands' were said to account for one third of the overseas trade of France, and were more important at that time to the economy of Britain than were either America or the East India Company.[1] As the King himself said, 'If we lose our sugar islands, it will be impossible to raise money to continue the war.'[2] Contraband trade with the islands in gunpowder and other war supplies was vital also to the American rebels, particularly trade with the Dutch island of St Eustatius, from which it is estimated that seven or eight ships a day sailed for America during thirteen months of 1778–9.[3]

Rodney, drawing on his past experience in the West Indies, had written to Sandwich in May 1778[4] urging on him the importance of capturing either Martinique or St Lucia, both of which had been returned to France in the peace negotiations at the end of the previous war. Of the two he favoured St Lucia, mainly because of the excellence of its careenage harbour, which was capable of taking the biggest ships, and because of its favourable strategic position. Holding it would put Martinique in the same position as British-held Dominica, namely lying between two enemy islands (Dominica lay between Guadeloupe and Martinique, and Rodney's proposal would put Martinique between Dominica and a British-held St Lucia). Furthermore, in the prevailing easterly winds St Lucia was further to windward than most of the other West Indian islands and therefore well placed either to support friendly islands or to prevent help getting to those held by the enemy.*

In March 1779 Rodney submitted a short paper both to Sandwich and to Lord George Germain, the Secretary of State with responsibility for the land war in America, on how best to deploy British ships across the Atlantic on the assumption that 'in all probability the great stress of war will be carried on in the West Indies and on the coasts of America.'[5] His proposal essentially was that ships should be transferred from the West Indies to America in the hurricane season (July to November) and back again when it was over. There was a natural logic in this proposal since the roughest weather off the American coast tended to occur in the earlier part of the year, which was a good time for naval operations in the West Indies.[6]

After his return to England in May 1778 Rodney took lodgings at 4 Cleveland Row, close to St James's Palace. It was no coincidence that this proximity to a royal palace carried with it immunity from the service of writs, thus affording Rodney some protection from his creditors.[7] His financial problems were a spur to obtaining employment, but they were also an impediment to his doing so. However, at the end of that year he reached an

---

* Dominica was lost to the French in September 1778 and St Lucia was captured for the British by Admiral Barrington in December 1778.

accommodation with his creditors and shortly afterwards money due to him from the Navy Board was released.[8] His loan from the Maréchal de Biron had been repaid soon after his return to England with the aid of Drummond's Bank.[9]

With that obstacle to employment out of the way other factors were also working in his favour. In January 1778 he had been promoted Admiral of the White, making him one of the most senior British admirals. Apart from his proven ability he was a supporter of the government at a time when political allegiance was an important factor in naval appointments. In an age when professional ability alone was not enough to guarantee success, connections and patronage were essential in a naval career. For their part, those bestowing patronage looked for something in return. Political allegiances, therefore, tended to be a matter of public knowledge, and indeed Rodney, like other senior naval and army officers, had been a Member of Parliament for many years. As a result the Navy was politicized to a degree which would be unthinkable today, and appointments were both declined and withheld on political grounds, although an officer, once appointed, tended to do his duty regardless of politics.[10] Rodney, once a Whig, was now a Tory and a supporter of the government, unlike most senior officers whose key promotions had occurred during the long period of Whig ascendancy. At this time of Rodney's search for employment two events had magnified political differences within the Navy. Firstly, the Whig opposition was against the attempt to suppress the American rebellion by force and senior naval officers of that persuasion were either reluctant to serve or were regarded as unreliable by the government. Rodney's robust views on the need for firm action in America commended him to those who mattered and to the King in particular. Secondly, an indecisive battle against the French off Ushant on 27 July 1778 had resulted in two controversial courts martial in which the principal protagonists, Admirals Keppel and Palliser, were prominent supporters respectively of the opposition and the government. Rodney managed to remain fairly detached from the bitter hostilities stirred up by these events, but he was later to blame political faction for operational inefficiencies both in the fleet and in the dockyards. The Battle of Ushant is itself of interest in connection with his career since two of his future opponents in the West Indies, the Comtes de Guichen and de Grasse, fought in the battle as divisional commanders (*chefs d'escadre*) under d'Orvilliers.

When, late in 1779, there was a need to replace Admiral Byron after his failure to save Grenada, Rodney was an appropriate choice as Commander-in-Chief in the Leeward Islands, enjoying as he did the support of the King, Lord Sandwich and Lord George Germain, although Sandwich found it necessary to reassure the King that there were arrangements which would limit Rodney's involvement in financial transactions:

> If Sir George Rodney should from his indigence have any temptation to make advantage of purchasing stores or anything else of that sort, he will have no means of doing it at present, as there will be a Commissioner on the spot thro' whose hands all that business must be transacted.[11]

The commissioner in question, appointed in November 1779, was Captain John Laforey, who was promoted by Boscawen to the rank of Captain in 1758 for his gallant service at the siege of Louisbourg. As captain of the *Echo* (24) he served under Rodney in the capture of Martinique in 1762. Most recently he had taken part in the Battle of Ushant as captain of the *Ocean* (90). Sandwich's comment to the King could be taken as implying that the purpose of Laforey's appointment was to keep an eye on Rodney, but that appears not to be the case as his primary and important responsibility was to expedite the repair and cleaning of ships at English Harbour, Antigua, the main repair base on the Leeward Islands station. On an official level he had a reasonably harmonious relationship with Rodney, who made him a commodore in August 1780 to reinforce his authority in dealing with ships' captains, but they disagreed in April 1781 about naval stores seized in St Eustatius.[12]

Another appointment which may have been intended as a way of keeping an eye on Rodney was that of his Flag-Captain, Walter Young, who was recommended to him by Sandwich, but who like Laforey was a friend, or a least a close acquaintance, of Sir Charles

Middleton,* the Comptroller of the Navy.[13] Young was a newly promoted captain, middle-aged and probably a Scot, who most recently had been working as a transport agent at Deptford while on half-pay as a commander. While there he had a working relationship of sorts with Middleton. Earlier in his career Young had served as a Lieutenant in the *Guadeloupe* on the Jamaica station when Rodney had been Commander-in-Chief. What he lacked in experience as a captain he made up for with robust common sense. However, in some of his many letters to Middleton written during his time as Flag-Captain he was highly critical of Rodney, who, unaware of his disloyalty, esteemed him greatly.[14]

In November 1779 Rodney hoisted his flag in the *Sandwich* (90) and on 27 December sailed from Spithead with a large escort force accompanying a convoy of 300 merchant ships. Some of the latter were for the West Indies and some for Gibraltar and Minorca which he had orders to relieve before crossing the Atlantic to his new appointment (Gibraltar had been under blockade by the Spanish both on land and at sea since June 1779).[15] The escorts were joined by other warships from Plymouth bringing the total to twenty-eight ships of which twenty-one were ships of the line.[16] The trade for the West Indies, escorted by four warships, were detached on 7 January 1780 when 300 miles west of Cape Finisterre. Rodney was soon able to show that he had not lost his touch during his prolonged unemployment. On 8 January he encountered a convoy of sixteen store ships out of San Sebastian and captured them all together with their escort of seven warships. The largest of these was the *Guispuscuano* (64), a newly built and fully fitted ship which Rodney renamed the *Prince William* in honour of the King's third son, Prince William Henry, who was serving in the flagship of the second-in-command as a midshipman. Some of the merchant ships were loaded with naval stores and provisions for the Spanish Navy at Cadiz and others with bale goods belonging to the Royal Caracas Company. Those loaded with provisions (flour and wheat) Rodney sent on to Gibraltar under escort of the newly renamed *Prince William* and the remainder he sent to England.[17]

* Later Lord Barham.

49

On 16 January, as he approached Cape St Vincent, Rodney received a warning of a large force of Spanish warships to the south. Having rounded the Cape he was 12 miles south of it at 1.00 pm, when his leading ship reported Spanish ships to the south-east. Rodney immediately ordered his fleet to bear down on the enemy in line abreast, but before this could be accomplished the Spanish ships were seen to be trying to form line of battle ahead on the starboard tack. With the wind coming from the west this would have put them on an approximately southerly course. At 2.00 pm Rodney hauled down the signal for line abreast and ordered a general chase, to engage as the ships came up 'by rotation', meaning presumably that his leading ships should attack the sternmost Spanish ships and that the pursuing British ships should successively take on the first available disengaged Spanish ship.[18] He also ordered his ships to take the lee gage (i.e. to get on the leeward side of their opponents) to prevent the enemy's retreat into their own ports. The Spanish fleet, consisting of eleven ships of the line and two frigates, was commanded by the 42-year-old Don Juan de Lángara y Huarte, one of the brightest officers in the Spanish Navy. It was his misfortune to have become separated from the rest of the Spanish fleet, commanded by Admiral Cordoba, which had been driven into Cadiz by heavy weather.[19] Two of his own eleven ships of the line were out of sight so that his effective strength was nine. His first perception of Rodney's fleet was that it was in two columns which intended to double his outnumbered fleet (i.e. to attack it on both sides). After consultation with his captains he resolved to make a run for Cadiz, 100 miles to the south-east, where he could be reinforced by Cordoba's twenty ships at anchor there in company with four French ships, hence his attempt to get into line of battle on a southerly course.[20] But he had lost time on his consultation and had reckoned without the speed advantage which coppering had given some of Rodney's ships. By 4.00 pm the British leaders, *Defence*, *Bedford*, *Resolution* and *Edgar* had caught up and opened fire, Rodney having made the general signal to engage and close. At 4.40 pm the *San Domingo* blew up with the loss of all hands, having been engaged by three British ships, and just as a fourth, the *Bienfaisant* (Captain Macbride), was coming up. The latter was only half a cable astern and was showered with debris. The battle continued during the night with the help of a full moon. Outnumbered and prevented by heavy seas from opening their lower-deck gun ports on the lee side, from which the British were attacking, the Spanish ships surrendered or were disabled as the night wore on. The heavy weather made it difficult to board them. De Lángara's flagship lost her mizzen mast while engaged by three British ships and surrendered at 8.30 pm after the *Bienfaisant* came up and shot down her main topmast. At 2.00 am on the following day Rodney ordered his fleet to heave to after the *Monarca*, the headmost Spanish ship, had struck. Earlier she had shot away the main topmast of the *Alcide*, which had been pursuing her but she had then been forced to haul down her colours by the frigate *Apollo* (Captain Pownoll), just as the *Sandwich*, unaware of this, came up and put a broadside into her. Rodney subsequently conceded the honours to Pownoll. Of the nine Spanish ships of the line engaged in the action only two escaped, as did the two frigates; de Lángara became a prisoner of the British. However, two of the captured ships, the *San Julian* (70) and the *San Eugenio* (70), were driven ashore. The heavy weather of the previous night continued during the 17th and put several British ships, including the *Sandwich*, dangerously close to the shoals of Sanlucar. They did not get back into deep water until the following morning, when Rodney made Cape Spartel. At sunset the British fleet entered the Straits of Gibraltar.[21] Rodney anchored in Gibraltar Bay on 23 January having sent on a squadron to relieve Minorca. He got into Gibraltar on 27 January and estimated that his capture of the supplies bound for Cadiz added two years' provisions to the beleaguered garrison.[22] With him were four of the Spanish ships captured in the Moonlight Battle which, like the previously captured *Guispuscuano* (renamed *Prince William*), were taken into service in the Royal Navy. De Lángara's flagship, the *Fenix* (80) was renamed the *Gibraltar*. The *Diligente* (70), the *Monarca* (70) and the *Princesa* (70) all retained their names. Rodney said of these additions to the British Fleet,

The Moonlight Battle 16–17 January 1780

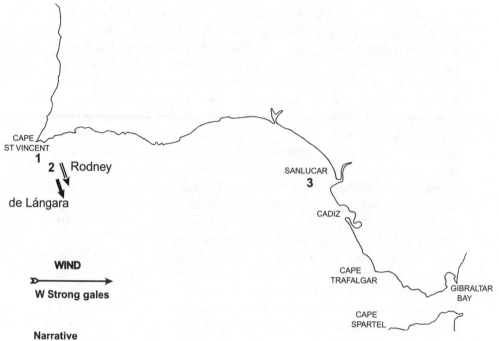

Narrative

16 January

1. 1.00 pm   The British fleet, 12 miles south of Cape St Vincent, sights the Spanish fleet to the south-east. Rodney gives the signal to bear down on the enemy in line abreast.
   Spanish ships are seen to be trying to form line of battle on the starboard tack.
   2.00 pm   Rodney hauls down the signal for line abreast and orders a general chase, to engage as the British ships come up by rotation, and to take the lee gage to prevent the enemy's retreat into their own ports.

2. 4.00 pm   As his leading ships close the enemy Rodney makes the general signal to engage and close. The four leading British ships engage shortly afterwards.
   4.40 pm   The Spanish ship, the *San Domingo,* blows up with the loss of all hands.

17 January

2. (continued)
   2.00 am After the surrender of the *Monarca,* the furthest ahead of the Spanish ships, Rodney orders his fleet to heave to.

3. The heavy weather of the previous night continues all day and puts several British ships, including the *Sandwich,* dangerously close to the shoals of Sanlucar. They do not return to deep water until the next morning (18 January), when Rodney rejoins the convoy and makes Cape Spartel. The British fleet enters the Straits of Gibraltar at sunset.

'the five Spanish men of war are as fine ships as ever swam and far superior to our seventy-four gun ships.'[23]

The relationship between Rodney and de Lángara was cordial and Rodney told Sandwich that the Spanish were 'extremely thankful for the humanity shown the prisoners'. Captain Macbride of the *Bienfaisant*, who had accepted the surrender of de Lángara, had shown particular consideration by allowing the Spanish admiral, his officers and his men to remain in the *Fenix*, in return for suitable undertakings, because of the presence of smallpox in his own ship.[24] However, Rodney used his custody of his Spanish prisoners to negotiate vigorously for the release of British prisoners held by Spain.

From a tactical point of view Rodney drew two main conclusions from the outcome of the Moonlight Battle. Firstly, it confirmed his belief in the advantage of attacking from to leeward: 'when the British fleet take the lee gage, the enemy cannot escape. This event has proved it, and I am fully convinced that every ship of the enemy struck and would have been taken possession of had the weather permitted.'[25] Secondly, it convinced him of 'the infinite utility' of copper-bottomed ships, without which, he believed, the enemy could not have been brought to action. He asked Sandwich to add a number of such ships to the West Indies squadron.[26]

While Rodney had praised his officers in his official report he told Sandwich of his concern about the effect of 'Faction and Party' in the fleet:

It is with concern that I must tell your Lordship that my brother officers still continue their absurd and illiberal custom of arraigning each other's conduct. My ears have been attempted to listen to the scandal; I have treated it with the contempt it deserved. In my opinion every officer did his duty to King and country. I have reported it so, and I hope to the satisfaction of your Lordship and the nation. The unhappy difference between Mr Keppel and Sir H. Palliser has almost ruined the Navy. Discipline in a very great measure is lost, and that eager willingness of executing the orders given by the Board of Admiralty, or by those acting under their authority, is turned into neglect; and officers presume to find fault and think, when their duty is implicit obedience. [27]

Throughout the battle Rodney, suffering from severe gout, had been confined to his cabin, where he received news from and relayed orders through his Flag-Captain, Walter Young. The most controversial aspect of the action was the claim made by Young, several months later, not only that he had masterminded the action but that it would have been even more successful if Rodney had accepted all his advice. Writing to Middleton from St Lucia on 28 June he confirmed that when the Spanish fleet was sighted only nine of de Lángara's eleven ships of the line were present. He went on to complain that by not taking his advice on the best method of sailing Rodney had wasted time in rounding Cape Finisterre and consequently nearly missed the enemy altogether. Of the action itself he wrote:

When the *Bedford* made the signal for the number she discovered, I wished to have had the signal for a general chase, as night was coming on. This the admiral opposed and ordered the signal for a line of battle ahead at two cable's distance. This I opposed in turn, conscious that a great deal of time and distance would be lost, and proposed the signal for a line of battle abreast at a cable's distance.

The admiral's ill state of health and his natural irresolution occasioned our shortening sail frequently, which prevented me from bringing the *Sandwich* so early into battle as I could have wished; and so it was with difficulty that I succeeded at last, as he attempted several times to have the ships called off from chase.[28]

Rodney was at a great disadvantage by being confined to his cabin and there is little doubt that Young, who was a sensible man, would have given him sound advice. Rodney said as much to Sandwich: 'He proves himself the very man I could have wished, excellent, diligent, brave, good officer, endued with every quality to assist a commander-in-chief. I think myself much indebted to him for the late action, and am not ashamed to acknowledge it.'[29] However, it is highly unlikely that Rodney, of all people, would have delegated his responsibility for the fleet and the convoy to a man who had not previously commanded a ship of the line, let alone a battle fleet. The responsibility was Rodney's alone and there is no doubt as to who would have taken the blame if things had gone wrong. Historians, on the whole, have not taken Young's claims too seriously.

By his achievements in the Moonlight Battle and the relief of Gibraltar Rodney had justified the faith of those who had recommended his new appointment. Sandwich was quick to congratulate him and to take the credit: 'I scarcely know how to find words to congratulate you enough upon your late glorious successes, and upon the eminent services you have done your country. The worst of my enemies now allow that I have pitched upon a man who knows his duty and is a brave, honest and able officer.' He reported that he had obtained for Rodney the thanks of both Houses of Parliament, and had made the motion in the House of Lords himself mentioning that Rodney had captured more line-of-battle ships in one action than had been taken in any one action in either of the two preceding wars.[30] Ten days later the euphoria had subsided a little and Sandwich felt compelled to take Rodney to task for leaving the *Edgar* in the Mediterranean contrary to his instructions.[31] However, that slightly sour note did not prevent the nation from showing its tangible appreciation of Rodney's achievements in due course by the grant of a pension of £2,000 per annum, and nomination as an extra Knight of the Bath.

If Rodney was acclaimed at home so too was de Lángara in his own country, where he was seen as having fought heroically against overwhelming odds despite having been seriously wounded (two head wounds and one to his right thigh).[32] His wounds were serious enough to keep him ashore until 1783 when he commanded the Spanish squadron in the West Indies, which was to have attacked Jamaica with the French, but peace intervened. His next appearance in British naval history was as an ally, when he helped Hood to capture Toulon in 1793. At the end of his career he became first the professional and then the political head of the Spanish Navy.

Chapter 4

De Guichen

On 15 February 1780, Rodney sailed from Gibraltar for the West Indies in the *Sandwich* in company with the *Ajax, Montagu* and *Terrible,* all coppered seventy-fours, together with the *Pegasus* (32) and the captured *San Vincente* (10). On arrival at Barbados on 17 March he was displeased to find no message as to a rendezvous with his second-in-command, Rear Admiral Hyde Parker,* but learnt from local merchants that he was in Gros Islet Bay, St Lucia. He also learnt that French reinforcements, under the Comte de Guichen, had left Brest on 3 February for the West Indies. He sent his three largest ships out from Barbados to look for the French ships, but they were unsuccessful, and de Guichen arrived at Fort Royal, Martinique on 22 March with 16 ships of the line, 4 frigates and 83 merchant ships. There he took under his wing the squadron of the Comte de Grasse, who had been in command in the West Indies.[1] Five days later Rodney arrived in Gros Islet Bay to join Hyde Parker, a tetchy sixty-six year old known in the Navy as 'Old Vinegar'. He had served under Rodney during the bombardment of Le Havre in July 1759 as captain of the frigate *Brilliant* (36). Thereafter he had served in the East Indies and off Manila during the remainder of the Seven Years' War and had then been un-employed for much of the interval between that war and the

---

* Later Vice Admiral Sir Hyde Parker (1714–1782), father of the admiral whose signal Nelson ignored at Copenhagen.

American War of Independence. He was promoted to the rank of rear admiral in 1778 and accompanied Byron to North America as his second-in-command. In that capacity he had been present at the action off Grenada on 6 July 1779, and when Byron was recalled a month later Parker had been left temporarily in command in the West Indies.[2] He had chosen Gros Islet Bay, a well-defended anchorage, in order to keep watch on the French, only 30 miles away in Fort Royal, their main West Indian base.

Luc-Urbain du Boëxic, the Comte de Guichen, had been at sea since the age of eighteen. He had a reputation as one of the foremost tacticians in the French Navy, but although six years older than Rodney had considerably less experience of high command. He had taken part in the inconclusive action off Ushant in 1778 which led to the Keppel and Palliser courts martial, but had served there as a squadron commander (*chef d'escadre*) under d'Orvilliers. The fleets at the disposal of Rodney and de Guichen were, on paper, more or less equal. Rodney had twenty-one ships of the line and de Guichen twenty-three. The French ships, because they were recently out of Brest, were generally in better condition than the British ships, particularly those which had been in the West Indies for some time. Shortly after his arrival de Guichen had approached St Lucia but had taken fright after seeing the defences and returned to Fort Royal.

From 2 April Rodney tried unsuccessfully for two days to lure de Guichen out to battle, taking his whole fleet off Fort Royal Bay and getting it close enough 'to count all their guns, and at time within random shot of some of their forts'.[3] De Guichen chose to remain in port but Rodney's opportunity came when his lookout ships reported the sailing on 13 April of de Guichen's fleet. On board, in addition to the ship's companies, were 3,000 troops under the command of the Marquis de Bouillé, the enterprising forty-year-old soldier and Governor of Martinique. He and de Guichen intended, having first seen on its way a convoy to St Domingo, to go round the north of Martinique and double back to attack Barbados before Rodney could get there to protect it.[4] Rodney set off in pursuit and sighted the French on the 16th about 24 miles west of the Pearl Rock, a large isolated rock off the north-western side of Martinique. By five in the evening he was able to

Rodney v. de Guichen off Martinique 17 April 1780
Rodney's First Attempt at Concentration

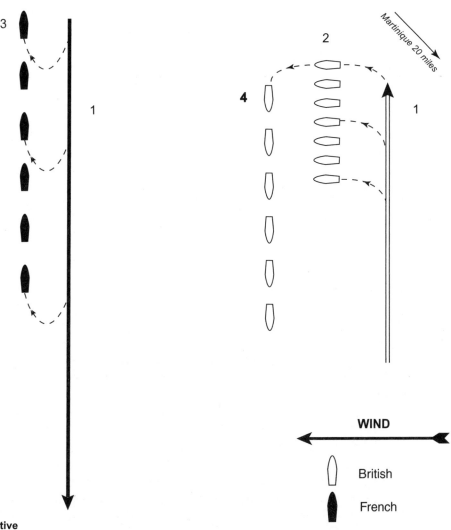

WIND

⬭ British

⬛ French

Narrative

6.45 am 1. Opposing fleets passing slowly on opposite courses in line ahead, French (22 ships) southbound and well extended, British (20 ships) northbound and more compact. Rodney signals his intention to make a concentrated attack on de Guichen's rear.

8.30 am 2. Rodney orders his fleet to form line of battle abreast and bear down on de Guichen's rear.

3. At about the same time de Guichen's fleet executes an order to wear together into line ahead northbound. As a result his threatened rear is now his van and can be supported by the rest of his fleet coming up astern.

9.00 am 4. His attack thwarted, Rodney orders his fleet to haul to the wind together into line ahead southbound. As a result the opposing fleets are again passing on opposite courses.

discern that the enemy fleet consisted of twenty-three ships of the line, one 50-gun ship and five small ships. At nightfall he formed his fleet in line of battle ahead and stationed two frigates to keep watch on the French fleet during the night.

At daylight on 17 April Rodney saw the French forming line of battle ahead and made a signal to his own fleet for line ahead at a distance of 2 cables (480 yards).[5] These were the opening moves in the Battle of Martinique, which Rodney later regarded as his most important action, although the results fell far short of what he intended. Having previously informed his captains of his intention to concentrate the whole of his fleet against part of the French Fleet,[6] he nearly achieved this on two occasions during the action. At 8.45 am and again around midday, he had his whole fleet, as a result of skilful manœuvring, opposite part of an overextended French line. On both occasions he was thwarted – on the first occasion by de Guichen's order to his fleet to change course, and on the second by the failure of some of his own captains to comprehend what was required of them.

Rodney's first attempt at concentration began at 6.45 am when he signalled his intention to attack the enemy's rear with his whole force. At 7.00 am, 'perceiving the fleet too much extended' he made the signal for line of battle at one cable's length only. At 8.30 am he ordered his fleet to form line of battle abreast and bear down on the French rear, now 12 miles to leeward,[7] but as his ships came round on to their new course de Guichen's fleet executed an order to wear together into line ahead northbound. As a result his threatened rear was now his van, which could be supported by the rest of his fleet coming up astern. Rodney assumed that de Guichen had ordered this manoeuvre as a counter-measure because he had discerned what the British intended, but according to the account of de Guichen's chief of staff he had decided to turn his fleet to the north before Rodney began his run down towards him and their respective manoeuvres had coincided.[8] His intention thwarted, Rodney ordered his fleet to haul to the wind into line ahead southbound, with the result that the British and the French were again on opposite courses (see diagram p. 59).

At 10.10 am Rodney began to position his fleet, for his second attempt at concentration, by ordering it to wear together on to the same course as the French and at 10.36 am ordered line of battle ahead at two cables, on the new (starboard) tack. At 11.00 am he made the signal to prepare for battle 'to convince the whole fleet I was determined to bring the enemy to an engagement'.[9] That signal was followed immediately by a signal to alter course to port, i.e. towards the enemy in a slanting direction.[10] Fifty minutes later Rodney's fleet, closed up to 2 cables, was opposite the centre and rear of the extended French line and therefore in an ideal position from which to launch a concentrated attack on that part of the line. Rodney was clear in his own mind as to what should happen next and assumed that it should be just as clear to his captains. 'At fifty minutes after eleven, A.M., I made the signal for every ship to bear down, and steer for her opposite in the enemy's line, agreeable to the 21st article of the additional fighting instructions.'[11] What he intended was a repeat of his manoeuvre aborted earlier that morning, namely that every ship should sail down towards the enemy line, now about 3 miles away,[12] towards the French ship then abreast of her. It was implicit in the idea of concentration that some French ships would be attacked by more than one British ship. That, indeed, was the whole point of Rodney's plan. Unfortunately, many of his captains did not understand the signal to mean that.

The key words of Article 21 were 'every ship in the squadron is to steer for the ship of the enemy, which, from the disposition of the two squadrons, it must be her lot to engage.' To captains schooled in eighteenth century naval tactics those words usually meant that each ship should steer for her corresponding ship in the enemy line, and in particular that the leading ship should steer for the enemy's leading ship. In many circumstances that was a prudent thing to do because failure to cover the leading ships in the enemy line as well as the rear ships would expose one's own line to being 'doubled', i.e. being attacked on both sides.[13] This, certainly, was how the signal was interpreted by Captain Robert Carkett, who commanded the British lead ship, the *Stirling Castle*. He set off towards the French lead ship which was then probably at least

61

Rodney v. de Guichen off Martinique 17 April 1780
Rodney's Second Attempt at Concentration

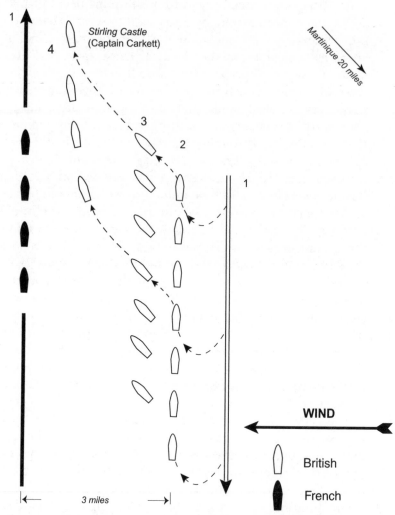

1

Stirling Castle
(Captain Carkett)

4

3

2

1

Martinique 20 miles

WIND

British

French

|← —   3 miles   — →|

Narrative

9.00 am 1. After the failure of Rodney's first attempt at concentration the opposing fleets are again passing on opposite courses with the French line much the more extended.

10.10 am 2. Rodney orders his fleet to wear together onto the same course as the French.

11.00 am 3. Rodney orders his fleet to alter course to port and then, at 11.50 am, to bear down on the enemy and steer for the 'ship which...it must be her lot to engage', intending an attack by his whole force on the French centre and rear.

4. The signal is misinterpreted by Captain Carkett in the leading British ship, the *Stirling Castle*, who, in accordance with orthodox practice, steers for his opposite number leading the French van, and is followed by other ships in Hyde Parker's Van Division seeking out their opposite numbers in the extended French line. As a result Rodney's second attempt at concentration is ruined.

3 miles ahead and was followed by the two ships astern of him and by the commander of the van division, Admiral Hyde Parker in the *Princess Royal*, who had interpreted Rodney's signal in the same way, as had Commodore Thomas Collingwood in the *Grafton*, the leading ship in the centre division. His master's log recorded: 'Bore away for our opponent, which bore N.N.W. [i.e. fine on the port bow] about two or three miles.'[14] Two captains in the van division, Captain Bowyer of the *Albion* and Captain Douglas of the *Terrible*, who appeared to understand what Rodney intended were ordered by Hyde Parker to conform to his interpretation.[15]

Rodney's second attempt at concentration was ruined, but it was too late to remedy the situation by signal and the British fleet was committed to action. The van division and the leading ship of Rodney's own centre division, seven ships in all, were opening out the distance between themselves and the rest of the British fleet as they steered towards their corresponding ships in the French line. Rodney had lost effective control of the action which developed into three separate actions. The headmost ships began to engage at around 1.10 pm, but at too great a distance.[16] Because of uneven station keeping in the vans of both fleets the three leading ships, *Stirling Castle*, *Ajax* and *Elizabeth* found themselves engaging five French ships, whereas the next three, *Princess Royal* (Admiral Hyde Parker), *Albion* and *Terrible* were opposed to only one French ship between them.[17] At about 3.30 pm Parker's division succeeded in driving some of the leading French ships out of the line and causing them to take refuge under the lee of their own centre.[18] Shortly afterwards he ordered all his ships to tack and they rejoined the centre.

Rodney's centre division did not go into action until about 1.45 pm because the enemy were further away in this part of the line.[19] Rodney in the *Sandwich* and the three ships astern of him, *Suffolk*, *Boyne* and *Vigilant*, attacked the ships immediately astern of de Guichen, driving three of them out of the line.[20] At 2.20 pm de Guichen, believing Rodney intended to lead some of his ships through the gap thus created, signalled his ships to wear together in order to cut Rodney off, but when he realized that this was not Rodney's intention he cancelled the signal.[21]

The *Sandwich*, however, did inadvertently go through the gap alone and Rodney found de Guichen's flagship, the *Couronne*, on his weather bow. Of the two ships ahead of Rodney in the British line, the *Cornwall* and the *Yarmouth*, the former was engaging the ship ahead of de Guichen, but was too far to windward, and the latter was even further to windward, laying to with her main and mizzen topsails aback.[22] It emerged later that her captain, Nathaniel Bateman, was so perplexed as to how he should respond to Rodney's signal that he was unable to decide to do anything, for which he was later court-martialled and dismissed the Service.

Seeing Rodney unsupported de Guichen's flagship and her seconds (i.e. the two ships closest to her) wore out of the line to engage the *Sandwich*, who fought them off for an hour and a half, taking considerable punishment before drawing away to windward.[23] She had seventy shots in her hull on the starboard side and extensive damage to masts and rigging. During the action she had used 160 barrels of powder and 3260 round shot.[24] It is not clear how the *Sandwich* came to sustain most of the damage on her starboard side. Accounts of this part of the action suggest that the *Couronne* and her seconds were to leeward of Rodney's flagship and this is consistent with Luny's painting (see Plate No. 12) which also shows all the ships involved on the same heading. For the *Sandwich* to be engaged on her starboard side and at the same time to be to windward of her opponents this heading must have been southerly, whereas the general heading of both fleets was northerly. If that was the case, one can only assume that the *Sandwich* turned either before or during the engagement.

The distance between the opposing rear divisions appears to have been too great for effective fighting, but at about 3.00 pm Captain John Houlton, commanding the *Montagu*, decided to get closer. The *Montagu* was raked twice in doing so, and on reaching the French line was unable to come back on to the starboard tack for lack of wind. Houlton therefore went round on the port (south-bound) tack in order to discharge his starboard guns against the enemy. At this point the *Triomphant*, flagship of the Comte de Sade, wore round to the south together with four other French ships. In the process three of these ships got entangled with one another and were fired on by the *Montagu*, but Houlton was wounded and left the deck. When the French ships had got clear they in turn fired on the *Montagu*, severely damaging her. The command devolved upon Lieutenant Robert Appleby, who, having consulted his wounded captain, decided to withdraw from the action and signal for assistance. He was later court-martialled but was honourably acquitted (see page 74).[25] Some time after 3.00 pm Admiral Rowley wore out of the line with some of his ships including the *Vengeance* (Commodore Hotham) in order to pursue the French southbound rear division (both sides soon wore back).[26] Rodney was incensed, first of all his van division and now Rowley's rear division had effectively abandoned him. This certainly seems to be how the French perceived it. According to the Marquis de Bouillé, who later met Rodney in London, one of his officers who was with de Guichen in the *Couronne* consoled the despondent French Admiral by exclaiming, 'Courage, General! The English desert their commander.'[27] Rowley's explanation, which Rodney demanded the next day, was that the enemy's rear having given way, and worn round on to the other tack,

> I conceived it to be my duty to follow them, therefore wore and brought them to action on the larboard [port] tack; soon after which they gave way and wore back to the northward, in which I likewise followed them, and made all the sail I possibly could to renew the engagement with them, but the shattered condition of my sails and rigging prevented my effecting it.
>
> These, Sir, are the reasons I have to offer for the movement you allude to, conceiving, from the signal you made previous to the action, that 'twas your intention to make the greatest impression upon their rear.[28]

Rodney's crushing response was that he required only obedience from inferior officers, 'the painful task of thinking belongs to me.' [29]

Rodney v. de Guichen off Martinique 17 April 1780
Closing Stages

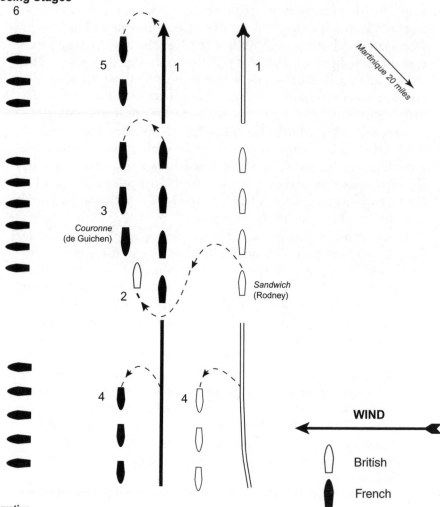

Martinique 20 miles

5

Couronne
(de Guichen)

Sandwich
(Rodney)

WIND

British

French

Narrative

2.00 pm   1. Both fleets generally engaged but the range between their respective rear divisions is too great to be effective.

        2. The French centre gives way and Rodney's flagship, the *Sandwich,* goes through the French line near de Guichen's flagship, the *Couronne.*

        3. The *Couronne,* supported by two other ships, wears out of line to engage the *Sandwich,* which keeps them at bay for 1 1/2 hours.

        4. Rodney is not supported by Rowley's rear division which wears out of line to engage the French rear division.

3.30 pm   5. The leading French ships take refuge from the British under the lee of their own line.

4.15 pm   6. The French Fleet withdraws to leeward.

De Guichen withdrew his fleet to leeward at about 4.15 pm and the battle was over. Casualty figures for the British were 120 killed and 354 wounded, and for the French 222 killed and 537 wounded.[30] Rodney, with his flagship badly damaged, and his fleet scattered to the north and to the south, was in no position to pursue but was left to contemplate the ruin of his well-conceived plan for a decisive victory.

Opinions vary as to what went wrong. Rodney attributed the failure to inattention to signals and suspected that in some cases there might even have been deliberate disobedience intended to harm the government. He said as much in a letter to Sandwich written shortly after the battle,[31] and writing to his wife three months later repeated his suspicion: 'Part, I am sure, was villainy, with the hope of upsetting the Administration. I have told them so, and if it is necessary can bring my charge home.'[32] Those suspicions seem far-fetched to us in an age when it would be highly unusual for serving officers to be motivated by party political consid-erations, but that there was an element of indiscipline within the fleet is suggested by an incident referred to by Sir Gilbert Blane.* He had been told by an officer of Marines on board the *Cornwall*, the ship immediately ahead of the *Sandwich* in the English line, that during the action, as the smoke cleared away, he saw the *Sandwich* at a great distance and remarked to one of the lieutenants, 'We have made a great mistake here. There is a signal flying for a close action at two cable's length asunder, and we are a league ahead of the Admiral. Pray tell the Captain.' To which the Lieutenant bluntly replied, 'No, damn him, let him find it out himself.' Blane goes on to say that while Rodney spoke in the highest terms of the bravery of his officers, he said that they were influenced by a spirit of party and that there was 'not a Captain on board his fleet who did not think himself capable of being Prime Minister of Great Britain'.[33] According to Blane Rodney had notified every captain, before the battle, either by written or oral communication, of his intention to concentrate his attack on part of the French Fleet.[34] It is clear from what happened that some captains did understand what was

* Rodney's Physician to the Fleet.

required of them and either acted accordingly or were prevented from doing so by their divisional commanders, but those who understood were in a minority. Most did not. This suggests that in the three weeks which had elapsed between Rodney's assumption of command and the action against de Guichen he had simply not had enough time to impress his will and his personality upon the fleet. With the wisdom of hindsight it also suggests that in the short time available he did not ensure that the key people were adequately briefed, of whom the most important were his sub-ordinate admirals and commodores and the captains who were to occupy the first and last places in the British line. In any concentration of force which involved bearing down on the enemy in or nearly in line abreast those two captains would effectively be in the position of sheepdogs ensuring that the flock kept together in a compact group. Having said that, Rodney was in a rather different position from Nelson whose painstaking briefing of his officers before Trafalgar is legendary. Nelson had a well-worked-out plan of attack, whereas Rodney had no more than an intention, namely to concentrate the whole of his fleet against part of the enemy fleet. His opponent, de Guichen, was reputed to be the foremost tactician in the French Navy and precisely how Rodney achieved his intended concentration of force would depend on how events unfolded on the day.

In analyses of what went wrong one key factor is sometimes overlooked. Rodney made two attempts to bring superior force to bear on part of the French fleet, the first starting at 6.45 am and the second at 11.00 am. It is the latter which has attracted the controversy, but in the earlier operation Rodney's subordinate admirals and captains did precisely what he wanted them to do. His fleet was bearing down in a concentrated pack on an over-extended French line when the attack was aborted by de Guichen's change of course. Rodney achieved the compliance of his fleet on that occasion by using unambiguous signals. He ordered a formation (line abreast) and a course to steer (towards the enemy). He began the second attempt in much the same way, ordering an alter-ation of course to port which resulted in his whole fleet approaching the enemy on a slanting course. From that point he could, by signalling further changes of course or formation as necessary, have 'conducted' his fleet to whichever part of the enemy line he wished to.[35] Instead he chose a signal fraught with ambiguity in that part of it which ordered captains to steer for the ship 'which . . . it must be their lot to engage'. Rodney intended that each captain should steer for the enemy ship which was then abreast of him, but the idea that they must mark their opposite number in the enemy line was so deeply ingrained in eighteenth-century tactical thinking that the offending captains probably failed to consider the rest of Article 21, which required them to preserve the distance between ships ordered in the signal for line ahead (in this case 2 cables). In full it read:

> If the squadron be sailing in line of battle ahead to windward of the enemy, and the commander-in-chief would have the course altered in order to lead down to them, he will hoist an union flag at the maintopgallant mast head and fire a gun; whereupon every ship in the squadron is to steer for the ship of the enemy, which, from the disposition of the two squadrons, it must be her lot to engage, notwithstanding the signal for the line ahead will be kept flying; making or shortening sail in such proportion so as to preserve the distance assigned by the signal for the line, in order that the whole squadron may, as near as possible, come into action at the same time.[36]

While the ambiguity in the middle part of the article may explain why some captains and Admiral Hyde Parker got it wrong, they were clearly in breach of the requirement to maintain a distance of 2 cables between ships placed on them by the latter part of the article. In some cases they allowed the distance to open out to a mile or more. Furthermore Rodney's 6.45 am signal of his intention to attack the French rear, although it had been hauled down after it had been answered, was still in force, but captains may have been confused on this point since four hours had elapsed and much had happened since it had first been hoisted. Rodney could have removed those doubts by repeating the signal. It is not clear why

Rodney chose the ambiguous Article 21 instead of the simpler and more effective combination of signals he had used in the morning. It may be because he believed, wrongly, that de Guichen had 'penetrated' his intention and altered course to thwart it and that to repeat the earlier signals would be to invite the same response. [37]

One curious aspect of this action is akin to the dog that did not bark. Rodney's Flag-Captain, Walter Young, usually critical of Rodney in his letters to Middleton, was on this occasion entirely supportive: 'confident I am, had the captains attended to the signals and the movements of the Sandwich, the day would have been a glorious one indeed.'[38] Clearly he thought that Rodney's choice of signal, in which he may have had a say, was appropriate.

Aggrieved as Rodney was by the conduct of several officers, he mentioned only one by name in his official despatch of 26 April, namely Captain Robert Carkett of the *Stirling*, of whom he said:

 Had Captain Carkett, who led the van, properly obeyed my signal for attacking the enemy, and agreeable to the 21st Article of the 21st Additional Fighting Instructions, bore down instantly to the ship at that time abreast of him, instead of leading as he did to the van ship, the action had commenced much sooner, and the fleets engaged in a more compact manner, and the enemy's centre and rear must have been taken or destroyed.

His penultimate paragraph was a stinging rebuke to the defaulters in general:

 I cannot conclude without acquainting their Lordships, that the French Admiral, who appeared to me to be a brave and gallant officer, had the honour to be nobly supported during the whole action – 'tis with concern inexpressible, mixed with indignation, that the duty I owe my Sovereign and my country obliges me to acquaint your Lordships, that during the action with the French Fleet, on the 17th instant, His Majesty's, the British flag was not properly supported.[39]

70

The last sentence of that paragraph was omitted from the Despatch as published by the Admiralty, as was the reference to Carkett, who learnt about it somehow and wrote to Rodney, whose reply was forthright but written more in sorrow than in anger. Carkett joined the Navy as an able seaman, probably in 1734, and was appointed to the *Plymouth* as a midshipman four years later. He was serving in her in that capacity when Rodney became her captain, in what was his first command, in 1742. In the Seven Years' War Carkett distinguished himself in an action off Cartagena in February 1758 in which the *Monmouth* (64) took on single-handedly the French *Foudroyant* (80). When Captain Arthur Gardiner of the *Monmouth* was killed the command devolved on Carkett as first lieutenant. He fought on for three hours until both ships had been brought to a standstill. When two other British ships came up in support the *Foudroyant* surrendered to Carkett. He was immediately promoted to command the prize and was confirmed in post rank shortly afterwards.[40]

Rodney wrote:

I have received your letter of yesterday, acquainting me, that you are credibly informed, that in my public letter to the Admiralty, relative to the action with the French fleet, on the 17th of April last, your name was mentioned.

It certainly was; and that you mistook, and did not properly obey my signal for attacking the enemy, agreeable to the 21st article of the additional fighting instructions, by not bearing down instantly to the enemy's ship then opposed to you, but led to the van ship, notwithstanding you had answered my signals, signifying that it was my intention to attack the enemy's rear, which signal I had never altered; of course, it behoved every officer to have paid the utmost attention to it.

Your leading in the manner you did, induced others to follow so bad an example; and thereby forgetting that the signal for the line was only at two cables' length distance from each other, the van division was led by you to more than two leagues distance from the centre division, which was thereby exposed to the greatest strength of the enemy, and not properly supported.

Could I have imagined your conduct and inattention to signals had proceeded from any thing but error in judgment, I had certainly superseded you, but God forbid I should do so for error in judgment only. I only resolved, Sir, not to put it in your power to mistake again upon so important an occasion as the leading a British fleet to regular battle.

You must now, Sir, however painful the task, give me leave fairly to tell you that during the time you have been under my command, you have given me more reason to find fault with your conduct as an officer, than any other in the fleet, (Captain Bateman excepted) by your inattention to signals, and, Sir, by negligently performing your duty and not exerting yourself as it behoved the oldest captain in the fleet, by setting an example of briskness, activity, and scrupulous attention to signals.

Did you do so? When, upon the first signal I made for a line of battle abreast, and then going down to provoke the enemy to come out to battle, you hauled your wind, instead of making all the sail you possibly could to get into your station, agreeable to the first article of the additional fighting instructions, and thereby set a very bad example to all the young captains.

Judge yourself what I must have felt, to observe, that the two oldest captains of the fleet I had the honour to command were the only persons I had just reason to reprimand by public signal, and let them know they had not obeyed. Your almost constantly keeping to windward of your station in sailing afterwards; the repeated signals made for the ship you commanded to get into her station; your being at an amazing distance from the fleet the night before the battle; my being obliged to send a frigate to order you down; your being out of your station at daybreak, notwithstanding the line of battle was out all night. All this conduct indicated an inattention which ought not to have been shown by an officer who had been bred in the good old discipline of the Western Squadron; and which nothing but the former service you had done your king and country, and my firm belief of your being a brave man, could have induced me, as commander of a great fleet, to overlook.

You may judge what pain it has given me to write this letter to an officer I have known so long, and have always had a regard for; but in great national concerns, and where the service of my king and country is intrusted to my care, it behoves me to do my duty, and to take care that those under my command do theirs. Both of which, without favour or partiality, I shall strictly adhere to.[41]

Carkett's attempt to put his side of the story to the Admiralty came to nothing as he and the *Stirling Castle* were lost off Cap Français, St Domingo in the violent hurricane of October 1780.[42] If other officers escaped personal criticism in Rodney's Despatch after the Battle of Martinique, they were not spared in a private letter to Lord Sandwich written on 31 May (in an earlier letter to Sandwich Rodney had referrred in general terms to 'barefaced disobedience to orders and signals').[43] He expressed his pleasure that Rear Admiral Hyde Parker was returning home:

He is a dangerous man with a very bad temper, hostile in the highest degree to the Administration and capable of anything, if he thinks he is within the pale of barely doing his duty . . . Mr Parker chose to lay with his whole for more than half the battle an idle spectator, and would not permit two gallant officers to do their duty,* but forced them to continue in-active with himself, although he saw the centre attacked by a superior force and in danger.[44]

Referring to Rear Admiral Joshua Rowley who had led the rear division away from the flagship in order to deal with the French rear he wrote:

I don't know which is of the greatest detriment to a State, a designing man or man without abilities entrusted with

---

* Captain Bowyer of the *Albion* and Captain Douglas of the *Terrible*.

command. Had not Mr Rowley presumed to think, when his duty was only obedience, the whole French rear and and the centre had certainly been taken. [45]

He criticized Commodore Hotham for following Rowley and finally referred, sympathetically this time, to Commodore Collingwood, who had served under him in the invasion of Martinique in 1762:

> The best and bravest officer under my command has taken his following Mr Parker's bad example so much to heart that it has destroyed him. Nothing that I could say, do or write to him could restore his peace of mind, and with the greatest concern I must acquaint your Lordship that that gallant officer has lost his senses for many days, and yesterday was put on board the Brilliant frigate to go to Lisbon, but it is impossible for him to arrive at that place.[46]

Collingwood died at sea on 2 June 1780.[47]

The courts martial of Lieutenant Robert Appleby of the *Montagu* and Captain Nathaniel Bateman of the *Yarmouth* took place respectively at St Kitts in August 1780 and in New York in October 1780. Both officers had incurred Rodney's wrath for withdrawing their ships from the action but the circumstances were very different. In the case of Appleby, who had taken over the command of the *Montagu* from his wounded captain, the Court found that the charge of withdrawing from the enemy without signal or order for doing so had been proved, but 'by no means to the great detriment of His Majesty's service; so far from it that it has been clearly proved to the Court that the ship must unavoidably have fallen into the hands of the enemy, had she not been withdrawn from the action at the time she was.' Appleby was honourably acquitted.[48]

Captain Bateman of the *Yarmouth* was less fortunate. Like Carkett, he was an elderly captain who had come up from the lower deck and who had originally been promoted for bravery, in his case in the action off Toulon on 11 February 1744.[49] On 17 April 1780 he was not the only captain who had difficulty interpreting

Rodney's signal at 11.50 am ordering every ship to bear down and steer for her opposite in the enemy's line. He decided to follow the ship ahead of him, the *Grafton* (Commodore Collingwood), as she followed the van division led by Carkett in search of the enemy van; but she was a much faster sailer and soon left the *Yarmouth* far behind. Uncertain as to what to do next Bateman drew out of the line to windward and hove to with his main and mizzen topsails aback. He spent an hour or more in that state and failed to support Rodney's flagship, the *Sandwich*, while she was heavily engaged, more or less abreast of the *Yarmouth*, with de Guichen's flagship, the *Couronne* and two other ships. This was the essence of the charge against him, coupled with failing to respond to Rodney's signals to get closer until towards the end of the action. The Court found against him and he was dismissed the service with a recommendation for clemency, it having appeared to the Court 'that Captain Bateman's misconduct did not arise from cowardice or disaffection, but from diffidence and error in judgment'. This recommendation availed him nothing. His applications in 1781 and 1792 to be reinstated were turned down by the Admiralty.[50] Rodney was dismayed both by the acquittal of Appleby and by the leniency of Bateman's sentence and he resolved in future to send 'high delinquents' home for trial. [51]

When the fighting was ended on 17 April by de Guichen's withdrawal Rodney was unable to pursue him because of damage to several of his ships and to the *Sandwich* in particular.

However, the French fleet was sighted three days later attempting to return to Fort Royal Bay in Martinique, the only place where de Guichen could repair his battle damage. Rodney succeeded in cutting him off and de Guichen, rather than face another action, took shelter under Guadeloupe. By 25 April the French were in the vicinity of Antigua.[52]

Believing it to be the only way to bring de Guichen to action Rodney decided to get to Fort Royal Bay before him.[53] He kept his fleet off that port for two days from 25 April until the condition of several of his ships, and the lee currents, made it necessary for him to put in first to Gros Islet Bay, St Lucia and then into Choc Bay nearby, in order to land sick and wounded men and to water and refit the fleet. He detached frigates 'both to leeward and to windward of every island, in order to gain intelligence of the motions of the enemy, and timely notice of their approach towards Martinique'.[54]

On 6 May, having refitted his fleet as best he could, Rodney received intelligence of de Guichen's fleet approaching Martinique from the east. Having replenished his stores in St Eustatius, de Guichen had set out with the intention of seizing St Lucia.[55] Rodney put to sea with nineteen ships of the line, two 50-gun ships and several frigates. He was obliged to leave behind the *Grafton* and the *Fame*, the former because her masts were totally unserviceable and the latter because she had been condemned as unseaworthy. After beating to windward between St Lucia and Martinique for four days Rodney sighted the French fleet on 10 May about 9 miles to windward. Pointe des Salines, the southernmost point of Martinique was then 15 miles away bearing NNE. Rodney was joined on that day by Captain Affleck in the *Triumph*, bringing him up to twenty sail of the line. De Guichen's fleet consisted of 23 ships of the line, 7 frigates and 4 smaller ships. For the next nine days Rodney pursued the French to windward, but having the advantage of the wind and faster sailing ships the French had no difficulty in keeping out of reach. However, each day at around 2.00 pm, when the prevailing easterly wind was steadiest, de Guichen teased the British by bearing down on them with his fleet in line abreast and then coming back on the wind at 'little more than random shot distance'.[56]

On the 12 May Rodney had hoisted his flag in the *Venus* frigate where he was to remain throughout the time that the two fleets were in contact, including during the brief engagements on 15 and 19 May. His object was by close supervision to instil the discipline which he had found lacking on 17 April:

As I had given public notice to all my captains, &c.,&c.,&c., that I should hoist my flag in one of my frigates, and that I expected implicit obedience to every signal made, under the certain penalty of being instantly superseded, it had an

Rodney v. de Guichen off Martinique 15 May 1780
Opening Stages

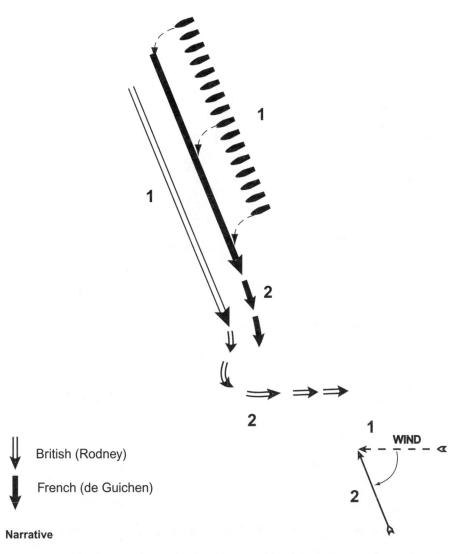

British (Rodney)

French (de Guichen)

Narrative

12.30 pm 1. Wind easterly, French to windward. Rodney, having sailed to leeward as if to withdraw has encouraged de Guichen to bear down in pursuit. Rodney hauls his wind into line ahead on the port tack (course SSE) and de Guichen does the same. The British van is about five ships ahead of the French.

2.00 pm 2. The wind veers to SSE enabling the British to weather the French line.

Rodney v. de Guichen off Martinique 15 May 1780
Closing Stages

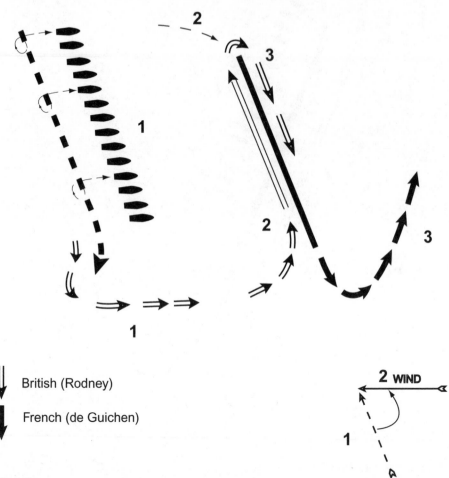

↓↓ British (Rodney)

↓ French (de Guichen)

Narrative

3.30 pm 1. The French, finding the British to windward, wear together in order to escape.

6.00 pm 2. The wind backs to easterly, allowing the French to weather the British by tacking to the south. The British bear away in succession on to a parallel and opposite course to the French.

8.00 pm 3. The British van, having reached the end of the French line, tacks in succession on to the same course as the French. The French respond with a similar manoeuvre, tacking in succession to the north to weather the British and make their escape.

admirable effect, as they were all convinced, after their late gross behaviour, that they had nothing to expect at my hands but instant punishment to those who neglected their duty. My eye upon them had more dread than the enemy's fire, and they knew it would be fatal. No regard was paid to rank – admirals as well as captains, if out of their station, were instantly reprimanded by signals, or messages sent by frigates: and, in spite of themselves, I taught them to be, what they had never been before – *officers*.[57]

On 15 May Rodney resolved to lure de Guichen into action by bearing away and making sail as if withdrawing. The French, bearing down as they had done every day, came much closer than usual, with their van ship abreast of Rodney's centre. At this point, at approximately 2.00 pm, the wind unexpectedly veered from E to SSE enabling Admiral Rowley's van division to tack and get to windward of the enemy (see diagram). The French responded by wearing together and attempting to escape on the starboard tack, but by this time the wind had backed to easterly, enabling the French to come about on to the port tack to windward of the British. In doing so they effectively crossed the 'T' of the British line. Rodney's lead ship, the *Albion*, commanded by Captain Bowyer, continued towards the French line reaching it at about 7.00 pm. In doing so she was exposed to the guns of fifteen ships taking considerable punishment before tacking to the north and leading Rowley's van division on a parallel and opposite course to the French line, which it engaged as it passed along it from centre to rear. The remainder of the British fleet was unable to get close enough to get into action 'without wasting his Majesty's powder and shot, the enemy wantonly expending theirs at such a distance as to have no effect'.[58] At about 9.45 pm, having passed the French rear, the van division tacked to south to come once to windward of the enemy. The French responded by tacking to the north to regain the windward advantage and withdrew.

The two fleets were again in contact on the 19 May. At daybreak both were in line ahead, the French 12 to 15 miles ahead and the

Rodney v. de Guichen off Martinique 19 May 1780
Opening Stages

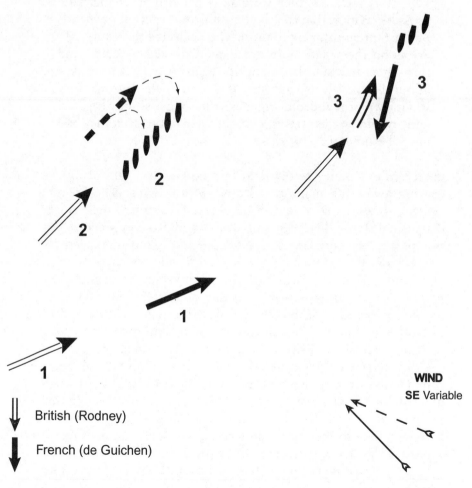

WIND
SE Variable

British (Rodney)

French (de Guichen)

Narrative

6.00 am 1. Wind south-easterly. Both fleets in line ahead on the starboard tack, the British following in the wake of the French and 10-12 miles astern. Rodney gains slowly on the French and attempts to get to windward.

12 noon 2. De Guichen orders his fleet to tack together and to cross ahead of the British line iin a starboard bow and quarter line with his ships half a cable (120 yards) apart.

1.30 pm 3. The French come into line ahead southbound,to windward of the British. From 3.15 to 4.30 pm the opposing fleets are engaged in a passing action. By closing up his fleet de Guichen has achieved a measure of concentration against the British van.

Rodney v. de Guichen off Martinique 19 May 1780
Closing Stages

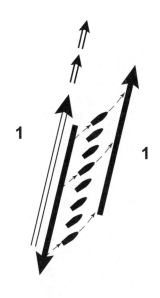

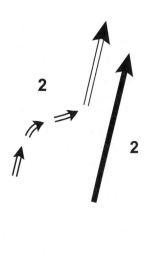

WIND
ESE Variable

 British (Rodney)

French (de Guichen)

Narrative

4.30 to 4.45 pm	1. When the British van passes the French rear de Guichen, to avoid being weathered, opens out the distance between the two fleets by ordering his fleet to tack together away from the British and then to turn together on to the same course as the British.
5.00 to 6.15 pm	2. Rodney's van and centre carry out a similar movement to close the gap but no further action ensues. During the night the French gradually draw ahead and by the next morning the British are 5 miles astern.

British following in their wake. Throughout the forenoon Rodney gained steadily on the French in an attempt to get to windward, but at midday de Guichen ordered his fleet to tack together into a line of bearing and, having crossed ahead of the British, to bear away on to a parallel and opposite course to windward of them and within cannon shot. The two fleets were then engaged for about an hour as they passed one another. As de Guichen had closed up his fleet his effort was concentrated on the British van, which passed his rear at about 4.30 pm. To prevent the British getting to windward of him de Guichen ordered his ships to come up into the wind together in order to open up the distance between the fleets and then to tack on to the same course as the British (see diagram). By a similar manoeuvre Rodney's van and centre closed the gap but there was no further action. During the night the French drew ahead and at daybreak on 20 May Rodney's fleet was 6 miles astern.[59] British and French casualties for the actions of 15 and 19 May were for the former 21 killed and 100 wounded, and for the latter 47 killed and 113 wounded.[60]

The French were out of sight by 21 May and Rodney, now 120 miles out into the Atlantic, had to reckon with the state of his ships. The *Cornwall* and the *Boyne* were signalling that they were in danger of sinking, while the mainmast of the *Conqueror*, Rowley's flagship, was irreparable and likely to go over her side at any moment. Rodney sent these ships to St Lucia before the wind and took the remainder to Barbados in order to put the sick and wounded ashore and carry out repairs.[61] After reaching St Lucia the *Cornwall* sank as did the *Fame*, which had been left behind. Writing to Middleton a month later Walter Young listed a further nine ships in Rodney's fleet which he predicted would share the same fate if they were not got home within four months.[62]

After the engagements of the 15 and 19 May Rodney had no complaints about the conduct of the senior officers whom he had censured after the action of 17 April, indeed Rowley's division, including Commodore Hotham in the *Vengeance*, had borne the brunt of the fighting in both actions. It may well be that Rodney's close supervision from a frigate had improved matters, but their feelings had been ruffled, perhaps irreparably, by Rodney's reaction to the 17 April fiasco, as illustrated by a letter from Hotham to Sandwich:

> I can no longer wish to serve in this country: for where the chief in command will assume merit to himself, and aim to aggrandise his own reputation by depreciating indiscriminately the character of every office below him, service will become irksome and all confidence must cease.
>
> The account published by authority of the affair of the 17th April, although ludicrous enough in itself, has nevertheless given much cause of discontent here.[63]

Parker, due to go anyway, returned to England in a fury and had to be restrained from conducting a pamphleteering war against Rodney;[64] Rowley was sent to Jamaica with ten ships to reinforce Sir Peter Parker, whom he later succeeded as Commander-in-Chief there. Hotham continued to serve under Rodney for another year, albeit at a distance for some of that time as he remained behind as senior officer in the Leeward Islands when Rodney went to America. In contrast to Rodney's reaction after the encounter of 17 April, de Guichen had nothing but praise for his own officers in all three engagements, citing their bravery and exact execution of signals.[65]

A French writer on eighteenth-century naval tactics saw Rodney's three encounters with de Guichen as classics of the genre. He acknowledged Rodney's planned concentration on 17 April as a concept well ahead of its time but dismissed it as an excellent idea, feebly applied.[66] Apart from that he listed a number of ways in which he thought that the encounters reflected the tactical thinking of the époque, including the sanctity of the line of battle, the prohibition of individual initiative, the lack of the offensive spirit and the failure to pursue after the engagement.[67]

Some of the criticisms are more fairly applied to de Guichen than to Rodney. The test of the offensive spirit must surely be the use made by each admiral of the advantage of the weather gage when he possessed it. Rodney had it for most of the action of 17 April and tried twice to put it to devastating effect, but was thwarted in the application. De Guichen had it for most of the encounters of 15 and 19 May but appears only to have played with it. The brief actions which took place on both occasions resulted from Rodney's attempt to seize the weather gage from him. While the results in tactical terms of all three encounters were stalemates (both sides claimed the advantage), Rodney gained the strategic prize since de Guichen was thwarted in his designs on Barbados in April and on St Lucia in May.

The arrival early in June of Spanish ships to join de Guichen gave him a significant numerical superiority over Rodney whose promised reinforcements from England and America had been delayed, but the Spanish arrivals were of little use to the French because of the extent of illness on board the Spanish ships. Rodney's fear of an attack by the combined fleets on St Lucia and other British islands proved to be unfounded. Apart from the ill health of his sailors, Don Solano, the Spanish admiral, had little inclination to join the French in aggressive action. Having joined forces off Dominica the allies had gone to Fort Royal in Martinique, where they remained inactive until 5 July. They sailed that night, without lights, and remained together until they reached the eastern end of Cuba. There they parted company, the Spanish going to Havana and the French to Cap Français in St Domingo. There de Guichen received letters from the Marquis de Lafayette and the French Minister to the United States imploring him to operate in North American waters, but he chose to obey his orders from home which required him to take his fleet to Europe. Earlier de Guichen, who had lost a son in one of the engagements with Rodney and was exhausted by the campaign, had asked to be relieved. 'The command of so large a fleet,' he had written, 'is infinitely beyond my capacity in all respects.'[68]

Unaware of this, Rodney had received false intelligence to the effect that de Guichen was to take twelve ships of the line to America.[69] Following the arrival in the West Indies on 12 July of Commodore Walsingham with a reinforcement of five ships, Rodney had made a preliminary disposition of ships in advance of

the onset of the hurricane season. Hotham remained behind with
six ships of the line, and frigates, for the protection of St Lucia and
other British possessions. Rowley and Walsingham went to
Jamaica with ten ships, initially to provide protection for that
island as required, and thence to return to England both in order
to escort the home-bound trade and to enable the warships themselves to be refitted. Rodney kept under his own control ten
coppered ships to be available, outside the hurricane zone, for
whatever contingency might arise. He took these ships to America
arriving off Sandy Hook, New Jersey on 15 September 1780.[70] De
Guichen had sailed for Europe with twenty-four ships of the line
on 16 August.

Chapter 5

De Grasse

When de Guichen sailed for Europe on 16 August 1780 he was accompanied by the Comte de Grasse who had served as one of his squadron commanders (*chef d'escadre*) during the encounters with Rodney earlier in the year. De Grasse was to return to the West Indies before long and to play a dominant part in French naval operations there and on the coast of North America. François-Joseph-Paul Comte de Grasse-Tilly was born on 13 September 1722 in the Castle of Bar, 6 miles from the town of Grasse in Provence. His family, one of the oldest in France, traced its descent back to 993 from Rodoard, the Prince of Antibes. When he was not yet twelve he entered the Seminaire de la Marine in Toulon (the normal minimum age for entry was fifteen, but he was big for his age and his family obtained a special dispensation). After only a year at the school he was appointed a page to the Grand Master of the Knights of St John. The ships of the Knights of Malta, mainly employed in protecting merchant ships from pirates, were regarded as one of the best training schools for young noblemen in the art of marine warfare and in the etiquette of a gentleman.[1] Shortly before the start of the War of the Austrian Succession in 1740 de Grasse left Malta to serve in the French Navy as a *Garde-marine* (midshipman) in the *Ferme* (74) and the *Diamant* (50). In the latter he took part in the indecisive action between a British fleet commanded by Admiral Thomas Mathews and a Franco-Spanish fleet off Toulon on 11 February 1744. Three years later, as an ensign in the *Gloire* (40) in a squadron commanded by M. de la Jonquière, de Grasse was wounded and taken prisoner in an unequal action off Cape Ortegal on 3 May 1747 against Admiral Anson's Western Squadron. Rodney, who commanded the *Eagle* in that squadron, had been detached to cruise independently and did not take part. The *Gloire*, whose captain was decapitated by a cannonball at the start of the action, surrendered after a three-hour fight against Anson's flagship, the *Prince George*, and two other ships. De Grasse spent three months in captivity in England.

Thereafter, de Grasse progressed up the chain of command but he did not reach the rank of *Capitaine de Vaisseau*, the prerequisite for commanding a ship of the line, until towards the end of the Seven Years' War (1756–1763) when he was nearly forty. He had little opportunity to distinguish himself during that war, part of which he spent in Indian waters and part in the campaign which led to the loss of Havana. He continued to serve during the long years of peace, a time of regeneration for the French Navy, which had fallen far behind the British Navy. Up to the start of the American War of Independence de Grasse's experience of command had been much inferior to that of Rodney, but in May 1778 he was appointed a *chef d'escadre* in the fleet of d'Orvilliers and in that capacity took part in the Battle of Ushant on 27 July. In January 1779 he sailed for the West Indies with four ships to reinforce d'Estaing and under his command took part in the Battle of Grenada on 6 July. He also served under d'Estaing in American waters and took part in the unsuccessful attempt to retake Savannah in the autumn of that year before returning with his division to the West Indies where he assumed temporary command. De Guichen joined him and took over the command in March 1780.

In an age when men were smaller than they are today de Grasse was a comparative giant of a man standing 6 ft 2 inches or more and well proportioned. There is a story to the effect that he was disobeyed by a soldier on board a ship when he was a sixteen year old with the Knights of Malta. He reputedly picked up the offender and threw him from one side of the ship to the other. Anxious that he might have been hurt, de Grasse immediately ran across to pick the soldier up, but was relieved to find that he had only a few bruises. His orders were obeyed promptly thereafter.[2]

Rodney arrived off Sandy Hook, New Jersey, on 15 September 1780 with ten ships of the line, all coppered. Although General Washington, who was expecting de Guichen, was said to be in despair at the news of Rodney's arrival[3] there was little Rodney was able to do in support of General Sir Henry Clinton's land forces. He was ashore ill for much of the time and frustrated by lack of co-operation on the part of Vice Admiral Sir Marriott Arbuthnot, a prickly sixty-eight year old who resented Rodney's assumption of command both as an affront to his dignity and, probably, as a dilution of his share of prize money. In going to America and superseding Arbuthnot, Rodney relied on the terms of the commission dated 1 October 1779 appointing him 'Commander-in-Chief of His Majesty's ships and vessels employed and to be employed at Barbadoes and the Leeward Islands and the seas adjacent'.[4] This was a flawed interpretation of his authority according to N.A.M. Rodger, who argues that there was no legal mechanism whereby Rodney could assume and Arbuthnot resign the command of the North American station. He concedes, however, that Rodney had real and good reasons for going to America and one cannot quarrel with his suggestion that he might have secured Arbuthnot's co-operation by leaving undisturbed the arrangements on the North America station for patronage and prize money.[5] Whatever the legal position the Admiralty supported Rodney in the dispute with Arbuthnot, as perhaps it was bound to, but before the dispute had arisen and when he had first learnt that Rodney was in readiness to go to America, Sandwich had written to him privately saying: 'It is impossible for us to have a superior fleet in every part; and unless our Commanders-in-Chief will take the great line, as you do, and consider the King's whole dominions as under their care, our enemies must find us unprepared somewhere, and carry their point against us.'[6] Much later, Sandwich rebuked Rodney privately for having interfered with appointments of officers in the local squadron, although acknowledging his right to do so, and asked him to refrain from doing so if he had occasion again to go to North

America, where Arbuthnot was about to be succeeded by Rear Admiral Robert Digby.[7]

Rodney got on well with Clinton, who had fallen out with Arbuthnot, but he was unable to persuade him to revive an abandoned project to attack Newport, Rhode Island. He was, however, instrumental in mounting a small expedition to the Chesapeake against enemy supply lines, in support of a planned invasion of North Carolina by Lord Cornwallis. Unfortunately it arrived too late, Cornwallis having been obliged to retreat to South Carolina following the defeat of part of his army in the Battle of King's Mountain on 7 October 1780.[8]

Rodney returned to the West Indies in November, arriving in Barbados on 6 December to find that in October a late hurricane of exceptional ferocity had devastated the islands and damaged many ships. He learnt on arrival that Rear Admiral Sir Samuel Hood was on his way with reinforcements and to serve as his second-in-command, Sandwich having informed him that it had not been easy to find officers of the requisite calibre to serve under him. Hood was a special promotion to the flag list on 26 September 1780, as was Rear Admiral Francis Samuel Drake, already serving with Rodney as a Commodore. Both had served under Rodney earlier in their careers, Hood as a midshipman in the *Sheerness* and the *Ludlow Castle* from 1743 to 1745, and later as captain of the frigate *Vestal* (32) in the bombardment of Le Havre in July 1759. It was in the *Vestal* in February of that year that Hood had fought and captured the French frigate *Bellona* (32) off Cape Finisterre. Otherwise, his naval service had been unremarkable and in February 1778 at the age of fifty-three he had been appointed Commissioner at Portsmouth and Governor of the Royal Naval Academy, appointments which normally would have signified the end of his active career, an expectation which would have been reinforced by the fact that on the occasion of the King's visit to Portsmouth in May 1778 he was created a baronet.[9] There was nothing, so far, in the career of the future Commander-in-Chief in the Mediterranean and mentor of Nelson that would have led anyone to anticipate Nelson's description of him as 'the greatest Sea-officer I ever knew'.[10] Drake, five years younger than Hood, was a collateral descendant of Sir Francis Drake (1540–1596). As a lieutenant he took part in the Battle of Quiberon Bay in 1759, and as captain of the *Falkland* (50) served under Rodney in the taking of Martinique in 1762. Latterly, he had been with Rodney since June 1780, having been sent to the West Indies from Arbuthnot's squadron in North America. He had then gone back to America with Rodney and returned with him to the West Indies.[11] By the same letter that informed him of Hood's and Drake's appointments he learnt that he had been elected as Member of Parliament for Westminster.[12]

One of the consequences of the hurricane was that large quantities of naval stores had been ruined in Barbados, St Lucia and Jamaica. Furthermore there were no docking facilities, so that ships with hull damage could only be repaired by the time-consuming process of careening. As a result Rodney faced considerable difficulties in repairing not only the ships damaged locally but also the ships which he had brought back from America, which had encountered a violent two-day storm on passage and suffered severely in their masts, yards, sails and rigging. Despite this and having heard that the fortifications in St Vincent had been almost destroyed in the hurricane he made preparations for a combined operation with General Vaughan to recapture the island, which had been taken by the French on 17 June 1779.[13]

Preparations began on 9 December in Gros Islet Bay, St Lucia and the expedition set out on the 14th, arriving off St Vincent the following day. It comprised nine ships of the line with the landing force, mostly marines, embarked in four smaller ships. General Vaughan was able to land unopposed because the French had withdrawn all their troops into the fortifications on high ground overlooking Warrawarrow Bay, where the British had landed, and the town of Kingston. It was soon apparent that contrary to the intelligence which had inspired the expedition the fortifications were intact and that there was no reasonable prospect of a successful assault. It also transpired later that during the preparations in St Lucia the Marquis de Bouillé had got wind of the intended expedition and sent much-needed stores and gunpowder from Martinique to St Vincent, which had got there the day before the British arrived. Captain Walter Young maintained that Rodney had delayed the preparations at St Lucia for two days in a fit of indecisiveness, but there does not appear to be any corroboration of this.[14]

Hood arrived in Barbados on 7 January 1781 with eight ships of the line and four frigates together with over a hundred merchant ships. All the newly arrived warships were coppered. Three weeks after Hood's arrival, Rodney received news that Britain was at war with Holland and orders to consult with the Army on attacking Dutch possessions in the West Indies. The most suitable target was St Eustatius, lying a few miles north-west of St Kitts. The flourishing entrepôt activities of this small island had long angered Rodney, because of their rôle in circumventing restrictions on trading with the French and the Americans, and his ire was directed in particular at British merchants involved in the trade, whom he regarded as traitors. Because of the quick passage made by the sloop which brought him his orders, the French in the West Indies were not yet aware that Holland had joined the war on their side and on 3 February Rodney was able, by a show of force, to demand and receive the surrender of the island with scarcely a shot fired. A convoy which had left St Eustatius for Europe thirty-six hours earlier was pursued and brought back providing, together with the remaining contents of warehouses ashore, booty whose value was out of all proportion to the size of the island. Here then was an opportunity for Rodney both to punish treachery and to ensure, through his share of prize money, that he would never again have to live in the shadow of bankruptcy. It is alleged against him that these twin temptations clouded his judgment and interfered with the proper execution of his duty as Commander-in-Chief. For the next three months he immersed himself in the practical and administrative measures needed to deal with the spoils and delegated to Hood the operational responsibility for intercepting French reinforcements believed to be on their way under de Grasse.

After leaving the West Indies in August 1780 de Guichen's first port of call was Cadiz where his eighteen ships of the line, including the squadron commanded by de Grasse, were absorbed into the fleet commanded by the Comte d'Estaing. Soon after his arrival the combined fleet, around forty strong, sailed for Brest where it arrived on 3 January 1781, there to be refitted for redeployment to various parts of the world. A month later de Grasse went to Paris on sick leave and while there called on the King at Versailles. Shortly afterwards he was selected to command the French fleet in the West Indies. In addition to his responsibilities there his orders required him to co-operate as necessary with Generals Washington and Rochambeau in North America. At the same time Suffren was appointed to command in the East Indies and de Barras at Rhode Island. De Grasse apparently accepted his appointment with some reluctance, mainly because of ill health. He was promoted to the rank of *lieutenant général* on 22 March 1781 and on the same day he and Suffren sailed from Brest, escorting a large convoy. De Barras sailed four days later. On 29 March Suffren parted company taking five ships of the line and part of the convoy, leaving de Grasse with twenty ships of the line, including his flagship, the *Ville de Paris* (110), one of the largest and finest warships afloat. Also left with de Grasse were three frigates, a convoy of 150 ships for the West Indies and North America and the *Sagittaire* (50). The last named parted company on 5 April with 660 troops for America.[15] Accompanying de Grasse as a squadron commander (*chef d'escadre*) was Louis Antoine de Bougainville, noted explorer and mathematician. He had joined the Navy in 1763 having previously served with distinction in the Army during the Seven Years' War as Montcalm's aide-de-camp in Canada. He proved in due course to be less successful as a fighting admiral than he had been in his other careers.

De Grasse's arrival off Martinique on 28 April and the size of his fleet took Rodney and Hood by surprise. The speed of his passage across the Atlantic might have made it difficult to warn Rodney in time, but Hood thought that if a small, fast sailing vessel had been despatched from England up to two weeks after de Grasse left Brest if would have reached the West Indies before him.[16] In response to the earlier false intelligence Rodney had ordered Hood in February to cruise to windward of Martinique with seventeen ships of the line including Drake's squadron.[17] They were still to windward early in March, spread out from Martinique to Dominica with frigates dispersed to ensure that it was almost impossible for enemy ships to approach undetected. At the same time Rodney reported that a close watch was being kept on Fort Royal, on the lee side of Martinique, where there were four French ships of the line and four frigates.[18] However, by 15 March Rodney had concluded that the French squadron which he had been warned about in February was unlikely to arrive in the West Indies so he ordered Hood to move to leeward of Martinique and to maintain a close blockade of Fort Royal with part of Drake's squadron keeping watch on St Pierre, further up the coast.[19] He believed that the new dispositions had two advantages: firstly, that it would be impossible for the French to enter Fort Royal without giving Hood an opportunity of bringing them to action, assuming that he stationed frigates to windward to provide advance warning; and secondly, that since Hood would now be much closer to St Lucia it would be easier to detach ships for stores, provisions and water. He added also that from his long experience of Martinique and its navigation he was convinced that a British squadron could keep station off Fort Royal Bay for months without being driven to leeward.[20] Hood was unconvinced, believing that he should have remained to windward of Martinique, and wrote to Rodney on 1 April:

I begin to be extremely impatient for the honour of seeing and acting immediately under your flag, as I do not feel myself at all pleasant in being to leeward; for should an enemy's fleet attempt to get into Martinique, and the commander of it inclines to avoid battle, nothing but a *skirmish* will probably happen, which in its *consequences* may operate as a defeat to the British squadron, though not a ship is lost and the enemy suffer most.[21]

Rodney did not relent and the outcome was much as Hood predicted.

De Grasse's fleet and convoy were sighted to windward of Martinique at 7.00 am on 28 April by the frigate *Amazon* and Hood received her sighting report two hours later. The British fleet

Hood v. de Grasse off Martinique 29 April 1781
Opening Stages

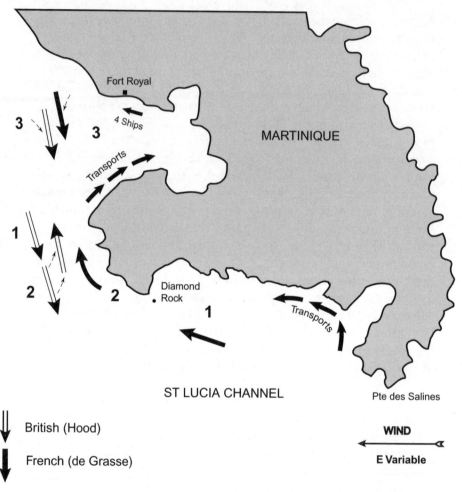

British (Hood)

French (de Grasse)

WIND
E Variable

Narrative

1. At 9.00 am the French fleet is seen between Pointe des Salines and Diamond Rock with the transports following astern and hugging the shore. Hood, standing to the southward signals for a close line and to prepare for action. At 9.27 am both fleets hoist their colours.

2. At 10.35 am the British tack together as the French round Diamond Rock, which brings them them on to the same course as the French, now heading for Fort Royal, with the French van opposite the British Centre. The French open fire at 11.00 am but Hood holds his fire.

3. At 11.20 am Hood tacks his ships together to the southward. De Grasse, his transports now secure, wears his ships together on to the same course as the British and is joined by the four French ships in Fort Royal Bay.

Hood v. de Grasse off Martinique 29 April 1781
Closing Stages

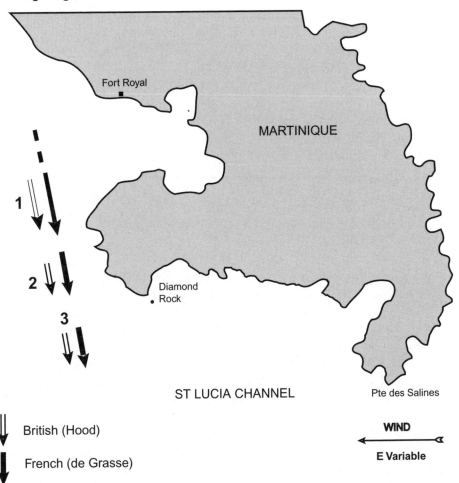

Fort Royal

MARTINIQUE

1

2

3

Diamond
Rock

ST LUCIA CHANNEL

Pte des Salines

British (Hood)

French (de Grasse)

WIND

E Variable

Narrative

1. The addition of four ships from Fort Royal Bay gives de Grasse 24 ships against Hood's 18.
   At midday, finding it impossible to get close to the enemy, Hood tries to entice the French
   towards him by bringing to under topsails.

2. The *Barfleur* (Hood) and the *Ville de Paris* (de Grasse) begin to exchange fire at 12.30 pm
   and the engagement becomes general, but at too great a range. Firing ceases at 1.34 pm.

3. The leading ships on both sides catch the stronger breeze in the St Lucia Channel and draw
   ahead. Four British ships are attacked by eight French and are much damaged.

was then apparently some distance to leeward of Martinique as Hood spent the whole of that day and the ensuing night getting as far as he could to windward with the intention of being close to Fort Royal at daybreak as he was uncertain from which direction the enemy would approach. At around 9.00 am on the 29th the French were seen between Pointe des Salines and Diamond Rock at the south-eastern and south-western extremities respectively of Martinique, with the transports astern of the fleet and hugging the shore. Hood, whose fleet was then standing to the southward, made the signals for a close line and to prepare for action and at the same time the enemy appeared to be forming line of battle. Shortly afterwards Hood was joined by the *Prince William* returning from St Lucia, bringing his strength up to eighteen ships of the line compared with de Grasse's twenty. However, in addition to his small numerical superiority de Grasse had much the greater weight of ordnance having three ships of 80 guns and fifteen of 74 guns in addition to the massive *Ville de Paris* (110). Furthermore he had potentially an overwhelming superiority if he were able to effect a junction with the four French ships of the line in Fort Royal Bay. Hood's only advantage was that all his ships were coppered and therefore faster sailers.

At 9.27 am both fleets hoisted their colours and as the French rounded Diamond Rock Hood tacked his ships together to the northward at 10.35 am, bringing them on to the same course as the enemy, now heading for Fort Royal, with the French van opposite the British centre. The French opened fire ineffectually at 11.00 am but Hood held his fire. At 11.20 am Hood tacked his ships together to the southward and shortly afterwards, observing that the enemy shot was passing overhead, hoisted the signal to engage. De Grasse, his transports now secure, wore his ships together on to the same course as the British and the four French ships in Fort Royal Bay, which had earlier slipped their cables, now joined the rear of his fleet, bringing his total strength up to twenty-four compared with Hood's eighteen. At midday, finding it impossible to get close to the enemy, Hood tried to entice the French towards him by bringing his fleet to under topsails. The *Barfleur* (Hood) and the *Ville de Paris* (de Grasse) began to exchange fire at 12.30 pm and the engagement became general, but at too great a range. Hood commented, 'I believe never was more powder and shot thrown away in one day before, but it was with Monsieur de Grasse the option of distance lay, and he preferred that of long shot. It was not possible for me to go nearer.' Hood repeated the order for close line of battle at 1.34 pm but ceased firing shortly afterwards finding that not one enemy shot in ten was reaching the British fleet. However the leading ships on both sides caught the stronger breeze in the St Lucia Channel and drew ahead of the rest of their respective fleets. Being closer together they continued the engagement for some time, in the course of which four British ships were attacked by eight French and were much damaged. Among them was the *Russell*, which received several shots in her hull and was being kept afloat with difficulty. Hood sent her off that evening to St Eustatius, 220 miles away, where she arrived on 4 May, bringing Rodney the first news of the action.

On 30 April variable winds denied Hood the opportunity of getting to windward of de Grasse and bringing him to action. In the late afternoon he found that two more of his ships, the *Centaur* and the *Intrepid* were leaking badly. Taking this into account and the fact that he had over 1,500 men sick and short of complement, he judged it 'improper to dare the enemy to battle any longer, not having the least prospect of beating a fleet of twenty-four sail of the line capital ships'. In the evening he sailed to the north as the currents to the south would have prevented his damaged ships from reaching St Lucia. Rodney, having received the news of de Grasse's arrival with a much larger fleet than expected, put to sea on 5 May in the *Sandwich* in company with the *Triumph* and the *Russell*, after hurried repairs to the latter. He met Hood between St Kitts and Antigua on 11 May, de Grasse having anchored at Fort Royal on 6 May. British losses were thirty-nine killed, including Captain Nott of the *Centaur*, and 162 wounded. According to a British source[22] the French losses were 119 killed and 150 wounded, but only 18 killed and 53 wounded according to a French source.[23] Hood had handled his fleet well against a superior enemy, but had been frustrated by his inability to gain the weather gage (i.e. to get to windward of the enemy). He thought that if Rodney had allowed him to remain to windward of Martinique he 'must have brought the enemy to close action upon more equal terms or they must have given up their transports, trade &c'.[24] De Grasse had achieved his main aim of getting his convoy safely into Fort Royal but, not for the last time, had thrown away the opportunity of using his superiority to destroy part of the British fleet.[25]

De Grasse and de Bouillé soon took advantage of the absence of the British fleet to launch attacks on St Lucia and Tobago, the former with a force of 1,200 under de Bouillé and the latter with a force of 1,300 under Captain d'Albert de Rions in the *Pluton*. Both expeditions sailed from Martinique on 9 May. De Bouillé landed in the north of St Lucia on the following day and on the 12th, de Grasse anchored his fleet in Gros Islet Bay believing that de Bouillé had mastered the local defences. He was soon disabused of this idea by heavy gunfire from the shore battery which Rodney had established on Pigeon Island. The local garrison had been reinforced by the timely arrival at the Carénage of three British frigates and a sloop in search of Hood and the landing of their crews. Unfortunately one of the frigates, the *Thetis,* had struck a rock coming in and sunk. De Bouillé concluded that the British defences were too strong to be taken. His troops were re-embarked and the expedition returned to Fort Royal. There de Grasse and de Bouillé increased their landing force to 3,000 and sailed for Tobago on or about 22 May.[26]

After his reunion with Hood on 14 May and after taking in stores at Antigua Rodney took his fleet south to Barbados where he learnt of the abortive attack on St Lucia and where late on 26 May he learnt that the French had landed in Tobago. He immediately ordered Drake to take six ships of the line and a small land force under General Skene to assist the local garrison, making it clear that he was to return if the main enemy fleet appeared off the island. Drake sailed in the evening of 28 May and arrived on 30 May as did de Grasse with twenty ships of the line. As ordered, Drake returned immediately to Barbados, arriving in the evening of 2 June. Rodney sailed with his whole fleet the following morning having, according to Hood, expressed his determination to give the

98

enemy battle. He reached Tobago in the afternoon of 4 June when large numbers of French ships were seen standing out from Great Courland Bay on the north-west side of the island. On the following day Rodney learnt that the island had surrendered when Drake had left. In the afternoon of 5 June twenty-four French ships of the line were seen sailing northwards and by 6.00 pm they were 9 or 10 miles to leeward. Rockets were seen during the evening but by 11.00 pm the French were lost to sight and there was no sign of them. Rodney returned to Barbados where he arrived on 8 June. He gave as his reasons for not seeking to engage the French on 5 June his reluctance to get entangled in the Grenadines, the chain of small islands between St Vincent and Grenada, and possibly to be caught up in the strong lee currents of the channel between Grenada and the Spanish Main. But his main concern was for the security of Barbados, whose defences had not yet been reinstated following the hurricane damage of October 1780. This, probably, was why he had not immediately taken his whole fleet to Tobago when he learnt that it had been invested, a decision of which Hood was highly critical. For his part Rodney was angry that Tobago had surrendered, apparently in response to a French threat to burn the plantations, and he was particularly incensed by the fact that cannon which he had delivered for the island's defence more than a year earlier were still unmounted on the beach where they had been landed. De Grasse returned to Fort Royal on 18 June.[27]

Chapter 6

St Eustatius

The orders by whose authority Rodney captured the Dutch island of St Eustatius could not have been issued to anybody who would have carried them out with greater zeal. He owed his appointment as Commander-in-Chief, in part at least, to his unequivocal disapproval of the American rebellion and he saw the trading activities based on the neutral island as providing valuable, if not vital, support to that rebellion, allowing as they did essential supplies to reach America. They also made it possible for Americans to export their produce and to exchange it for naval supplies and other goods from Europe. Not all exports were illicit, however, some having been sanctioned by Parliament in 1780 for the convenience of Britain herself and her sugar islands.[1] Six months before the seizure of the island, when Holland was still a neutral power, Rodney had stationed frigates off St Eustatius to intercept and destroy American ships. On 6 August 1780 some of those frigates had chased five American armed merchantmen into the roadstead of the neighbouring Dutch island of St Martin where, on anchoring, the 'piratical rebels' had hoisted their colours and, by putting springs* on their cables, had pointed all their guns at a British sloop. Rodney was enraged that the Dutch Governor had apparently tolerated this insult to the British flag and had despatched from St Kitts the

---

*Spring – a hawser between a ship's cable and the stern allowing the ship to be pulled round while at anchor.

Intrepid and a squadron of frigates to seize the American ships. He reported that this had had a good effect on the governors of the Dutch islands who now paid some attention 'to ancient treaties and acknowledge that they know no American colours, nor suffer any to be hoisted in their ports in the West Indies'.[2] Britain's sensitivity on the question of American rebel colours went back as far as 1776 when on 16 November Fort Orange in St Eustatius, with the authority of the Governor, returned the salute of the American warship *Andrew Doria*, an event which came to be known as 'The First Salute'.[3]

It was not only America which benefited from trade through St Eustatius. The French depended on it for the maintenance of their fleet in the West Indies, as reported by Sandwich in a cabinet paper in September 1779:

> There is one circumstance concerning the Leeward Islands that deserves our most serious attention; and without something is done in that point, the French will always maintain their fleets and islands in good condition, and be free from the innumerable distresses which we are subject to. From conversing with Admiral Barrington* and from what I knew before I am convinced that two-thirds of the provisions that we carry out under convoy from England and Ireland is, on its arrival in our islands, immediately shipped off for St Eustatius and from thence to Martinique, without which the French could not keep their fleet in a condition for sea.[4]

That much of the trade which passed through St Eustatius was harmful to Britain is self-evident but as mentioned earlier what was intolerable to Rodney was the suspected involvement of British merchants in supplying the French and the rebel colonies. In his opinion they were acting treasonably and he was determined that they should be punished.

The seizure of the island was preceded by thorough naval and military preparation and, with one lapse, proceeded without a

* Rear Adm. the Hon. Samuel Barrington, C-in-C Leeward Islands 1778–9.

hitch, the island authorities being unaware that Holland and Britain were at war. Rodney's partner in this enterprise, as in the unsuccessful St Vincent expedition, was Major General the Hon John Vaughan. Some twenty years younger than Rodney, he had served in 1762 under General Monckton in the capture of Martinique, in which Rodney had commanded the naval forces. In the American War of Independence Vaughan had served under both Cornwallis and Clinton, and under the latter had attempted unsuccessfully in October 1777 to relieve Burgoyne before his surrender at Saratoga. He returned to England in 1779 and at the end of that year sailed with Rodney's Gibraltar expedition in the convoy which was detached to the West Indies where he assumed command of the land forces.[5] The joint command in St Eustatius was mirrored at government level since Rodney reported to the Admiralty and Vaughan to Lord George Germain, the Secretary of State with responsibility for the war in America.

Rodney's ships, with 3,000 troops embarked, left St Lucia on 30 January 1781 and sailed up the west coast of Martinique, Rodney taking care to ensure the whole fleet was seen from Fort Royal and St Pierre 'to prevent the French penetrating our design'. Drake was left behind with four ships of the line and two frigates to watch the French ships in Fort Royal Bay and Hood's squadron was sent ahead to prevent any Dutch warships or merchant ships from leaving St Eustatius. When the main fleet arrived there on 3 February Rodney stationed his ships to neutralize the shore batteries. Before any troops were disembarked, 'in order to save the effusion of human blood', a summons to surrender was issued to the Dutch Governor, Johannes de Graaff, 'with which he instantly complied'. By the following day Rodney was able to report that the islands of St Martin and Saba had also surrendered, no terms whatever having been allowed them.[6] The only shots that were fired during the taking of St Eustatius were by the *Gibraltar* and the *Prince William* which, without orders, opened fire briefly on the Dutch frigate *Mars* (38), the only Dutch warship present. This brought down Rodney's wrath on at least one of the offending captains. He wrote the following day to Captain Stair Douglas of the *Prince William*:

You may easily imagine Sir what I must have felt at the time the firing commenced, and how much it must have hurt me to observe in the Sight of the Fleet, Army, (and an Island which a few minutes before had submitted to his Majesty's Arms,) such a wanton display of the Slackness of Discipline in a British Fleet. Trust it will never happen again, it is my Duty to prevent it, and no Consideration whatever shall induce me to overlook a breach of Discipline in the Fleet I have the honour to command.

Despite his reminder to Douglas that 'the Captain of every Ship is responsible for the Discipline of that Ship', Rodney accepted his lame excuse that the order had been given without his authority by a junior officer.[7] This was an uncharacteristicly lenient Rodney. He was less forgiving a month later when he allowed to proceed the sentence of death by a court martial on six sailors of the cutter *Sylph* who had conspired to rise in mutiny, kill the officers and take the vessel to a French or American port:

To have pardoned anyone after committing so heinous a crime as treason and mutiny, might have induced others to run the same risk . . . I have long experienced that where good discipline prevails, there is seldom occasion for punishment.[8]

The concentration of wealth which Rodney and Vaughan found at St Eustatius exceeded every expectation. Rodney told his wife that the riches were 'beyond all comprehension'. Some 130 merchant ships were seized in the bay, and in addition to the Dutch frigate *Mars* there were five smaller American warships. A 'richly loaded' Dutch convoy of thirty ships, which had sailed thirty-six hours earlier was pursued and brought back. Unfortunately the Dutch admiral in the single escorting warship was killed. On the waterfront below the town stone-built warehouses extending for a mile and a quarter were full, as were the magazines, and the extensive beach was covered with sugar, tobacco and cotton.[9] Rodney's initial estimate of the value of the booty was 'more than two millions sterling',[10] but the final estimate seems to have been around three million (equivalent to approximately £M300 at 2001 prices).* The sheer extent of the property seized posed a formidable task of investigation and classification in order to ensure that the various categories of goods were dealt with in the most appropriate way. The decision by Rodney and Vaughan to take this task upon themselves exposed them, and Rodney in particular, to allegations of neglect of more important operational responsibilities and to excessive interest in personal enrichment. Initially, the magnitude of the task and the need to secure the spoils against a possible French attack made their involvement unavoidable, but it is un-fortunate that they were unable to detach themselves and deal with the matter at arm's length once the essential work had been done. One of Rodney's more sympathetic biographers blamed the government for not foreseeing the problem:

> When ordering the capture of St Eustatius, the government, who were well aware of its importance and wealth, made a grave mistake in not sending out a civil commission to settle the multitudinous affairs and details consequent on its capture, and so relieve the commanders of the armed forces of the heavy responsibility that devolved upon them, to the detriment of their own duty.[11]

The point is well taken, particularly when one considers that at the time of Rodney's appointment as Commander-in-Chief in the Leeward Islands, Sandwich found it necessary to reassure the King that all important financial transactions on the station, such as the purchase of stores, would pass through the hands of a commissioner.[12]

Among the critics of Rodney's conduct was Hood. By impli-cation he blamed his own failure to prevent de Grasse from reaching Martinique on Rodney's absorption with St Eustatius. In a private letter of 21 May to George Jackson, Second Secretary of the Admiralty, he complained that 'never was a squadron so

---

* House of Commons Library Research Paper 02/44, 11 Jul 2002 – *Inflation: The Value of the Pound 1750–2001.*

unmeaningly stationed as the one under my command, and what Sir George Rodney's motive for it could be I cannot conceive, unless it was to cover him at St Eustatius, and it is equally as difficult to be accounted for by Mr Drake and every captain.'[13] That Rodney's insistence on Hood remaining to leeward of Martinique was related to his concerns about St Eustatius is clearly correct since in his instructions to Hood of 15 March he commented that the convoy which he had been assembling for some time to carry the booty from St Eustatius to England would be sailing within two days. Hence his insistence that Hood should prevent the four French ships of the line in Fort Royal Bay from getting out.[14]

Hood wrote to Jackson again on 24 June and it was clear that the de Grasse affair was not the only source of his dissatisfaction related to St Eustatius. A few days after the seizure of the island Rodney cancelled an expedition to capture Curaçao in which Hood was to command the ships and General Vaughan the land forces, and for which Rodney had promised Hood five sail of the line and some frigates. Vaughan, whose idea the project was and who had prevailed on Hood to enlist Rodney's support, suddenly decided that he could not spare the men. Rodney later gave his reason for the cancellation the intelligence received on 12 February of a French fleet heading for the West Indies. That intelligence, though it subsequently proved to be false, was sufficient reason for cancelling the expedition, but Hood was convinced that the true reason was the reluctance of Vaughan to be away from St Eustatius 'where he fancied there were three million of riches'. In Hood's opinion those riches 'were so bewitching as not to be withstood by flesh and flood . . . but tempting as they were, I am abundantly happy in being at a distance; and it would doubtless have been fortunate for the public had Sir George been with his fleet, as I am confident he would have been to windward instead of to leeward when de Grasse made his approach.' He went on to criticize the arrangements for dealing with the spoils of St Eustatius:

The Admiral and General have a great deal to answer for, which I told them long ago; and they now begin to be in a squeeze, as many of their actions will [not] well bear the

105

daylight. Had they abided by the first plan settled before I left them, [and] not have interfered, but have left the management to the land and sea folks appointed for that purpose, all would have gone smooth and easy, and to the perfect satisfaction of the two corps; but I now see much mischief may arise.[15]

The arrangements to which Hood was referring stemmed from a formal agreement signed between Vaughan and Rodney two days after the capture to the effect that all vessels, merchandise and public stores seized should be distributed according to the King's pleasure.[16] This acknowledged the legal position whereby all the spoils were the property of the King unless and until he relinquished any part of them to be available for distribution as prize money. It was also intended to bring everything into one account thereby forestalling the usual practice in respect of prize money whereby all captures on land went to the Army and all those at sea went to the Navy. There was clearly an early expectation that part at least of the booty would be available for prize money. To deal with that eventuality, as well as other matters arising out of the capture, it was decided at a meeting of senior officers to set up a joint commission on which the two services would be equally represented. The naval representatives, nominated by Hood, were four captains, including Walter Young and Joseph Hunt, Hood's secretary. A proposal to employ Arietas Akers, the agent for the prisoners of war at St Kitts, to manage the sales was rejected on the grounds of conflict of interest (he had substantial claims against traders at St Eustatius) and Rodney also confided to Hood that he was untrustworthy.[17] In mid-march Hood learnt with dismay that Rodney and Vaughan had replaced the joint commission with a new one and that the untrustworthy Akers had been appointed to manage the sales.[18]

The suddenness of the capture meant that many documents which might otherwise have been destroyed or sent away were available for inspection and Rodney's early investigations confirmed his suspicions about the nature of some of the trading activities in St Eustatius. He discovered, for instance, that after the Battle of Martinique on 17 April 1780, de Guichen had been joined under Barbuda by two vessels which had been sent from St Eustatius heavily laden with cordage and naval stores, accompanied by carpenters. In Rodney's estimation this had saved eight French ships of the line the necessity of going to St Domingo for repairs.[19] This was particularly galling because after the hurricane in October the St Eustatius merchants had refused to supply the British dockyard in Antigua with much-needed cordage, although their warehouses were now found to be full of it.[20] It was also discovered that twelve of the ships found at St Eustatius when the island was seized had slipped away from the convoy which Hood had brought out from England.[21] The most comprehensive source of information about the nature of trading activities was in the records of the firm of Curzon & Gouverneur, which had a wide range of contacts in America, Europe and the West Indies.[22] Samuel Curzon and Isaac Gouverneur Jr. were Americans (Curzon had been the local agent of Congress in St Eustatius since the beginning of the war) and were therefore presumed to be British subjects who owed their allegiance to the Crown. They were sent as prisoners of state to England where they were committed for high treason but released by the incoming Rockingham ministry after a 'rigorous confinement of thirteen months'.[23] Also sent to England were their records, less two chests of documents, which they admitted to having sent away, for use by the courts and Parliament when required. After reading them Germain* was satisfied that they showed a connection between British subjects and the enemy.[24]

This confirmation of Rodney's suspicions encouraged him, with the assistance of a compliant Vaughan, to pursue vigorously the policy of confiscation heralded by a proclamation of 6 February requiring all residents to give details of their possessions to the Quartermaster General.[25] His main targets were 'the perfidious Dutch, and the traitorous English, who had made themselves Dutch Burghers, purely for the base design of supplying the Americans with naval and military stores, and every necessity of life'. He told Vice Admiral Sir Peter Parker in Jamaica that 'all their property

---

* Lord George Germain, Secretary of State for the Colonies.

whatever has been seized, as have likewise all the goods in their magazines'.[26] The confiscations in some cases included personal possessions and cash carried on the person.[27] According to Captain Walter Young there was also widespread plunder 'for want of discipline . . . both by sea and land'.[28] Side by side with confiscations went a policy of deportation of those resident in the island, varying according to their nationality. The French, as respected enemies, appear to have been treated with the most consideration. They were allowed to leave with their household goods, as were the Dutch merchants. The Jews were despatched summarily to the island of St Thomas with fourteen days' provisions. The Americans were sent back to America, but their departure was delayed to prevent their warning others not to come to the islands.[29] (For the same reason Rodney had kept the Dutch flag flying over Fort Orange for the first month of the occupation.)[30] Bona fide planters in St Eustatius were exempt from confiscations and deportation.

The sale of seized ships and their cargoes had begun early on, the sale of the first fourteen ships realizing over £100,000. European and perishable goods were disposed of by public auction from 15 March onwards. West Indian and American produce was loaded into the Dutch ships taken at St Eustatius, and sent to England on 19 March in a convoy commanded by Commodore Hotham.[31] The cash proceeds of the various sales and of the confiscations were accumulated in the *Sandwich* and the suspected English property was kept locked up, in both cases 'to await His Majesty's pleasure'. The King's decision was published in England on 30 March. As anticipated he relinquished his interest in the spoils in favour of 'Our said Commanders-in-Chief, and Our land and sea forces under your respective commands'. Specifically excluded, however, were three categories of goods, namely the military stores and equipment necessary for the defence of the captured Dutch islands, the land and personal possessions of their settled inhabitants and finally 'such effects as shall be proved to be the property of British subjects, *lawfully exported thither, or which may be lawfully imported into Great Britain from thence*'.[32] The last-named category included American produce which enjoyed the protection of the 1780 Act of Parliament referred to above.[33] Also covered was

108

1. Rodney as a Rear Admiral by Sir Joshua Reynolds.
   (*By permission of Lord Egremont. Photograph: Photographic Survey, Courtauld Institute of Art*)

2. Rodney in his retirement by Sir Joshua Reynolds.
(*The Royal Collection ©2005, Her Majesty Queen Elizabeth II*)

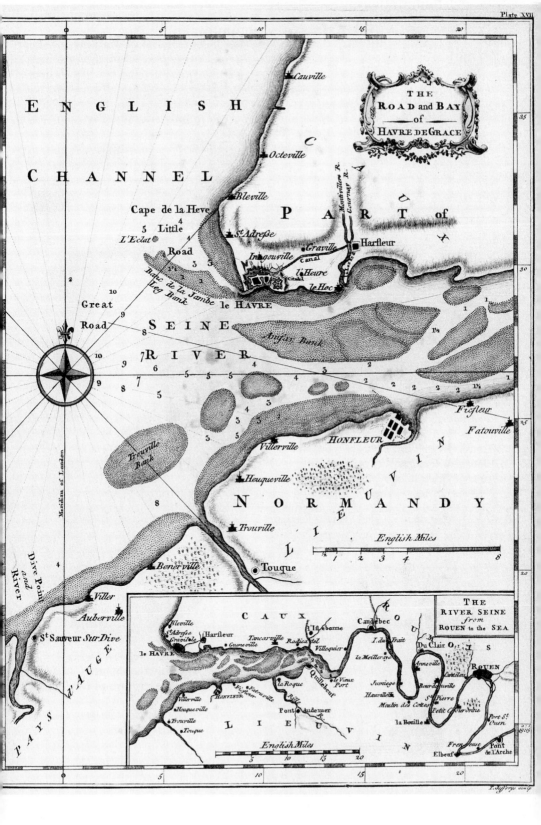

3. The road and bay of Havre de Grace (Le Havre) in 1761.
(©National Maritime Museum, London)

4. Rear Admiral Edward Hawke (later Lord Hawke, Admiral of the Fleet) who commanded the British fleet at the Second Battle of Finisterre on 14 October 1747.
(©*National Maritime Museum, London*)

6. Admiral Sir George Pocock, who, with Lieutenant General Lord Albemarle, captured Havana in 1762.
(©*National Maritime Museum, London*)

5. Major General Robert Monckton, Rodney's partner in the capture of Martinique in 1762.
(*The National Portrait Gallery, London*)

7. John Montagu, 4th
Earl of Sandwich,
after Johan Zoffany.
He was First Lord
of the Admiralty
during key periods
in Rodney's career.
(*The National Portrait
Gallery, London*)

8. Greenwich Hospital. Rodney was President from 1765 to 1771 and Hood
from 1796 to 1816. (*Author*)

9. The Moonlight Battle on 16-17 January 1780 by Francis Holman – the Spanish ship, the *San Domingo*, blowing up.   (©*National Maritime Museum, London*)

10. A view of Gibraltar after The Moonlight Battle.   (©*National Maritime Museum, London*)

11. Dr Gilbert Blane by J. Archer
    Shee. Blane was Rodney's
    Physician to the Fleet from
    1780 to 1782 and a pioneer
    in naval medicine.
    (*The Royal College of Physicians
    of London*)

12. The Battle of Martinique on 17 April 1780 by Thomas Luny – the *Sandwich*
    (Rodney) fighting off the *Couronne* (de Guichen) and other French ships during
    the final phase of the action.
    (*Berrington Hall, [The National Trust], ©Hammond Photography*)

13. Rear Admiral Hyde Parker by George Romney. Hyde Parker commanded the British van division during the Battle of Martinique on 17 April 1780.
(©*National Maritime Museum, London*)

15. Major General the Hon. John Vaughan, Rodney's partner in the capture of St Eustatius.
(*William L. Clements Library, University of Michigan*)

14. Rear Admiral Joshua Rowley by George Romney. Rowley commanded the British rear division during the Battle of Martinique on 17 April 1780.
(©*National Maritime Museum, London*)

16. The Comte de Guichen, reputed to be France's finest tactician, was Rodney's opponent in three actions off Martinique in 1780.
(©*Musée national de la Marine*)

17. The Comte de Grasse commanded the French fleet in the West Indies from 1781 to 1782 and was defeated by Rodney in the Battle of the Saintes on 12 April 1782.
(©*Musée national de la Marine*)

18. Rear Admiral Sir Samuel Hood by James Northcote. Hood was Rodney's second-in-command on the Leeward Islands Station from 1781 to 1782. (©*National Maritime Museum, London*)

19. Vice Admiral Marriot Arbuthnot, Commander-in-Chief of the North American Station from 1779 to 1781. (©*National Maritime Museum, London*)

0. Rear Admiral Thomas Graves by James
Northcote. Graves commanded the British
fleet in the Battle of the Chesapeake.
(©*National Maritime Museum, London*)

21. Charles 1st Marquess Cornwallis by
Thomas Gainsborough. His surrender at
Yorktown on 19 October 1781 effectively
ended the land war in America.
(*The National Portrait Gallery, London*)

2. The Battle of the Chesapeake on 5 September 1781. The Royal Navy's failure to regain
control of Chesapeake Bay from the French led to the surrender of Lord Cornwallis at
Yorktown six weeks later. (©*National Maritime Museum, London*)

23. The Marquis de Vaudreuil commanded the French rear division in the Battle of the Saintes on 12 April 1782, and assumed overall command after de Grasse was captured.
(©*Musée national de la Marine*)

25. Captain Sir Charles Douglas, a noted gunnery expert, was Rodney's Flag Captain in the Battle of the Saintes on 12 April 1782.
(©*National Maritime Museum, London*)

24. Louis Antoine de Bougainville, better known as an explorer, commanded the French van division in the Battle of the Saintes on 12 April 1782.
(©*Musée national de la Marine*)

26. The Battle of the Saintes on 12 April 1782 by Thomas Luny – Rodney's flagship, the *Formidable*, breaking the French line.
   (*Berrington Hall [The National Trust]*, ©*Ian Blantern*)

27. The Battle of the Saintes on 12 April 1782 by Thomas Luny – de Grasse's flagship, the *Ville de Paris*, striking her colours at sunset.
   (*Berrington Hall [The National Trust]*, ©*Ian Blantern*)

28. Captain Alan Gardner (later Admiral Lord Gardner), commanded the *Duke* in the Battle of the Saintes on 12 April 1782 and went alone through one of the gaps in the French line. (©*National Maritime Museum, London*)

30. Captain the Hon. William Cornwallis (later Admiral Sir William Cornwallis) commanded the *Canada* in the Battle of the Saintes on 12 April 1782. (©*National Maritime Museum, London*)

29. Captain James Saumarez (later Admiral Lord Saumarez) commanded the *Russell* in the Battle of the Saintes on 12 April 1782. (©*National Maritime Museum, London*)

Hamilton delin.   Thornton sculp.

31. A contemporary print purporting to show de Grasse surendering his sword to
    Rodney. (In fact, Rodney sent Captain Lord Cranstoun across to accept the surrender).
                                                                        (Author)

32. John Clerk of Eldin by James Saxon. He and others thought that his theories on naval tactics had influenced Rodney, but the evidence is unconvincing. (*The Scottish National Portrait Gallery*)

33. Rodney near the end of his life, painted by Jean Laurent Mosnier. (©*National Maritime Museum, London*)

property sent by merchants in British islands for secure storage in St Eustatius for fear of a French attack on those islands.

The news of the King's decision arrived in the West Indies too late for the British traders whose legitimate possessions were excluded in the final sentence. Hood heard about it informally from Jackson, without details, on 17 May,[34] but Vaughan did not receive the full text until 30 May and it is not known when Rodney received it because he was absorbed in the attempt to save Tobago from 30 May to 8 June. On 13 June he instructed Akers to dispose of the property either because he was not yet aware that it was protected or because he believed on the evidence of seized records that it was connected with trading with the enemy and therefore not possessed legitimately. The goods in question were sold by auction at a fraction of their value without the owners having the opportunity to bid for them.

There can be little doubt that Rodney's objectivity, and therefore his effectiveness as Commander-in-Chief, was impaired by his obsession with St Eustatius. The conventional wisdom is that he was driven by greed. On the day after the capture of the island he made this statement in a letter to the Secretary of State for the Home Department:

It is a vast capture; the whole I have seized for the King and the state, and I hope will go to the public revenue of my country. I do not look upon myself entitled to one sixpence, nor do I desire it; my happiness is having been the instrument of my country in bringing this nest of villains to condign punishment. They deserve scourging and they shall be scourged.[35]

His disclaimer of any interest in prize money was almost certainly ritual and expected to be read in that context. Based on precedent there was a strong possibility that the King would make at least part of the booty available for prize money and on 6 February, only two days after his disclaimer, Rodney made a settlement of £800 per annum in favour of his son, George, in anticipation of his marriage to Anne Harley.[36] The pension of £2,000 a year, which he had been granted in recognition of the Moonlight Battle,[37] might have covered that settlement and his living expenses but his debts remained,[38] and it is inconceivable that a man who had been in desperate financial straits for over a decade would not be interested in the prospect of restoring his fortune. However, that does not mean that such an interest would necessarily have been his only, or indeed his main preoccupation in dealing with St Eustatius. Prize money was a legitimate and accepted reward for the hazards of a precarious profession. Even Hood, who was reputed to have little interest in it, was moved to write to Rodney two years after the event, complaining bitterly about the poor prospects of any prize money resulting from the capture of the island and lamenting the fact that he might 'after all my fatigue and trouble return home as poor as I came out'.[39] However, if Rodney was keenly interested in personal enrichment, as many of his contemporaries believed, he was also determined to punish treachery. If anything impaired his judgment as Commander-in-Chief it is likely to have been his obsessive vendetta against what he saw variously as a 'nest of villains',[40] a 'nest of vipers',[41] a 'nest of thieves',[42] or 'this iniquitous island'.[43] Cynics might argue that this was synthetic anger designed to justify his plunder of the island for personal gain, but his obsession had its roots in the past. A year earlier he had written to John Robinson, the First Secretary of the Treasury, referring to the 'pernicious traffic' between St Eustatius and St Lucia, and other British islands, which resulted in the diversion to France, Holland and America of produce and revenues which belonged properly to Britain. He had given orders to his ships to seize all vessels loaded with produce from St Lucia which were not cleared out and actually bound for Britain and this had had a good effect. He added that he had put an end by this method to the same 'pernicious practice' after the conquest of Martinique in 1762.[44] Again, those who take the bleakest view of Rodney's character might suggest that all this was a pretext for capturing ships for prize money, but his anger seems to have been genuine.

Unfortunately, in his determination to punish those he considered guilty of treason, Rodney usurped the function of the courts, where, in due course, he and Vaughan found themselves involved in no less than sixty-four lawsuits brought by traders alleging wrongful confiscation of their goods. Many of those cases went against them.

In the end the seizure of St Eustatius brought little benefit to Britain and it was captured by France within six months. For Rodney the ultimate consequence of his involvement was that he ended his days in genteel poverty, a fate he might have avoided but for two disasters. Firstly, the convoy taking the booty back to England, on which his hopes of prize money chiefly depended, was intercepted in the Channel approaches on 2 May 1781 by La Motte Picquet, who captured many of the merchant ships,[45] and secondly, the books of account and other trading documents which he had so carefully assembled to justify his actions and which he entrusted to government ministers at home could not be found when he needed them to defend himself in court against claims for wrongful confiscations.

Chapter 7

The Chesapeake

After the capture of Tobago, de Grasse had returned on 18 June to Fort Royal in Martinique. He sailed thence on 5 July for Cap Français in St Domingo via Grenada where he was joined by the *Hector*, which had been disabled in the Tobago expedition. He took with him twenty-three ships of the line, one 50-gun ship and a convoy of 160 merchantmen. At Cap Français, where he arrived on 16 July, he found an additional four ships of the line under Monteil.[1] He also found waiting for him three letters from the Comte de Rochambeau, the senior French General in America, urgently requesting his presence in what he described as a critical situation. As well as ships Rochambeau asked him to bring money (1.2 million livres) and troops. The letters, in part prompted by Washington, outlined two possibilities for the next offensive operation, namely an attack against the British garrison at New York, which Washington favoured, or an intervention on the Chesapeake against Cornwallis. Since neither was possible without his support the choice was left to de Grasse who responded decisively to the requests for assistance. Having failed to raise the money in St Domingo against the security of his own and another officer's property there he succeeded in raising it in Havana without security.[2] He arranged to borrow until November 3,300 French troops and their artillery who had been allocated to the Spanish. Despite the fact that ten of his ships of the line had been in the West Indies for a long time and had been ordered home for repair, he postponed the sailing of the trade convoy to Europe which they were to have escorted and decided to take his whole fleet to America.[3] It is a measure of the boldness of this decision that Rodney did not contemplate its possibility and based his own disposition of ships on the assumption that de Grasse would take half his fleet to America, an assumption shared by Hood. Mahan commented that 'it was not the least among the fortunate concurrences for the American cause at that moment, that de Grasse, whose military capacity was not conspicuous, showed then a remarkable energy, politic tact and breadth of view'.[4]

De Grasse sailed from Cap Français for America on 5 August. Including the *Hector* and the *Bourgogne* which joined him two days later his fleet consisted of twenty-eight ships of the line. To minimize the chance of detection by the British but also to rendezvous with the frigates *Aigrette* and *Railleuse* which were to bring the money from Havana, he took his fleet through the little used and difficult Old Bahama Channel between Cuba and the Great Bahama Bank, 'the famous dreaded channel, where no French Fleet had ever passed'.[5] After meeting the two frigates on 17 August off Matanzas on the north-west coast of Cuba he sailed for the Chesapeake via the Straits of Florida. During the passage north four small British ships were sighted and captured with the result that the movements of the French fleet were not detected.[6] In one of those ships was General Lord Rawdon, former British commander at Savannah and Charleston.[7] De Grasse reached the mouth of Chesapeake Bay on 30 August and anchored in Lynnhaven Bay, immediately west of Cape Henry. The following day he arranged for the 3,300 troops he had brought from Havana to be taken by boat 40 miles up the James River to join the Marquis de Lafayette.[8]

Four days before his departure from Cap Français de Grasse had sent the frigate *Concorde* to Rhode Island with letters for Rochambeau and de Barras confirming his decision to go to the Chesapeake and leaving de Barras with discretion either to operate independently on the American coast or to go south to join him. He confirmed also that he would have troops with him. Having learnt on 14 August of de Grasse's intentions, Washington abandoned his plan for an attack on New York and turned his attention to the Chesapeake,[9] where Cornwallis, with 8,000 men, was preparing a defensive position based on the village of Yorktown between the York and the James Rivers. Charles, Earl Cornwallis had served with distinction in subordinate roles in the early part of the war and, following the capture of Charleston on 12 May 1781, had commanded the British army in the south. His incursions from South Carolina into North Carolina and Virginia had met with limited success and had been bedevilled by his difficult relationship with Sir Henry Clinton, the British Commander-in-Chief in America based in New York. His entry into Virginia had been without specific orders and against Clinton's wishes,[10] but Clinton refused his request to be allowed to return to Charleston. The choice of Yorktown as a base was in part prompted by the desire of the Royal Navy for a southern anchorage during the freezing months[11] and its value as a defensive position depended entirely on British control of sea communications. Near the Yorktown peninsula, with nearly 5,000 men, was the young French general, the Marquis de Lafayette, whose force was soon to be augmented by the 3,300 men, commanded by the Marquis de St Simon, brought from the West Indies by de Grasse.[12]

On 19 August Washington and Rochambeau set out on a 400-mile march from the Hudson to the Chesapeake with 2,500 American and 4,000 French troops, leaving behind a small defensive force at West Point. After a detour designed to give the impression that he planned to attack New York from the south, Washington reached Philadelphia on 2 September, where he was joined the following day by Rochambeau. Soon after leaving Philadelphia on 5 September he learnt in Chester, Pennsylvania, that de Grasse had arrived at the Chesapeake.[13] At 8.00 am on the same day de Grasse received a report from a frigate cruising off Cape Henry of an approaching fleet. It was not de Barras as he hoped, but the British.[14]

At the time of the St Eustatius interlude Rodney was very ill. In addition to his crippling gout he was afflicted with a stricture the symptoms of which would today suggest prostate problems. He applied for and was granted leave to return to England during the hurricane season in order to recuperate. Early in May he suffered a loss with the death of Captain Walter Young, his Flag-Captain, who died in St Eustatius, having been ill with a fever for some time. Notwithstanding his habit of criticizing Rodney behind his back, he had been a source of strength and support; Rodney had praised him generously in his despatches after the Moonlight Battle, and after the action against de Guichen on 17 April 1780. An anonymous note found in Middleton's papers said of him: 'The fleet has experienced a loss in Captain Young's death,* for I believe there is not another man breathing so calculated to control and guide to fame a character [Rodney] that Nature never intended should be either a hero or a man of business.'[15] His death at this time can only have added to the pressures on Rodney, who while anxious to go home for medical treatment felt unable to do so with so much to be attended to. Hood was not only irritated by his indecision but suggested that there were other reasons why Rodney was reluctant to return to England:

It is quite impossible from the unsteadiness of the commander-in-chief to know what he means three days together; one hour he says his complaints are of such nature that he cannot possibly remain in this country, and is determined to leave the command with me; the next he says he has no thought of going home. The truth is I believe he is guided by his feelings on the moment he is speaking, and that his mind is not at present at all at ease, thinking if he quits the command he will get to England at a time that many mouths perhaps may be opened against him on the top of Tobago, and his not fighting the French fleet off that island after the public declarations he made to every one of his determined resolution to do it; and again, if he stays much longer, his laurels may be subject to wither.[16]

News of de Grasse's departure from Fort Royal in Martinique reached Rodney at Barbados on 8 July. It had long been expected

* Died 2 May 1781.

that part at least of the French fleet would go to America in the hurricane season and assumed that the usual movement of British ships there at that time should be in sufficient strength, taking into account the number of French and British ships already in America, to meet the threat. Rodney's estimate of the likely number of French ships to go, reinforced by advice from the administration at home, was fourteen.[17] Hood did not disagree with this, but if anything his own estimate was lower. As late as 29 August his secretary, Joseph Hunt, suggested to Middleton that the number was unlikely to be more than 'twelve sail (about the number they had coppered)'.[18]

Of the twenty-four ships of the line under Rodney's command after Hood's arrival in January 1781, three had gone home with convoys between January and May, leaving twenty-one now on the station (see Appendix 7). Two of these, the *Triumph* and the *Panther*, an old-fashioned 60-gun ship, were sent home as escorts to the convoy sailing in August. Both were in need of refitting and coppering. The *Sandwich*, too unfit for the voyage home, was sent with the Jamaica convoy for refitting there. The *Torbay* and the *Prince William* were also sent with the Jamaica convoy with orders to proceed to America as soon as they had discharged their escort duty. Rodney's request to Sir Peter Parker was unambiguous:

> As the enemy have a very great naval force in North America, I must beg you will dispatch the *Torbay* and *Prince William* without detaining them a single moment, and also that you will add to their force by sending to that country every line of battle ship you can possibly spare from your station.[19]

Having decided that he must go home with the August convoy he chose to sail in the *Gibraltar*. She was in some need of repair and was said to have too deep a draught (27 feet) to go over the bar at Sandy Hook, a factor which would restrict her usefulness in America, but both these justifications were questioned later when Rodney's dispositions came under review. Of the remaining fifteen ships the *Russell* was still undergoing repairs in Antigua following the damage to her in the action of 29 April between Hood and de

116

Grasse. That left fourteen ships all of which Rodney ordered Hood, as his successor in command, to take to America.[20] Rodney sailed from St Eustatius on 1 August in the *Gibraltar,* accompanied by the *Triumph* and *Panther,* the frigate *Boreas,* two bomb vessels and the 150-ship convoy for England, having the previous day given up the command of the Leeward Islands station to Hood. In attendance, as far as the latitude of Bermuda, was the frigate *Pegasus* with the intention that, if Rodney's health had improved by then in cooler weather, she would take him to America. As this did not happen he sent her to New York and continued on the voyage to England.[21]

Hood went initially to Antigua with ten ships where he embarked troops requested by Clinton and sailed on 10 August for America. Shortly after leaving he was joined by Drake with four ships from St Lucia where he had been sent to investigate a report, which proved to be false, of four French ships of the line in Fort Royal, Martinique. Unlike de Grasse, Hood went by the most direct route to the Chesapeake and made his landfall on 25 August just south of Cape Henry, five days before de Grasse arrived there. Finding no sign of the enemy in the Chesapeake he made for New York via the capes of the Delaware, again without seeing any sign of a hostile fleet, and reached Sandy Hook on 28 August.[22] Arbuthnot had resigned the command of the North American station in July and gone home leaving his second-in-command, Rear Admiral Thomas Graves, in charge pending the arrival of his successor Rear Admiral Digby. Graves was only just senior to Hood and like him had commanded a frigate under Rodney during the bombardment of Le Havre during the Seven Years' War. More recently he had served under Byron in North America and the West Indies before returning home on promotion to flag rank. He had hoisted his flag in the *London* in the Channel Fleet under Sir Charles Hardy, before returning to America in July 1780 with reinforcements to join Arbuthnot, under whom he took part in the action off the Chesapeake on 16 March 1781.[23] He was not as able a commander as Hood and it has been suggested, in the light of subsequent events, that Hood resented serving under him.

On arrival at Sandy Hook, Hood received a letter from Graves requesting him to bring his fleet over the bar to join his own ships in New York harbour. Hood declined to do so but went by ship's boat to join Graves and Clinton at a meeting on Long Island, at which they discussed a project to attack Rhode Island where de Barras had his squadron of eight ships at Newport. The scheme was not without merit because it was desirable to prevent a junction between de Barras and de Grasse but Hood persuaded Graves that time was precious and that, whatever he did, he should move his ships across the bar to Sandy Hook (that evening they learnt that de Barras had sailed from Newport three days earlier).[24] On the first favourable wind Graves crossed the bar at Sandy Hook during the afternoon of 31 August with the five of his ships that were fit for service. As the senior of the two admirals he took command of the combined fleet of nineteen ships of the line (see Appendix 7 for details) which sailed immediately for the Chesapeake.[25]

On the morning of 5 September 1781 de Grasse's fleet lay at anchor in three lines in Lynnhaven Bay as the British fleet approached the Chesapeake with the wind blowing from north-north-east. The French were first sighted at 9.30 am when Cape Henry was approximately 20 miles away to the west. Although the exact number of ships could not yet be ascertained it was apparent by 11.00 am that the enemy was present in some force and Graves made the signal for line of battle ahead at 2 cables, which he shortened to one cable at 12.45 pm shortly after observing that the enemy fleet was getting under sail. By deduction from the log of the *London*, Graves's flagship, the fleet was now sailing somewhat north of west towards the Middle Ground, a shoal in the entrance to Chesapeake Bay about 5 miles north of Cape Henry. At 1.00 pm he hauled down the signal for line ahead and hoisted the signal for an east and west line of bearing at one cable.[26]

On receipt of the first report from an outlying frigate of ships approaching, the French fleet in Lynnhaven Bay rejoiced, believing that it must be de Barras with his eight ships from Rhode Island; but having left Newport on 25 August de Barras had gone out into the Atlantic to avoid detection, with the intention of working up to the Chesapeake from the south-east, and he did not arrive until

10 September. It was soon clear that the approaching fleet was too large to be anything but British, consisting as it did of nineteen ships of the line, one 50-gun ship, six frigates and a fire ship. The strength of de Grasse's fleet in Lynnhaven Bay was twenty-four ships of the line – on arrival he had sent four ships to block the entrances of the York and James Rivers. He was also short of 1,800 men who had manned the boats which took St Simon's troops ashore and were now collecting water for the fleet. The disparity in numbers of French and British ships was reflected in the number of guns mounted, 1,800 to 2,000 guns in the twenty-four French ships and 1,400 to 1,500 in the nineteen British.[27] The British fleet was also in rather worse condition than the French. The *Terrible* had come all the way from the West Indies with her pumps working and the *Ajax* was also leaky. However, all the British ships were coppered as opposed to about half of the French. Having established that the approaching fleet was British, de Grasse decided to go out to sea to fight. At 11.30 am he ordered his ships to slip their mooring cables, and when the ebb tide made just before noon they started tacking out against the north-north-easterly wind in some disarray in order to get out of the Bay. Although the mouth of Chesapeake Bay between Cape Henry to the south and Cape Charles to the north is 10 miles wide, the only navigable part is the channel between Cape Henry and the Middle Ground. Because of the urgency de Grasse ordered his ships to get into line of battle on an easterly course in order of speed (*par rang de vitesse*), i.e. without reference to their appointed positions in the line. In the race to get to sea de Bougainville's squadron took the van position and found itself some way ahead of the rest of the French fleet. There are conflicting accounts of the precise order in which particular ships joined the line but one French witness recorded that a gap of over a mile separated the first four ships in the line from the next two, and that those two were about two and a half miles ahead of the *Ville de Paris*, de Grasse's flagship. The same witness observed that the English 'were in the best possible order, bowsprit to stern, heading down on us and consequently to our windward'. He added that the three British Admirals (Graves, Hood and Drake) 'made an immense number of signals to each other before engaging us'.[28]

As the *Ville de Paris* cleared Cape Henry at about 1.45 pm the British fleet was getting close to the Middle Ground. It was not until 2.00 pm that the full strength of the French fleet became apparent. Since, at that time, neither Graves nor Hood were aware that de Grasse had brought his whole fleet from the West Indies, it was a natural assumption that de Barras had already joined him and that it was their combined fleet whose van the British now saw 3 miles to the south and sailing east on the port tack. At 2.11 pm Graves made the signal to wear together and his fleet came round on to an easterly course nearly parallel to that of the French.[29] Hood, whose division had led the approach to the Middle Ground, was now in the rear and Drake's division was in the van, with the *Shrewsbury* leading. Graves now faced an enemy fleet whose van was separated by a large interval from the rest of its fleet. This presented him with an opportunity of attacking the French van with his whole fleet and destroying it, probably before support could come up. However, because the French centre and rear were so far behind and because the French had five more ships, their rear was a long way behind the British rear, or in Graves's own words 'we were by no means extended with their rear'.[30] In classic line-of-battle tactics this was a situation to be avoided because it gave the enemy the opportunity of 'doubling' one's rear, i.e. attacking it on both sides. It was this factor rather than the opportunity of attacking the French van which Graves decided must be dealt with and accordingly, immediately after wearing, he ordered his fleet to bring to 'in order to let the centre of the enemy's ships come abreast of us'.[31]

It is not clear from the *London*'s log when the fleet got under way again, but according to Captain Thomas White, then a midshipman in Hood's flagship, the *Barfleur*, this was at 2.30 pm, when the French van had got nearly abreast of the British van.[32] At that time Graves ordered the leading ship, the *Shrewsbury*, to lead more to starboard in order to approach the enemy, and a fatal flaw in the command arrangements began to manifest itself. The fourteen captains who had come with Hood from the West Indies were accustomed to Rodney's signals and instructions, while Graves's five captains had been issued with the signals and instructions which he had inherited recently from Arbuthnot.

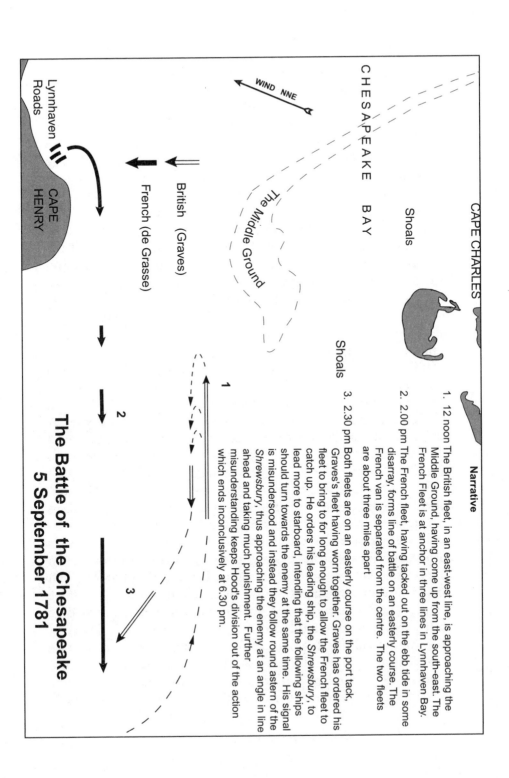

The Battle of the Chesapeake
5 September 1781

CAPE CHARLES

CHESAPEAKE BAY

Shoals

The Middle Ground

Shoals

WIND NNE

Lynnhaven Roads

CAPE HENRY

British (Graves)

French (de Grasse)

Narrative

1. 12 noon The British fleet, in an east-west line, is approaching the Middle Ground, having come up from the south-east. The French Fleet is at anchor in three lines in Lynnhaven Bay.

2. 2.00 pm The French fleet, having tacked out on the ebb tide in some disarray, forms line of battle on an easterly course. The French van is separated from the centre. The two fleets are about three miles apart

3. 2.30 pm Both fleets are on an easterly course on the port tack, Graves's fleet having worn together. Graves has ordered his fleet to bring to for long enough to allow the French fleet to catch up. He orders his leading ship, the *Shrewsbury*, to lead more to starboard, intending that the following ships should turn towards the enemy at the same time. His signal is misunderstood and instead they follow round astern of the *Shrewsbury*, thus approaching the enemy at an angle in line ahead and taking much punishment. Further misunderstanding keeps Hood's division out of the action which ends inconclusively at 6.30 pm.

Hood's captains were also issued with these after they came under Graves's command,[33] but there was very little time available for briefing or tactical exercises on the way from Sandy Hook to the Chesapeake. According to an authoritative analysis, what Graves intended by his 2.30 pm signal, consistent with Arbuthnot's signals and instructions, was that the whole fleet should alter course together to starboard in conformity with the movement of the leading ship, enabling the fleet to run down 'on a lasking course to engage', i.e. on a slanting course on a line of bearing parallel to the enemy line, so that all ships engaged at the same time.[34] What actually happened was that the ships astern of the *Shrewsbury*, all West Indies ships, misunderstood the signal and altered course not together but in succession, following in the *Shrewsbury's* wake. The result of this misunderstanding was that the British van approached the French van in line ahead at an angle and were thus unable to use their own guns although exposed to enemy fire.

Graves repeated the misunderstood signal twice and at 3.46 pm made the signal for line ahead at one cable followed by the signal for all ships to bear down and engage their opponents. At 4.11 pm the signal for line ahead was hauled down 'that it might not interfere with the signal to engage close'. That should have removed any misunderstanding as to what Graves intended. Ships began to bear down on the enemy, but unfortunately the *Montagu*, eighth in the line (in reverse order) and two ships ahead of the *London*, luffed up and opened fire at too great a range, forcing the ships immediately astern of her, including the *London*, also to luff up to avoid getting between her and the enemy. To restore an orderly formation and to push forward the ships which had luffed up prematurely Graves hoisted the signal for line ahead at 4.22 pm and at the same time hauled down the signal for close action. Five minutes later he restored the signal for close action and according to his own account hauled down the signal for line ahead.[35] However, Hood was adamant, and his assertion was corroborated by White, that the signal for line ahead was not hauled down until about 5.30 pm and that it remained hoisted together with the signal for close action. He decided that the signal for line ahead must prevail and called back the ships in his rear division which had begun to bear down on the enemy.[36] He ordered them to bear down again when he perceived that the signal for line ahead had been hauled down at 5.30 pm, but the French were then too far to leeward to enable him to achieve anything before firing ceased. According to the *London*'s log the signal for close action was repeated at 5.20 pm and it confirms that the rear division bore down to engage at 5.30 pm but it does not support Hood's contention that the signal for line ahead had remained in force until then. The signal in question was a union flag at the mizzen-peak and it has been suggested that Graves saw it hauled down but that it was rehoisted as a national emblem by an overactive signalman.[37]

The British van had engaged the first four ships in the French van shortly after 4.00 pm and because of the method of its approach had sustained considerable damage. The *Shrewsbury*, the lead ship, was beaten out of the line but the French were also severely punished and de Grasse signalled them to bear away to leeward. At 6.23 pm Graves hauled down the signal for close action and hoisted the signal for line ahead at one cable. Firing ceased at 6.30 pm shortly after and de Grasse took his fleet away to leeward. Nine British ships out of nineteen and about thirteen French ships out of twenty-four had played virtually no part in the action.[38] The British casualties were 90 killed and 246 wounded, of which over a third in total were in the *Shrewsbury* and her next in line, the *Intrepid*. Total French casualties were about 200.[39]

At the end of the action Graves had sent frigates to the van and rear with orders to the ships to keep in a parallel line with the enemy and well abreast during the night, with a view to resuming the action in the morning. They returned with reports of extensive damage, particularly in the case of the *Shrewsbury* and the *Intrepid* referred to above. The *Montagu* was in danger of losing her masts and the pre-existing leaking of the *Terrible* and the *Ajax* had worsened. In all only five ships, four of them in Hood's division, were undamaged. The fleets remained in sight of one another for five days and came near at times, but Graves considered that his 'mutilated' fleet lacked the speed to attack and de Grasse, who was to windward for much of the time, showed no inclination to do so. According to his own account Hood felt strongly that the British fleet should take possession of the Chesapeake while de Grasse was out but appears not to have urged it on Graves soon enough. On 11 September de Grasse took his fleet back into Chesapeake Bay where he found de Barras's squadron at anchor, having arrived the day before. Including the four ships previously left behind the French now had a combined fleet of thirty-six ships of the line. Following the burning of the *Terrible* on 11 September because she was likely to sink, the British fleet had been reduced to eighteen.[40]

Graves learnt on 13 September from the frigate *Medea* of the arrival of the French fleets in Chesapeake Bay and summoned Hood and Drake to a council of war in the *London*. In the light of the new intelligence, together with 'the present condition of the British Fleet, the season of the year so near the Equinox, and the impracticability of giving any effectual succour to General Earl Cornwallis in the Chesapeake', it was resolved to proceed with all despatch to New York to repair and replenish the fleet.[41] The fleet arrived at New York on 20 September, but because of a shortage of stores and provisions there it was a month before it was able to sail again. Four days after arrival, at a conference of generals and admirals it was agreed that the Navy should embark troops under the command of Sir Henry Clinton and attempt to force its way through the Chesapeake to relieve Cornwallis. The fleet sailed from Sandy Hook on 19 October with 7,000 troops. It now numbered twenty-five ships of the line having been reinforced by the arrival from England with Rear Admiral Digby on 21 September of the *Prince George*, *Canada* and *Lion* and the long-delayed arrival from Jamaica on 11 October of the *Torbay* and the *Prince William*. In addition two of Graves's own ships, the *Prudent* and the *Robust*, which had missed the last expedition, were now with the fleet. There were also two 50-gun ships and a number of frigates and fireships. At Digby's invitation, Graves was again in command until completion of the business in hand. On passage to the Chesapeake on 24 October Graves learnt from three men who had escaped by boat from Yorktown that Cornwallis had capitulated on the 18th. (The formal surrender took place the following day, the day Graves sailed from Sandy Hook.) After verifying this intelligence the fleet returned to New York to disembark the troops and to put the West Indies squadron in a position to leave America as soon as possible.[42]

The surrender of Cornwallis at Yorktown destroyed the will of Britain to continue the land war and led in due course to the loss of her American colonies. Since a key factor in his entrapment was the seizure by de Grasse of control of Chesapeake Bay, in combination with the advance from the north by Washington and Rochambeau, the Royal Navy was seen as bearing a heavy burden of responsibility for having failed to stop de Grasse from reaching the Chesapeake in the first place, and then, at the eleventh hour, in having failed to wrest control of the Bay from him in the action of 5 September. When the full implications of those two failures came to be considered at home there was an inevitable search for scapegoats, but long before that, indeed the day after the battle, recriminations began about the tactics used and the conduct of Graves and Hood.

On that day Hood wrote a memorandum, sent later to Jackson, which began, 'Yesterday the British fleet had a rich and most plentiful harvest of glory in view, but the means to gather it were omitted in more instances than one.' He elaborated on what he saw as three lost opportunities. Firstly, the French fleet should have been attacked as it came out of Lynnhaven Bay 'by no means in a regular or connected way'. Failing that, when the French van was out and far ahead of the centre and rear it should have been attacked with the whole force of the British fleet. 'There was a full hour and a half to have engaged it before any of the rear could have come up' and the isolated van could have been destroyed in half an hour. Finally, when the British van got into trouble, the centre should have been brought up in support. By implication he blamed the failure to achieve this, and his own inaction, on the fact that the signal for line ahead was kept flying, although he thought that this could have been remedied if Graves 'had set the example of close action, even with the signal for the line flying'.[43]

Graves also wrote a memorandum on 6 September, addressed to all flag officers and captains:

When the signal for the line of battle ahead is out at the same time with the signal for battle it is not to be understood that the latter signal shall be rendered ineffectual by the strict adherence to the former, and the signal for the line of battle is to be considered as the line of extension, and the respective Admirals and captains of the fleet are desired to be attentive not to advance or fall back, so as to intercept the fire of their seconds ahead and astern, but to keep as near the enemy as possible, whilst the signal for close action continues out, and to take notice that the line must be preserved parallel to that of the enemy during battle without regard to a particular point or bearing.

Hood took this as a personal rebuke, as he was intended to, and endorsed his copy of the memorandum, 'It is the first time I ever heard it suggested that too strict an adherence could be paid to the line of battle . . . According to Mr Graves's Memo, any captain may break the line with impunity when he pleases'.[44] Despite Hood's protestation, the principle that the fleet might bear down on the enemy notwithstanding the fact that the signal for the line was flying was not foreign to the West Indies squadron. Article 21 of Additional Fighting Instructions used by Rodney in the action against de Guichen on 17 April 1780 included just such a stipulation as did the very similar Article 17 of the Additional Fighting Instructions used in his 1782 campaign.[45]

Graves and Hood both have their champions and the arguments as to who should have done what on 5 September have never been resolved.[46] However, if Graves did indeed intend by his signal at 2.30 pm that the whole fleet should turn to starboard together and bear down on the enemy,* then much of the argument is sterile because had the fleet complied at that time, parts two and three of Hood's 'rich and most plentiful harvest of glory' might have been reaped. In other words, the fiasco was more a matter of a misunderstood signal than the failure of any individual. Graves said as much when he wrote to Sandwich, 'The signal was not understood. I do not mean to blame anyone, my Lord. I hope we all did our

* See p. 122 above and endnote 34.

best'.[47] That leaves to be considered what Hood saw as the first of the three missed opportunities, namely the possibility of attacking the French fleet as it emerged in disorder from Lynnhaven Bay. There is no evidence that Graves even considered this possibility. With fourteen of his nineteen captains having been under his command for only five days it is not surprising that he preferred a more controlled and conservative approach. It is a matter of speculation as to whether Hood or Rodney, if he had been there, might have risked it and succeeded.

Rodney, having heard the news from the Chesapeake, wrote to Jackson on 19 October. Not in the best of health he complained of 'a very violent pain in my stomach, which has continued these four days and reduced me much, which the news from America and Mr Graves's letter has increased'. His criticism of the tactics in the battle itself was relatively uncontentious. Like Hood he argued that Graves should have concentrated the whole of his fleet against part of the French fleet, which, in his own way, is what Graves was trying to do. Rodney reminded Jackson of his own unsuccessful attempt to do this against de Guichen on 17 April 1780. (Although Rodney did not say so the comparison was apt since on both occasions failure was linked to a misunderstood signal.) He conceded that Graves had fewer ships than de Grasse, but argued that if he had ensured that all his own ships had been in a state of readiness before Hood's arrival, and that if Sir Peter Parker had not detained two ships in Jamaica, he would have had twenty-five ships against de Grasse's twenty-four. He wrongly accused Graves of having failed to prevent a junction between de Barras and Graves by lying idle at Sandy Hook before Hood's arrival. That junction took place six days after the battle, not before it. He was also at pains to pre-empt criticism of his own role in the events which led up to the battle, and in particular the extent to which he had foreseen the threat posed by the movement of de Grasse's fleet to America and had issued the necessary warnings and instructions:

Had Mr Graves attended to the intelligence I sent him six weeks before I left the West Indies, as likewise two expresses

I sent him pressing his junction with his whole squadron with Sir Samuel Hood off the Capes of Virginia, he had been on that station long before de Grasse, and, of course, prevented the latter landing his troops in Virginia.[48]

Rodney repeated part of this statement in the House of Commons when replying to Edmund Burke's motion on St Eustatius on 4 December:

As to the disaster in America, he would tell the House what steps he had taken to prevent it. He had sent to the commander in chief at Jamaica, to send the *Prince William* and *Torbay* to America with the greatest dispatch; and he had sent also to the commander in chief in America, desiring he would collect his whole force, and meet him with it off the Capes of Virginia; and if he could not meet him, that he would let him know it by one of his frigates: but no answer had been sent to him or to sir Samuel Hood, for he himself was then so ill that he was coming home. He had sent twice to the admiral at Jamaica, and three times to the admiral at New York: one of his three dispatches miscarried, the vessel that carried it being forced on shore by some privateers; and from that circumstance he had learned always in future to keep copies of every dispatch, for of that he had none. If the admiral in America had [not] met sir Samuel Hood near the Chesapeak, the probability was that de Grasse would have been defeated, and the surrender of Lord Cornwallis prevented.[49]

On the premise that the Royal Navy's failure on the Chesapeake led directly to the surrender of Cornwallis at Yorktown, which in turn led to the loss of Britain's American colonies, it is inevitable that Rodney should attract his share of blame. The most serious charge against him is that he failed to defeat de Grasse in the West Indies, firstly by stationing Hood on the wrong side of Martinique to intercept his arrival from Europe, and secondly by not forcing an action after the loss of Tobago when he had the advantage of the weather gage and moonlight. The first alleged failure on his part is linked to his entanglement in the affairs of St Eustatius. Lord Shelburne said in the House of Lords on 27 November 1781 that 'he solemnly believed that the capture of Lord Cornwallis was owing to the capture of St Eustatius'.[50] Not everybody was convinced by Rodney's reasons for not fighting de Grasse after Tobago,[51] but the security of Barbados seems to have been uppermost in his mind.

Sir Henry Clinton blamed Rodney for sending too few ships to America, as have others. Of the twenty-four ships of the line under Rodney's command after Hood's arrival in January 1781, three had gone home with convoys between January and May, leaving twenty-one on the station, all of which were nominally available to send to America in August, apart from the *Russell* which was undergoing repairs of battle damage (see page 116 and Appendix 7). If de Grasse could take all his ships to America why did Rodney send only fourteen out of twenty? Two modern-day historians have considered this in detail. A.G. Jamieson concluded that Rodney sent all the ships he reasonably could have, with the possible exception of the *Gibraltar* in which he went home.[52] Kenneth Breen thought Rodney should have sent the *Gibraltar*, and that he should have sent the *Torbay* and the *Prince William* to America direct and not via Jamaica where they were detained by Parker.[53] Whether three more ships would have made a difference is hard to say. Their presence might have made Graves bolder, but it would not have resolved the signalling difficulty that lay behind his failure.

Rodney has also been criticized for sending Hood to America knowing that he would be subordinate to an admiral of inferior ability (Arbuthnot, Graves or Digby).[54] The implication of this criticism is that Rodney should have gone himself. While there may well have been other reasons for his going home, for instance to deal with matters arising from St Eustatius, there is little doubt that he was seriously unwell. Sandwich thought that his decision to come home was determined 'by his own bad state of health, which undoubtedly made him unfit at that time for service that required activity both of body and mind'.[55] That he wanted to go to America if possible is evident from the fact that he delayed a final decision until he reached the latitude of Bermuda. Furthermore he was accompanied on the voyage home by his personal physician, Gilbert Blane, later a pillar of his profession, and it seems reasonable to assume that there were compelling medical reasons for his return. Hood had no doubt that Rodney's presence at the Chesapeake would have made a difference. 'I am persuaded,' he wrote to Middleton, 'had that admiral led his Majesty's squadron from the West Indies to this coast, the 5th of September would I think have been a most glorious day for Great Britain.'[56]

Rear Admiral Thomas Graves was the younger brother of William Graves, a barrister and active Member of Parliament, who believed that his brother had unfairly received most of the blame for the misfortune on the Chesapeake. In 1783 he published two letters in defence of the admiral's reputation.[57] He had been particularly concerned by a speech in the House of Lords on 27 November 1781 by Lord Denbigh. This anticipated Rodney's statement in the House of Commons during the St Eustatius debate on 4 December, but the content was somewhat different apart from references to three despatches from Rodney and to a recommendation to the Commander-in-Chief in North America that he should collect his whole force and meet the squadron coming from the West Indies off the Capes of Virginia. Denbigh's speech was more critical of Graves than Rodney's and included the untrue statement that Hood had waited for Graves for nine days off the Chesapeake before going on to New York. He also alleged that Graves had disregarded warnings from the Admiralty similar to those sent by Rodney.

When William Graves encountered Rodney during a division in the House of Commons, he asked for copies of the three despatches (3 May, 7 July and 13 Aug 1781). Rodney agreed 'with great frankness and politeness' that he should have them and added that the July despatch was 'the most material of all'. He received copies of the May and August despatches after the St Eustatius debate, but a copy of the July despatch was more elusive. Rodney said that it was in his letter book in Plymouth and suggested that Graves ask the Admiralty for a copy, but the letter could not be found there. In a final attempt to get a copy Graves sent a friend to Plymouth

130

where Rodney was preparing to return to America, but he failed to get a copy before Rodney sailed. At some point, however, Rodney had given Graves a précis of the missing despatch. When he eventually obtained a copy of the despatch he found that it differed materially from the précis, which gave the impression that Rodney was better informed about French intentions than appeared to be the case from the despatch itself. The précis was a private note which came into the public domain when Graves published it two years later. More important is a comparison of the three despatches with Rodney's letter to Jackson of 19 October, a quasi-official document, and his speech in the St Eustatius debate on 4 December, which was a public statement.[58]

All three despatches were addressed to Arbuthnot and the relevant parts of them are quoted below. The first was written on 3 May and sent by the *Garland*, arriving in New York on 19 June. Rodney wrote:

> A very considerable French squadron, having arrived at Martinique from Europe on the 29th of last month, I think it is my duty to give you information thereof, that you may be on your guard should they visit the continent of America, in which case I shall send you every reinforcement in my power.[59]

The second, written on 7 July, and described by Rodney to William Graves as 'the most material of all', was sent by the *Swallow*, commanded by Captain Wells, who was ordered to proceed 'without one moment's loss of time' but was not told specifically of the importance of the sealed letter that he was carrying. He arrived at New York on 27 July, six days after Graves had set off in pursuit of a reported French convoy. Commodore Edmund Affleck took a copy of the despatch and sent Wells after Graves who was in the vicinity of Boston Bay. Just after the *Swallow* had left New York she chased a rebel privateer in the hope of making a prize but three more privateers appeared and forced her onto the rocks. Wells prudently threw the despatch unopened into Long Island Sound and Graves did not see Affleck's copy until he returned to New York on 18 August.[60] Rodney had written:

As the Enemy has at this time a fleet of 28 Sail of the Line at Martinique, a part of which is reported to be destined for North America, I have dispatched his Majesty's Sloop *Swallow* to acquaint you therewith, and inform You that I shall keep as good a look out as possible on their motions, by which my own shall be regulated.

In case of my sending a Squadron to America I shall order it to make the Capes of Virginia, and proceed along the coast to the Capes of the Delaware, and from thence to Sandy Hook, unless the intelligence it may receive from you should induce it to act otherwise.

The Enemy's Squadron destined for America will sail I am informed in a short time, but whether they call at Cape François, I cannot learn: however, you may depend upon the Squadron in America being reinforced, should the Enemy bend their forces that way.[61]

The third and last despatch was written on 13 August when Rodney headed for home in the latitude of Bermuda and was sent with the *Pegasus*, which did not reach Graves until 8 September, three days after the battle, having been delayed by an encounter with the French fleet. Rodney wrote:

Herewith I have the honour to enclose you intelligence which I received from St Thomas's the night before I sailed from St Eustatius, and to acquaint you that I left Sir Samuel Hood preparing to sail with all dispatch with 12 Sail of the line, 4 frigates, and a fireship, for the Capes of Virginia, where I am persuaded the French intend making their grand effort. Permit me therefore to recommend it to you to collect all the force you can, and form a junction with Sir Samuel there. You will I hope, ere this reaches you, have heard of his approach, by his fastest sailing frigate, which I directed him to dispatch for the purpose of looking out for intelligence off the Chesapeak and Delaware.

The French fleet under Monsieur de Grasse, when they left the Grenades to collect their convoy, consisted of 26 sail of the line and two large ships armed en-flûte; and I imagine, at least 12 of those ships, and in all probability of part of Mr de Monteil's squadron, will be in America; and it is not impossible they may be joined by some Spanish ships.[62]

The most important part of the intelligence report referred to in Rodney's letter was as follows:

A Mr . . . . arrived this Afternoon, the 31st July, from Saint Thomas's reports, that he left that Island on Saturday last; – six Days previous thereto, a Fleet of Merchantmen arrived in nine Days from the Cape where a French Frigate had arrived the Day before their sailing, with thirty Pilots for the Chesapeake and Delawar, which together with a Number of North Americans [vessels] Collected there and awaiting Convoy, to the number of Sixty or upwards, made it looked on as certain, that the French Fleet, which was hourly expected there from Martinique, would proceed immediately to America.[63]

Comparing these three despatches with Rodney's letter to Jackson of 19 October and his remarks in the St Eustatius debate in the House of Commons there are self-evident discrepancies. In particular, Rodney should have been aware that the August despatch, sent in the *Pegasus* and the only one to contain his recommendation that Arburthnot/Graves should meet Hood off the Capes of Virginia, did not reach Graves until after the battle.[64]

There is also in Rodney's letter to Jackson a reference to his instructions to Hood which appears to be at odds with the record:

I advised Sir S. Hood by all means to guard the mouth of the Chesapeake, to anchor in the Hampton Road if [there was] occasion, to keep his frigates cruizing off the coast to the southward, that he might have timely notice of the enemy's approach, and to despatch one of his frigates to Mr Graves, acquainting him with his arrival, and pressing a speedy junction, no one thing of which has been regarded.[65]

Rodney's last recorded communication with Hood before he sailed for England merely instructed him to proceed to New York via the Chesapeake and the Delaware, which he did, and left him a large measure of discretion if circumstances required it.[66] Did Rodney set out deliberately to mislead in his references to Graves and to Hood in order to portray himself in a better light, or had ill health played havoc with his memory? Perhaps William Willcox was nearest the mark when he commented that 'Sir George's memory was the servant of his interests.'[67]

On one charge, however, Rodney can be acquitted altogether, namely that he failed to pass on to Hood the intelligence report from St Thomas's which he enclosed with his August despatch to Arbuthnot (see above).[68] Hood enclosed a copy of the report, decribed as 'Intelligence No.1. Received 31 July 1781', with his despatch to the Admiralty from New York on 30 August, nine days before the copy of the report sent by Rodney to Arbuthnot reached America.[69] Both Rodney and Hood were accused of having failed to deduce from that report and its reference to thirty pilots that de Grasse intended to take his whole fleet to the Chesapeake, but it was a reasonable assumption that some of those pilots were for the sixty merchant ships also referred to in the report. In any event it would have never have occurred to Rodney or Hood, or, for that matter, to the Admiralty, that de Grasse would detain the home-bound trade at Cap Français so that he could send his whole fleet to America. As Thomas White commented, 'If the British government had sanctioned, or a British Admiral had adopted such a measure, however necessary to carry out an important political operation, the one would have been turned out, and the other would have been hung: no wonder that they succeeded and we failed'.[70] Yorktown was a British defeat, but it was also a French and American victory, brought about by a brilliant, if fortuitous, combination of land and sea forces and, not least, by the boldness of de Grasse.

Chapter 8

The Saintes – Preliminaries

De Grasse left America for the West Indies on 4 November 1781, taking with him thirty-four ships, including seven of de Barras's, and one 50-gun ship. On 29 October Congress had passed a resolutions of thanks to him and to Rochambeau, and Washington had written to him expressing his warm personal appreciation, coupled with the hope that he would return the following year.[1] De Grasse had declined his request to support immediate operations against Charleston or Wilmington in the Carolinas because of his pressing need to get back to the West Indies to prepare for the next year's campaign there.[2] One consequence of the Battle of the Chesapeake was that de Bougainville had been restored to de Grasse's favour after their estrangement following the encounter with Hood off Martinique at the end of April.[3] On reaching St Domingo de Grasse detached four ships to escort the delayed home-bound trade and took the rest of his fleet to Martinique, arriving at Fort Royal on 26 November. On that very day, having taken advantage of the absence of all major British warships from the West Indies, the Marquis de Bouillé had recaptured St Eustatius. Once he had overcome the initial difficulties of getting a fleet of eight small ships there against contrary winds and of landing troops in rough seas at night on a rocky shore, the operation had been absurdly easy. The defending garrison had been taken by surprise on the parade ground early in the morning and the Governor had been captured soon afterwards. In all 700 British troops were taken prisoner and some £250,000 in cash seized, the remaining proceeds of the St Eustatius confiscations, which according to Rodney had been intended to pay the Army in America. Saba and St Martin were also recaptured before de Bouillé returned to Fort Royal.[4]

Six days after de Grasse, Hood left America on 11 November with eighteen ships of the line, including four of Digby's, which was all he was prepared to spare at this time from his new command. The *Prince William* was left behind for repair and followed later. After a stormy passage, during which two ships became separated from the rest of the fleet, Hood arrived in Barbados on 5 December. There he found and appropriated the *St Albans*, newly arrived with a convoy from England. By January, with the extensive repairs to the *Russell* completed and with the arrival of Commodore Edmund Affleck from America with two more of Digby's ships, Hood had twenty-two ships of the line against de Grasse's thirty.[5] The imbalance would have been greater but for Rear Admiral Richard Kempenfelt's interception on 12 December of a French fleet and convoy commanded by de Guichen, 150 miles south-west of Ushant. This comprised nineteen ships of the line, of which five were destined for the West Indies, accompanied by a large number of transports, nineteen of which were captured before the fleet was scattered in a storm. Only two ships of the line and five transports eventually arrived in the West Indies.[6]

On 17 December de Grasse set out with de Bouillé and 6,000 troops embarked to attack Barbados but stormy weather in the St Lucia channel thwarted their attempt to get to windward and they returned to Fort Royal a week later.[7] They tried again on 28 December but once more returned after a week of heavy sailing. Frustrated in their attempts to get to Barbados de Grasse and de Bouillé now settled for St Kitts, which lying 190 miles to the north-west was more easily accessible with a prevailing easterly wind. They sailed on 5 January, with 6,000 troops embarked as before, and anchored at Basseterre, the principal port of St Kitts on the 11th. The whole island was taken, apart from Brimstone Hill in the north-west of the island, to which General Shirley, the Governor, had retired and which was defended by General Fraser with 1,200 troops.[8]

136

Apart from having fewer ships than de Grasse, Hood was having considerable difficulty obtaining enough bread for his fleet and he was also concerned about the condition of some of his ships. Nevertheless when he heard on 14 January from Governor Shirley that French men-of-war and transports had been sighted off Nevis, he put to sea at once with twenty ships (he was joined later by two more) and made for St John's Road, Antigua where he intended to make his base for the protection of St Kitts, but he heard on passage that St Kitts had been invested. After he reached Antigua on 22 January he learnt that de Grasse had anchored his fleet at Basseterre in an east-west line and not in particularly good order. In the prevailing wind this made the easternmost ships vulnerable to a surprise attack because it would be some time before the remaining ships could get up to windward to support them. Basseterre was only 60 miles from St John's Road, via the southern end of Nevis, and Hood sailed on the 23rd with the intention of attacking at first light the following day. Unfortunately, during the night the frigate *Nymphe* collided with his leading ship, the *Alfred*, and the resulting delay ruined his planned surprise attack. When the British fleet was sighted de Grasse put to sea. He believed that Hood was making for an anchorage further up the coast from which he could support the garrison on Brimstone Hill and he intended to use his numerical superiority to prevent this.[9]

The two fleets were in sight of one another for the whole of the 24th, with the British to windward, and on the following day Hood decided to occupy the anchorage which de Grasse had vacated. Shortly after 6.00 am he formed line of battle at one cable's length and by noon his fleet was sailing under Nevis on the approach to Basseterre keeping close to the land to deny access to the French. This was too close for the frigate, *Solebay,* which squeezed between a ship of the line and the shore went aground and was wrecked. So far, de Grasse had been unable to force an action but at 2.00 pm his flagship, the *Ville de Paris*, led an attack on the British rear where a gap had opened up which isolated the rearmost four ships. The three ships ahead of the gap dropped back to support their threatened consorts and by 3.30 pm the leading British ships were beginning to anchor in succession on an

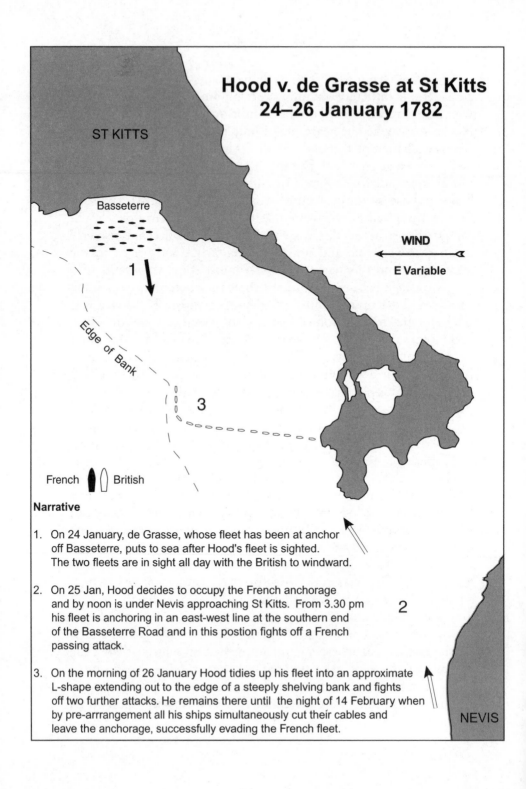

Hood v. de Grasse at St Kitts
24–26 January 1782

ST KITTS

Basseterre

1

Edge of Bank

3

WIND

E Variable

French ⬤ ◗ British

Narrative

1. On 24 January, de Grasse, whose fleet has been at anchor
    off Basseterre, puts to sea after Hood's fleet is sighted.
    The two fleets are in sight all day with the British to windward.

2. On 25 Jan, Hood decides to occupy the French anchorage
    and by noon is under Nevis approaching St Kitts. From 3.30 pm
    his fleet is anchoring in an east-west line at the southern end
    of the Basseterre Road and in this postion fights off a French
    passing attack.

    2

3. On the morning of 26 January Hood tidies up his fleet into an approximate
    L-shape extending out to the edge of a steeply shelving bank and fights
    off two further attacks. He remains there until the night of 14 February when
    by pre-arrrangement all his ships simultaneously cut their cables and
    leave the anchorage, successfully evading the French fleet.

    NEVIS

east-west line in the Basseterre Road and they were able to engage
the French fleet as it passed down the line before sailing away. The
next morning Hood tidied up the line of anchored ships into an
approximate L-shape with sixteen ships on the long leg lying east
and west and with the westernmost six ships lying north and south.
This arrangement provided all-round defence against another
French approach and springs on their cables gave individual ships
a wide arc of fire. By anchoring his ships on the edge of a steeply
shelving bank Hood ensured that the French could not anchor
outside him.

This defensive arrangement proved its worth on 26 January
when the French fleet made two passing attacks, the first at 9.00
am on the eastern end of the British line, and the second in the
afternoon on the western end. Neither was successful and there
were no further attacks. The French remained in sight, cruising to
leeward and awaiting developments ashore. The casualties
resulting from the engagements of 25 and 26 January were 72
killed and 244 wounded on the British side and 107 killed and
207 wounded on the French.[10] On the 28th, in an attempt to help
the beleaguered Brimstone Hill garrison, Hood landed 1,000 men
under General Prescott. They achieved initial success against de
Bouillé's much larger force and managed to occupy a
commanding position, but as there was no prospect of their
getting through to reinforce the garrison on Brimstone Hill they
were withdrawn and returned on 1 February to Antigua. Hood
had hoped to hold on long enough at Basseterre for de Grasse to
tire of keeping his fleet off St Kitts, but on 12 February Shirley
and Fraser surrendered. One factor in their decision had been
their inability to mount enough guns at Brimstone Hill, the local
inhabitants having refused assistance to haul up eight
24-pounders, two 13-inch mortars, 1,500 shells and 6,000
cannonballs, all of which fell into the hands of de Bouillé.

There being no further reason to remain at Basseterre, and
having seen the enemy preparing to position mortars to attack his
ships, Hood decided that he must withdraw and deliver his fleet in
as good condition as possible to Rodney, whose arrival from
England with reinforcements was imminent. On the evening of 14

February he summoned all his captains on board the *Barfleur* and announced his intention of quitting Basseterre that night. They synchronized their watches and returned to their ships. At 11.00 pm all ships cut their cables and, when clear of the anchorage, set course for Antigua via the north of St Kitts. The following morning the French, who had been at anchor off Nevis, saw an empty anchorage and no more than the tops of the rearmost departing British ships. De Grasse, short of ammunition and provisions, and with sickly crews, chose not to pursue.[11] Hood arrived at Antigua late on 19 February to take in provisions and on the 22nd sailed for Barbados where Rodney had arrived three days earlier. De Grasse's fleet had been reinforced shortly before Hood's departure by the arrival of the Marquis de Vaudreuil with the *Triomphant* and the *Brave*, the only warships to reach the West Indies after the interception and dispersal of de Guichen's fleet off the French coast on 12 December. De Grasse returned to Martinique on the 26th having detached de Barras on passage to capture Montserrat, which surrendered to him on 22 February.[12]

Hood's conduct at St Kitts was and has been much admired and is one of the episodes upon which his high reputation rests. It certainly excited the admiration of at least one of his captains who described the seizure of the anchorage at Basseterre as 'the most masterly manoeuvre I ever saw'[13] and wrote of the operation as a whole: 'it was well conducted, and has given the enemy a pretty severe check, and if you give him half the credit the enemy does, Sir Samuel Hood will stand very high in the public estimation.'[14] Rodney was less impressed. He criticized Hood's failure to station frigates to windward of Barbados to meet him, maintaining that if he had received the necessary intelligence de Grasse could have been brought to battle on his return to Martinique and the loss of Montserrat prevented. Commenting on Hood's escape from the anchorage at Basseterre he argued that with twenty-two ships of the line, well manned and copper-bottomed, Hood could have weighed anchor at noon day, even in the face of the enemy, and by standing out with his ships in a close-connected line, could have been in a position either to give or to avoid battle.[15]

Despite Rodney's criticism of his method of leaving it, Hood's seizure of the anchorage was a virtuoso performance. In Mahan's view, 'Whether regard be had to the thoughtful preparation, the crafty management of the fleet antecedent to the final push, the calculated audacity of the latter, or the firm and sagacious tactical handling from the first moment to the last, Nelson himself never did a more brilliant deed than this of Hood's.'[16] Impressive as it was, Hood's manœuvring at Basseterre achieved nothing in tangible terms. St Kitts was lost and the French fleet remained intact. It must, however, have raised considerably the morale of the British fleet after the depressing outcome of the Battle of the Chesapeake, and have contributed to the remarkable fighting efficiency of that fleet which characterized the forthcoming Battle of the Saintes. If the French fleet remained intact after the St Kitts encounter, so did Hood's, and Rodney was on the way with re-inforcements which would give the British more ships than the French. De Grasse had failed to use his temporary numerical advantage to destroy part, at least, of the British fleet. The eventual consequence of that failure, as Mahan put it, was that de Grasse 'had won a paltry island and lost an English fleet'.[17]

The *Gibraltar*, with Rodney on board, had arrived at Plymouth on 19 September, two weeks after the Battle of the Chesapeake and a month before the surrender at Yorktown. He was cheered by sailors in the dockyard when he left Plymouth and greeted by an enthusiastic crowd when he arrived in London on 24 September to take up residence in Lord Powys's house in Albemarle Street.[18] At official level his reception was muted as a result of the failure to recapture St Vincent, the loss of Tobago and looming legal problems following the capture of St Eustatius. When news of that capture had first reached London the guns of the Tower had been fired and government stocks had risen 1.5 per cent.[19] There had been talk then of a peerage for Rodney but that idea had been quietly dropped. For a time it seemed unlikely that he would be returning to the West Indies.[20]

On the day of his return to London Rodney had gone to Windsor seeking an audience with the King, who had just returned from hunting. Knowing that his loyal subject was under a cloud he pleaded fatigue and deferred the audience to another day.[21] Rodney's most urgent need was to get medical treatment and during October he left London for Bath to consult the eminent surgeon Sir Caesar Hawkins about the stricture that was preventing him 'making water'. As we do not know precisely what the problem was we can only speculate on the nature of Sir Caesar's treatment. It was certainly very painful. Rodney wrote to Sandwich on 4 November: 'May your Lordship never experience the pain and torture I have undergone since my coming to Bath, but Sir Caesar Hawkins assures me that in a short time my health will be perfectly restored.'[22]

News of the surrender at Yorktown did not reach London officially until 25 November but it had arrived six days earlier in Paris[23] and may have filtered across unofficially before the 25th. However, the news of Graves's failure on the Chesapeake had arrived in mid-October (Rodney had written to Jackson from Bath about Graves's despatch on 19 October) and around this time the government seems to have decided that, whatever his faults and health permitting, Rodney must resume his command in the West Indies. Following the death of the incumbent, Lord Hawke, on 17 October Rodney was appointed Vice Admiral of Great Britain, confirming his position at the head of his profession. This was an honorary appointment in the gift of the King, but Rodney suspected that it had been made on the recommendation of Sandwich.[24] The preparation of ships to accompany him as reinforcements was put in hand and the *Formidable* was chosen as his flagship. He returned to London in mid-November and busied himself with much official correspondence on a wide range of topics including gunnery, personnel matters and the health of seamen.[25]

On 4 December Rodney and Vaughan were present in the House of Commons for the debate on Edmund Burke's motion on St Eustatius. Essentially the debate was on their conduct, but technically the motion was for:

a committee of the whole House to examine into the con-fiscation of the effects of His Majesty's new subjects of the island of St Eustatius as well as goods and merchandize the property of His Majesty's British subjects, and into the sale and conveyance of the same to places under the dominion of His Majesty's enemies, and to other places, from whence his said enemies might be easily supplied therewith.

The latter part of the motion reflected Lord Shelburne's assertion a week earlier in the House of Lords that far from preventing the supply of essentials to the American rebels, the capture of St Eustatius and the ensuing sales of confiscated goods had facilitated the supply. However, the main thrust of Burke's argument was based on two premises: firstly, that British subjects by conquest were entitled to the same protection of the law as other British subjects; and secondly, that the confiscation of goods of those suspected of trading with the enemy must follow and not precede conviction in a court of law. He also criticized Rodney's failure to recapture St Vincent and to prevent the loss of Tobago, and argued, as Shelburne had done, that his preoccupation with St Eustatius had led to the disaster on the Chesapeake.[26]

Rodney responded in the only reported speech of his parliamentary career. He did not address the legal issues which Burke had raised, but repeated his familiar argument about the need to cut off supplies to Britain's enemies and to punish the friends of those enemies, including British traders who were supplying them. He stressed that when he seized all the property in the island it was not for his own use, at the time he believed that it would all belong to the King, and that he considered it to be his duty to make the most of it for the benefit of the public treasury. He rejected vigorously the allegation that confiscated goods had found their way into enemy hands. He pointed out that all stores and provisions had been sent to the Royal Navy's yard at Antigua, and that all ships leaving St Eustatius had been searched and relieved of provisions in excess of what was necessary for the voyage. He denied that he had been inactive for three months at St Eustatius and defended his actions related to the loss of Tobago, mentioning his concern for the safety of Barbados. He also sought to establish that he had taken adequate steps to warn and reinforce the North America station during the events leading up to the Battle of the Chesapeake.* Vaughan, also making his only reported speech in Parliament, referred to the common belief that he had made a great fortune as a result of the St Eustatius affair, but he stated on his honour, and was ready to confirm it on oath, that 'neither directly nor indirectly, by fair means or foul means, had he made a single shilling by the business'. He defended his conduct in relation to the deportation of the inhabitants and of the Jews in particular. He asked leave to lay on the table an appreciative address from their synagogue, but the Speaker ordered him to read it. Because of poor eyesight or inadequate lighting he was unable to do so and Rodney read it for him. Lord George Germain, for the government, said that because litigation was pending on the subject of the motion, he must vote against it. Despite an amendment which took some account of this objection the motion was defeated by a substantial majority.[27] The voting was on party lines and the result a foregone conclusion. Burke's motion was an attack on the government as much as on Rodney and Vaughan and, in any event, there was no possibility that the government would sacrifice an admiral urgently required to resume his command in the West Indies. It has been suggested that Burke may have been briefed in part by Middleton using information derived from Hood.[28]

Four days after the debate Rodney was in Portsmouth. He had left London earlier than he had intended, accompanied by Dr Gilbert Blane and his secretary, following an audience with the King, who had expressed concern about the safety of the West Indies.[29] At Spithead he embarked in the *Arrogant* (74) and on 17 December anchored in Cawsand Bay near Plymouth where the *Formidable* and other ships destined for the West Indies were being got ready for departure. There he was held up for three weeks by contrary winds and dockyard delays. He railed against the inefficiency of those responsible for preparing the ships, seeing in it the hand of 'party and faction'.[30] While he was there Sandwich wrote to him with news of Kempenfelt's interception of de Guichen and told him, 'The fate of this empire is in your hands.'[31] On 8

* See Chapter 7, pp. 127–34.

144

January Rodney set sail with his squadron of twelve ships of the line and two small ships, but they were no sooner out of Plymouth Sound than the wind backed to westerly and he put into Torbay to avoid being driven further back down the channel. He was able finally to sail on 14 January and rounded Ushant in a severe north-westerly gale on the 17th.[32]

Rodney's new Flag-Captain was Sir Charles Douglas, who lacked Walter Young's sharp intelligence but had considerably greater experience of command. He had served most recently in the Channel fleet as captain of the *Duke* (90) and was a noted gunnery expert whose innovations were to play an important part in forth-coming events. He was a suave and cultivated man and if he was somewhat pompous he had the great virtue of loyalty. Unlike Walter Young he kept any criticism he might have of Rodney mostly to himself.

Rodney arrived in Barbados on 19 February and joined Hood to windward of Antigua on the 25th. They were too late to prevent de Grasse reaching Fort Royal in Martinique.[33] There, while repairs to the French fleet were put in hand, belated celebrations took place to mark the birth of the Dauphin and the capture of Yorktown. At this time the British sloop *Alert* (Captain Vashon) arrived from St Lucia under flag of truce returning French prisoners of war under an exchange agreement negotiated between de Grasse and Hood. Her captain brought delicacies from Rodney for de Grasse and his officers, who reciprocated with local 'liquors' and an invitation, tongue in cheek no doubt, to Rodney and his officers to come and join in the celebrations.[34]

Apart from Barbados, only St Lucia, Antigua and Jamaica remained under British control. It was the last-named, Britain's largest and richest West Indian possession which for the French was the most sought-after prize, but it lay 1,000 miles across the Caribbean to the west (i.e. to leeward) of the Lesser Antilles. To go that far downwind was a risky business for a French fleet on its own, and attacking it would best be carried out in partnership with a Spanish fleet, taking advantage of French and Spanish territory near Jamaica. It was just such a project which was now in preparation and in which de Grasse was to command the naval forces and Lieutenant General Don Galvez (Spanish) the land forces.[35] It is said that the Spanish were so confident of success that, before he left Havana, Don Galvez was referred to in council as the Governor of Jamaica.[36]

The Franco-Spanish plan required de Grasse to join twelve Spanish ships of the line and 15,000 troops at Cap Français, St Domingo.[37] One estimate put the expected total strength of the combined force at 32,000 regular and 8,000 irregulars.[38] Rodney for his part was determined to bring de Grasse to battle in the seas around the Windward Islands, but realized that if he failed he would have to do so in the vicinity of Jamaica. He wrote on 5 March to the Governor of Jamaica, Major General John Dalling, and to Admiral Sir Peter Parker, the Commander-in-Chief, assuring them of his determination to protect the island, and told the Governor that he had given orders that a hundred 'stout Seamen with proper officers' from each ship of the line should be disciplined and trained in the use of small arms to act as soldiers ashore should the need arise, together with the marines of the fleet, troops and militia already in Jamaica and troops expected from home. He asked Parker to hold the small squadron under his command in readiness to join him off the east end of Jamaica or off the islands of St Domingo, and to procure and then employ fast sailing vessels to keep in touch with him.[39]

De Grasse was unable to leave Fort Royal during March for lack of essential stores and provisions, which he still awaited from Europe. Rodney intended to prevent the convoy carrying them from reaching him, but not for the first time he and Hood disagreed on how best to intercept enemy ships bound for Martinique. Both agreed that the British fleet should be positioned to windward but Hood, believing that the convoy would come in from the north, asked for his squadron to be allowed to cruise off Desirade, near Guadaloupe, and between that island and Dominica, while Rodney took care of the southern approaches. Rodney was not persuaded and when Hood put to sea on 16 March, he was ordered to remain between 15 to 30 miles to windward of the southern end of Martinique. On the 20th Rodney relented, allowing Hood to patrol as far north as Dominica, while he and Drake covered Martinique, but on the 22nd, concerned that Hood was too far north, and concerned also to protect Barbados, St Lucia and the trade, he closed up the fleet again off Martinique. As it turned out Hood had been right. The convoy, escorted by three sail of the line commanded by Mithon de Genouilly, had made Desirade and then slipped down between Guadaloupe and Dominica to Fort Royal where it had arrived on 20 and 21 March.[40]

Reinforcements had brought the opposing fleets nearly to numerical equality. Rodney had 36 ships of the line (a further 4 had been detached on convoy duties) and de Grasse 33. The advantage was not as great as those figures would suggest because individually the French ships were, on the whole, more powerful, but in terms of morale and fighting efficiency the British were greatly superior.[41] Sir Charles Douglas's innovations greatly increased the firepower of three of Rodney's ships, the *Formidable, Duke* and *Arrogant*, by making it possible for their guns to be traversed through 90° as opposed to the usual arrangement whereby guns could only fire at targets directly abeam. The result of this innovation was that the ships concerned could come into action sooner against a passing ship and remain firing for longer.[42] It also meant that at a range of up to a quarter of a mile it was possible to engage two ships in line ahead if they were up to 2 cables (480 yards) apart. This innovation was used in conjunction with improved arrangements for checking the recoil, and the use of goose quill priming tubes ignited by a flintlock on a lanyard, thus improving the safety of firing and also giving better control of the timing of firing, which allowed more accurate aiming than was possible with tapers.[43] Not attributable to Douglas, and probably more important, was the mounting on the upper deck of British ships of carronades,* large-calibre, short-barrelled guns capable of inflicting considerable damage at close range. Assuming that a list issued in July 1782 accurately reflected the situation two months earlier, 16 of the ships of the line which fought in the Battle of the Saintes and 4 out of the 10 frigates were equipped with carronades.[44] A proposal

---

* Named after their Scottish manufacturer, the Carron company.

to fit similar weapons to French ships had been studied but not implemented.[45]

If Sir Charles Douglas had improved the gunnery efficiency of the British fleet, Gilbert Blane was largely responsible for the remarkably good health of its sailors. In January 1780, when Rodney was in Gibraltar after the Moonlight Battle, he had appointed Blane, his friend and personal medical adviser, as Physician to the Fleet,[46] an appointment described by Christopher Lloyd as 'a piece of jobbery which had the most beneficial consequences'.[47] With Rodney's backing Blane embarked on systematic and comprehensive record-keeping to ascertain the state of health in the West Indies fleet and to devise ways of improving it, with the emphasis on prevention as much as cure. He had found Parker's fleet in very good health in a part of the world where life ashore was notoriously unhealthy and where many soldiers died of disease. In so far as one can generalize from detailed and meticulous observations, he identified a number of patterns in the health of the fleet. The unhealthiest ships tended to be those most recently arrived from home waters, where a common source of infection was from taking on pressed men who had been confined in guard ships.[48] Although scurvy, as one would expect, was more common in ships which had been at sea for some time because of the lack of fresh provisions, there was less scurvy in ships which had been in port for the same length of time, despite the fact that in most of the West Indian islands it was not possible to obtain fresh meat and vegetables. This, Blane suggested, was because when in port men tended to consume more sugar, which he believed had anti-scorbutic properties, and also because life in harbour was less dreary than at sea.[49] In another manifestation of the effect of morale on health he observed that when men were buoyed up by the prospect of battle, for instance during the encounters with de Guichen in April and May 1780 and immediately before the Battle of the Saintes in April 1782, the effect of illness was reduced.[50]

When Blane accompanied Rodney on his return to England on sick leave in August 1781, he embodied as recommendations in a memorandum to the Admiralty a number of measures based on his experience in the West Indies. These were as much administrative and practical as they were medical. He emphasized the crucial importance of cleanliness and dryness, and the effectiveness in achieving these conditions of the divisional system – the subdivision of the ship's company into squads or divisions each under the supervision of its own officer. This system was in use in a number of ships on a discretionary basis, but he recommended that it be made universal by regulation. He noted the value of fresh vegetables and fruit in combating scurvy and recommended that small ships should be employed to collect these on behalf of the fleet. He noted that wine was more conducive to good health than rum, and recommended the provision of special food for the sick. His final recommendations related to hospitals in which overcrowding was a problem in the West Indies because the fleet had outgrown the available facilities. This led to poor hygiene and the spread of disease so that sick sailors were often better off remaining in their ships if suitable food could be provided for them. He recommended a minimum of 500 cubic feet of space per patient in hospitals, strict control of cleanliness, the separation of diseases and the provision of hospital ships.[51]

Blane recorded that during the twelve months to July 1781 there were 12,109 men serving in twenty ships on the Leeward Islands station. Of these, excluding fifty-nine who died in or as a result of battle, there were 1,518 deaths, equal to 12½ per cent of the total.[52] During the month of April 1782, the month during which the Battle of the Saintes took place, the deaths from illness amounted to twenty-four in a total of 21,608 men serving in thirty-six ships, equivalent to an annualized mortality rate of only 1.3 per cent.[53] On Blane's own admission this was an exceptionally good month, both because of the recent arrival of fresh provisions including sauerkraut, molasses and essence of malt, all helpful as anti-scorbutics, and because of the extraordinarily high state of morale in the fleet – but they do suggest that there had been a considerable improvement. Healthiest of all ships at this time was the *Formidable,* Rodney's flagship, in which there were no deaths for the first four months after she left England in January 1782 and during which only thirteen men were sent to hospitals.[54] By contrast, based on Blane's observations in captured ships, the state of health in the French fleet at the time of the Saintes was poor and there was an increase in sickness and mortality in the British fleet in the month following the battle resulting from infections contracted by British officers and men sent to take charge of the prizes. He rated the 'discipline and internal economy' of the French ships as greatly inferior to those of the British. Apart from defects in cleanliness and ventilation he noted:

> There are not even scuppers opened on the lower decks as outlets to the water and filth, which necessarily accumulate there, and for which the only vent is a pipe contrived on purpose, passing from that deck along the ship's side into the hold, which becomes thereby a common sink, inconceivably putrid and offensive.[55]

Thus, at the end of March 1782, advantages of health and morale reinforced the superior fighting efficiency of the British Fleet, and it remained only to be seen whether the French could be brought to battle.

Chapter 9

The Battle of the Saintes

At the beginning of April 1782 the opposing fleets lay 30 miles apart, the French at Fort Royal, Martinique, and the British in Gros Islet Bay, St Lucia. On 5 April Rodney received intelligence that de Grasse had embarked 9,000 troops in transports and intended to sail on 8 April in order to join the Spanish fleet for an attack on Jamaica.[1] De Grasse was in a difficult position. He knew that he could not leave unobserved and get a head start on Rodney because of the British frigates stationed off Fort Royal to watch him. He knew also that when he did leave he would be encumbered with 150 merchant ships, consisting of the transports for Jamaica and a trade convoy for St Domingo. His orders made it clear that the Jamaica expedition was to have overriding priority.[2]

On the evening of 7 April Rodney dined ashore with some of his officers and a variety of civilians including staff from the hospital and victualling clerks. Amongst those present was Captain William Cornwallis, later a close friend of Nelson and a distinguished admiral in his own right. He related that towards the end of the evening the captain of one of the frigates patrolling off Fort Royal came up to Rodney and told him that part of the French fleet had sailed that morning and that the remainder were ready to go with the next offshore wind. Instead of thanking him for the information Rodney upbraided him for leaving his station in such robust terms that some of the civilians at the bottom of the table concluded that it was time for them to leave, and the frigate captain was obliged to plead 'a sprung bowsprit' as his excuse for having come into harbour bringing Rodney the news 'that an inferior fleet clogged with a convoy, if he chose to sail immediately, would be in his power next morning'. After the captain left Rodney came over to Cornwallis, whose indignation and astonishment he had observed, and said, 'He is one of my own making, I never spare them, by God.'[3] (The captain in question was Edward Tyrell Smith of the *Endymion* who had been sent into Gros Islet Bay by Captain George Byron of the *Andromache*, the senior frigate captain off Fort Royal, in order to repair a sprung mizzen mast.)[4] Rodney's displeasure does not appear to have done the young captain any harm as he ended his life a full admiral.[5] Cornwallis also criticized Rodney for allowing a punishment to be carried out (a flogging round the fleet of a man who been sentenced by court martial) before sailing the next morning.

At daylight on 8 April Captain Byron sent news via the *Alert* that the enemy were coming out and standing to the north-west. Rodney gave the signal to weigh, outermost and leeward-most ships first, and by midday all of his thirty-six ships were out of the bay. Having established by early afternoon that no French ships remained in Fort Royal, he set off in pursuit, his ships acting under a signal for a general chase, with divisions keeping together as much as possible so as to be able to get into line of battle when required.[6] By the following day both fleets had got as far as the north-western end of Dominica. At daylight about fifteen ships of the French Fleet had the advantage of the trade wind in the channel between that island and the small group of islands south of Guadeloupe, known as les Îles des Saintes, but the remainder and all the merchant ships were becalmed in the lee of Dominica near St Rupert's Bay. Lying further south, most of the British fleet, with Hood in the van, Rodney in the centre and Drake in the rear, was also becalmed but at about 7.30 am Hood's eight leading ships caught the breeze and began to move slowly northwards. North-west of them were two French ships, the *Auguste* (80), the flagship of de Bougainville, *chef d'escadre* of the third (Blue) squadron, and the *Zélé* (74). Separated from the rest of their fleet and in danger of being cut off, they caught the breeze at the same time as Hood's ships so that they were

The Battle of the Saintes 12 April 1782
Start of Action

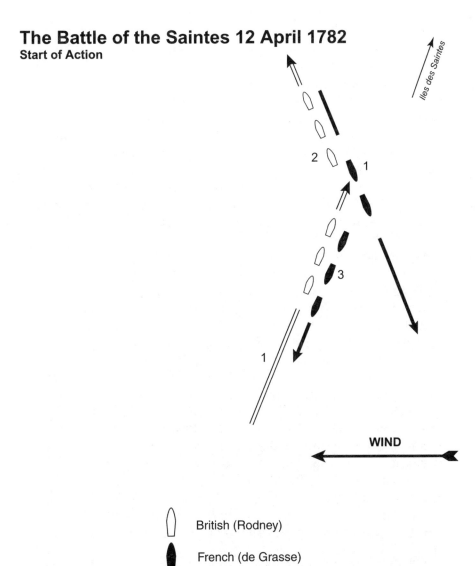

WIND

⬭ British (Rodney)

⬬ French (de Grasse)

Narrative

1. At 7.40 am the leading ship in the British Line, the *Marlborough*, engages the 9th ship in the French line. At this time both fleets are close hauled in line ahead in reverse order, the French sailing SSE on the port tack, and the British sailing NNE on the starboard tack.

2. As they come up successive British ships bear away on to a parallel and opposite course to the French.

3. The leading French ships bear away to engage the remaining British ships as they come up.

narrowly able to pass ahead of them and rejoin their fleet without the British opening fire. Rodney had hoisted the signal to engage earlier in the morning but had hauled it down. Captain Thomas White, who was a midshipman in Hood's flagship at the time, thought that Hood did not wish to take responsibility for bringing the French into action prematurely.[7] Up to this point the French ships in the Saintes channel had been sailing north, their number gradually increasing, but at 8.30 am de Grasse ordered them to tack and stand south to get between the British and his merchant ships which he sent to take refuge under the guns of Basse-Terre, Guadeloupe. When his leading warships were abreast of Hood he detached the Marquis de Vaudreuil, his second-in-command, with fifteen of them to engage Hood's eight ships.

The 59-year-old Marquis, son of a former Governor of Canada, had been in the Navy for over forty years. When captain of the frigate *l'Arethuse* at the start of the Seven Years' War in 1756 he had been captured by the British in an unequal contest off the French coast. In recognition of his gallantry he was allowed to keep his sword and return to France without exchange. In the present war he had fought in the Battle of Ushant under d'Orvilliers in 1778 in de Guichen's squadron and in the following year in the battle off Grenada under d'Estaing in the squadron commanded by de Grasse. Between those two engagements he had declined the governorship of St Domingo on the grounds that in time of war a naval officer's place was at sea. In the encounters between Rodney and de Guichen in April and May 1780 he served as *chef d'escadre* of the centre division and his flagship, the *Fendant*, was one of the four ships which Rodney in the *Sandwich* fought off for 1½ hours.[8]

Coming round onto a northerly course de Vaudreuil passed Hood, who was under easy sail to avoid getting too far ahead of the rest of the British fleet, engaging him ineffectually at long range, fearful of getting too close to the British carronades.[9] Then tacking and wearing to come round in a circle back onto a northerly course he engaged Hood's ships again, this time badly damaging the rigging on three ships. One of these was the *Royal Oak*, which had been becalmed and had missed the first engagement (9.48 am to 10.25 am) but had arrived in time to take her place at the head of Hood's division in time for the second engagement which lasted from 14 minutes past noon until the French disengaged at 1.45 pm. By this time Rodney's centre and rear had begun to move up and to engage the enemy, but at too great a range, and Rodney gave the order to cease firing in order to save ammunition.[10] All but sixteen of his ships had been engaged with the enemy. Captain Bayne of the *Alfred*, who had led the British line until the arrival of the *Royal Oak*, was killed in the action and one French ship, the *Caton* (64), had to be sent to Guadeloupe for repair. During this action de Grasse had sent a tender to order his convoy to leave Guadeloupe and proceed to St Domingo and by six in the evening it was out of sight.[11] He had thus saved his convoy and rid himself of its encumbrance but had thrown away an opportunity of bringing overwhelming force to bear on Hood's isolated van division. He paid dearly for his half-heartedness three days later.

If, so far, the advantages had lain with de Grasse, the balance now changed and this was partly due to the misfortunes of the French ship *Zélé* (74) which over the next three days was to be involved in two collisions. Her captain, the Chevalier de Gras Préville, had been promoted *capitaine de vaisseau* five years earlier despite reservations about his lack of professional experience.[12] However, since then he had had ample opportunity to make good that deficiency having served as captain of the frigate *l'Engageante* under d'Estaing, and as a Flag-Captain to the Comte de Sade in de Guichen's fleet during the encounters with Rodney. He transferred to the *Zélé* under de Grasse in 1781 but his previous experience as a captain does not appear to have improved his ship-handling ability and under his command the *Zélé* had been involved in a large number of collisions.

At the end of the day on 9 April Rodney wrote to Hood informing him that he proposed to lay to for the night and to look into Guadeloupe the following the day. If the enemy were not there he proposed to get to Cap Français, where the French were to rendezvous with the Spanish, before de Grasse. Hood, asked what he thought, replied:

155

De Grasse will certainly avoid you all he can, and when you know not where he is, you will, in my humble opinion, be perfectly right to push for the enemy's appointed rendezvous; but while you can keep him in sight, or know that he is not gone to leeward, I think you can on no account quit him, and will, I imagine, keep your fleet as much collected as possible, and avail yourself of every opportunity of getting to windward.[13]

Rodney took his advice. That night he reversed the order of sailing in order to put Hood's damaged division in the rear and Drake's division in the van. For the whole of that night and for the whole of the 10th Hood's ships were repairing their rigging and on the 11th the lack of wind in the lee of Dominica gave Rodney no opportunity of battle. There was more wind in the Saintes channel between Dominica and Guadeloupe where de Grasse spent the day in beating to windward. However, the previous night the *Zélé* had collided with the *Jason* (64). The latter had been so badly damaged that she had to be sent to Guadeloupe for repair, and the *Zélé* herself had lost her foretopmast and began to drop astern.[14] When, late on the 11th, she was threatened by British ships to leeward of the Saintes Channel, de Grasse felt compelled to come to her rescue, thus giving up much of his hard-won windward advantage. At 2.30 am on the morning of 12 April the *Zélé* repaid his chivalry by colliding with his flagship, the *Ville de Paris*, and had to be sent to Guadeloupe under tow for repair. The collision was apparently caused by the officer of the watch in the *Zélé* misinterpreting de Grasse's rules of precedence for ships approaching on different tacks.[15] According to a Swedish officer serving with the French fleet this was the fourteenth collision in which the *Zélé* had been involved during the previous thirteen months, a record exceeded only by the *Caton* with twenty-five collisions in twenty-one months.[16] Another source recorded that this the *Zélé's* fourth collision in as many days.[17] With 3 ships of the line now out of action (*Caton*, *Jason* and *Zélé*) the fighting strength of the French was down to 30, with Rodney's restored to 36 after repairs to damaged rigging were carried out at sea.

156

At 5.00 am on 12 April both fleets were on a southerly course on the port tack with the wind south-easterly, the French close to the Saintes and the British some 10 miles further south and west, off the north-west coast of Dominica. Neither fleet was formed up and the French fleet was spread over a great distance – estimates varied from 7 to 12 miles.[18] After the collision at 2.30 am there had been a considerable delay while the frigate *Astrée* attempted to pass a tow rope to *Zélé* in the darkness and the two ships were not under way to Guadeloupe until about 5.00 am. Half an hour later they were only 6 miles from the *Barfleur*, Hood's flagship, now in the rear of the British fleet, and therefore the nearest to them of the flagships. On instructions from Rodney to detach ships to chase them he sent the *Monarch, Valiant, Centaur* and *Belliqueux*.[19] De Grasse once again felt obliged to take his fleet to leeward to support the *Zélé* and by this decision effectively committed himself to a fleet action with Rodney. Constrained both by the narrowness of the Saintes Channel and by his proximity to the Saintes themselves, de Grasse could no longer make his escape to windward on the starboard tack,[20] and attempting to escape by running to leeward would have put him at the mercy of the British. At about 6.00 am he chose the only viable course of action, maintaining his southerly course and forming a line of battle. At 6.15 am Rodney recalled the ships pursuing the *Zélé* and ordered his fleet to form a line of bearing NNE to SSW, effectively to come on to the starboard tack in succession, and to close the distance between ships to one cable. This manoeuvre had the effect of putting Drake's undamaged rear division into the van, and Hood's slightly damaged van division into the rear with Rodney himself remaining in the centre. Had the wind remained south-easterly the British might have passed ahead of the French and gained the weather gage, but it backed to east-south-east soon after the start of the manoeuvre and the French passed ahead of the British. The leading ship in the British line, the *Marlborough* (74), engaged the ninth ship in the French line at 7.40 am and as they came up to the enemy line in succession British ships bore away onto a parallel and opposite course to the French. At 8.00 am de Grasse ordered the leading French ships to bear away both to get them out of the calms and variable winds off Dominica

157

and to engage the British ships still coming up.[21] The resulting shape of the line of battle was a dog-leg, with the northern part on a line NNW and SSE and the southern part NNE and SSW.

For the next hour and a quarter the two fleets passed each other slowly and at close range, with the French to windward and about 9 miles west of the northern end of Dominica. Like Rodney's fleet the French fleet was in reverse order with de Bougainville's third (Blue) squadron in the van and de Vaudreuil's second (White and Blue) in the rear. De Grasse in his flagship, the *Ville de Paris,* was with the first (White) squadron in the centre. The British applied their much superior gunnery to good effect with French casualties aggravated by the fact that in addition to their ship's companies they were carrying over 5,000 troops embarked for the intended assault on Jamaica.

At about 8.15 am de Grasse, wanting both to concentrate his attack on the British van and to keep his ships out of the lee of Dominica, attempted to reverse the direction of his fleet by signalling it to wear together on to the same tack as the British. The order was to some extent obscured by smoke but it was not obeyed by the ships which saw it and it was not repeated, as it should have been, by de Bougainville or de Vaudreuil. Justifying his decision after the event, de Vaudreuil maintained that, apart from four or five ships, the fleets were within musket shot of one another and that an attempt to wear in such close proximity, necessitating turning towards the enemy while under fire, would have been disastrous. The closeness of the fleets is corroborated by a witness in the *Northumberland,* in de Bougainville's squadron, who relates that it was possible to hear the British commands above the noise of gunfire and that fires were started in the French ship by wads from the British guns.[22] At 8.45 am de Grasse tried to reverse the direction of his fleet by another method. He now signalled ships to wear not together but in succession (starting with the leading ship), or to use the more descriptive French term, 'by countermarch'. Again the signal was ignored.

By about 9.00 am Rodney's centre division was engaging the French centre and part of the rear, when the wind veered from easterly to south-easterly, taking aback the French ships and

The Battle of the Saintes 12 April 1782
The Breaking of the Line

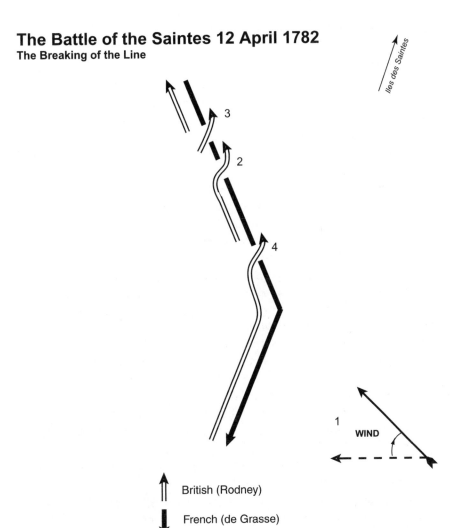

British (Rodney)

French (de Grasse)

Narrative

1. At 9.30 am the wind veers from Easterly to South-Easterly (light breeze), taking aback the ships in the French centre and rear and causing gaps to appear in the French line as they turn to starboard to keep their sails filled.

2. Rodney, in the *Formidable*, goes through the gap between the French ships *Diadème* and *Glorieux*, followed by five ships.

3. Captain Alan Gardner in the *Duke*, on his own, goes through a gap ahead of Rodney.

4. Commodore Edmund Affleck in the *Bedford* goes through a gap astern of Rodney and is followed by the whole of Hood's squadron of 12 ships.

forcing them to turn to starboard in an attempt to fill their sails (there was no comparable effect on the British ships because they were sailing off the wind). This effectively put the French ships into a bow and quarter line and caused bunching in places with a consequent opening up of gaps. The first British ship to confront this development was the *Duke* (Captain Alan Gardner), the next ahead of the *Formidable*. Emerging from dense smoke she saw an enemy ship right ahead and apparently standing towards her. Each ship tried to get to leeward of the other, the *Duke* turning to port and the French ship, probably the *Diadème*, turning to starboard. The *Duke* succeeded and continued passing along the French line, but the action of the *Diadème* caused the French ships immediately astern of her to bunch up and left a gap between her and her next ahead, the *Glorieux*. (The *Diadème* was the nineteenth ship in the French line and the leading ship in de Vaudreuil's rear squadron; the *Glorieux* was the twentieth in the line and the last ship in the French centre.) This was the gap which confronted Rodney in the *Formidable*. Much has been written about what happened next and to whom the credit is due, but in essence the *Formidable* led the five ships astern of her (*Namur*, *St Albans*, *Canada*, *Repulse* and *Ajax*) through a gap between the *Glorieux* and the *Diadème*.[23] At the same time, and apparently unaware of what Rodney was doing, Alan Gardner in the *Duke* went alone through the gap between the *Réfléchi* and the *Conquerant* (twenty-third and twenty-fourth respectively in the French line). He had little choice because the *Conquerant* had appeared on his port bow, but he was apprehensive about what might be seen later as the impropriety of quitting his own line.[24] Also apparently independently, because smoke obscured what Rodney and the ships following him were doing, Commodore Edmund Affleck in the *Bedford*, followed by the whole of Hood's division, went through the gap between the *César* and the *Dauphin-Royal* (twelfth and thirteenth respectively in the French Line).

As the British ships passed through their respective gaps they inflicted considerable damage on their opponents. Worst hit was the *Glorieux*, immediately to starboard as Rodney and his small group of ships passed through the gap. Gilbert Blane describes her as being within pistol shot of the *Formidable*, and Cornwallis as being as close to the *Canada* as it was possible to be without actually touching. As the *Canada* passed, her masts were tottering and soon after she was clear her bowsprit and all the masts fell. She did not return the *Canada*'s fire and nobody was seen on board except for one person who looked out of a lower-deck port in the bow and disappeared. Later she became a motionless hulk without masts or ensign staff, but with her flag nailed to the stump of a mast.[25] Also badly damaged were the *César* and the *Hector*, the two ships immediately to starboard as Hood's division followed Affleck in the *Bedford* through the gap astern of Rodney. Like the *Glorieux* both were captured later in the day.

On the *Formidable*'s port hand and between her and the *Duke* were four ships bunched together (*Diadème*, *Destin*, *Magnanime* and *Reflechi*). One of them had failed to come round to starboard to fill her sails when the wind shifted and had paid off on the opposite tack to her consorts. These four were pounded by the *Duke*, the *Formidable* and the *Namur*, all 90-gun ships, and the three ships astern of the *Namur*. The *Duke* and the *Formidable* had both been fitted with Sir Charles Douglas's traversing arrangements which greatly increased their destructive power. Furthermore, according to Douglas, the *Formidable* having discharged her port-side batteries into the group, then wore round to discharge her starboard guns before resuming her course.[26] It is remarkable that despite all this punishment none of the four ships concerned was among those captured later in the day.[27]

In all twenty British ships, over half of Rodney's fleet, passed through the enemy line and thereby ended up to windward of their French opponents. The remaining sixteen British ships had continued to the north, eventually passing the end of the French line the whole of which, apart from those ships which were disabled, was now free to escape to leeward, which it sought to do. Accounts of what happened during the rest of the day are fragmented and not always consistent as between one source and another. In the absence of wind there was a dense pall of smoke which meant that while ships on both sides were aware of what was happening in their vicinity they were ignorant of what was happening elsewhere. When the smoke cleared around the middle of the day firing had largely ceased except for the rearmost of Hood's ships which were still engaged but which were probably to windward of the enemy. By early afternoon both fleets were in three separated groups corresponding broadly to the squadrons or division they had occupied in the line of battle. Close to de Grasse's flagship, the *Ville de Paris*, were her seconds, *Languedoc* and *Couronne*, together with four other ships. De Vaudreuil's second squadron was 4 miles to the north and to leeward, and de Bougainville's third squadron was 2 miles to the south and to windward. The three crippled ships, *Glorieux*, *Hector* and *César*, were all to windward of their own fleet, *Glorieux* near the centre between the ships around Rodney and de Grasse respectively, and the other two between Hood's ships and de Bougainville's squadron.[28] By midday de Bougainville had removed his flagship, the *Auguste*, from the action and was repairing her damage.

The *Glorieux* was briefly under tow by the frigate *Richmond* from 11.00 am but Lieutenant Trogoff de Kerlessi, in command of the *Glorieux* after her captain the Vicomte d'Escars had been killed, cut the tow when British ships approached in order to save the *Richmond* from certain capture.[29] The first of those British ships to reach her was the *Canada*, commanded by Cornwallis, to whom she struck at 1.30 pm. Cornwallis left the *Royal Oak* to take possession of her and went off in search of further quarry. At 4.00 pm he came up with the *Hector* and compelled her to strike after an action of twenty minutes. Once again Cornwallis left it to another ship, the *Alcide*, to take possession of the prize and pressed on to engage the *Ville de Paris*. Earlier, after a chase of at least an hour and a half, Captain Inglefield in the *Centaur* had compelled the *César* to strike at 3.15 pm. At 5.00 pm Captain Sutherland in the *Belliqueux* engaged the *Ardent* (captured from the British in 1779) which struck after fifteen minutes.[30]

Rodney had hauled down the signal for close action at 11.00 am effectively leaving subordinate commanders to exercise their initiative. Hood got his boats out and towed the *Barfleur* round towards the enemy. He was then energetic in chivying his ships to take advantage of what wind there was to pursue the enemy. By contrast, according to Hood, Rodney's pursuit was leisurely, under the *Formidable*'s topsails only (sometimes with foresail set, and at others her mizzen topsail aback).[31] He hoisted the signal for close action at 1.00 pm but hauled it down again half an hour later. Judging from his signals[32] his main preoccupation during the late morning and early afternoon appears to have been to keep his fleet together and in particular to call back the leading ships (mostly Drake's van division) which had sailed past the French rear (de Vaudreuil's squadron). Two of those ships had worn out of the line on their own initiative in order to get to windward of the French. These were the *America*, Captain Samuel Thomson, the lead ship in Rodney's centre division, and the *Russell*, commanded by the 25-year-old James Saumarez, which was the rearmost ship in Drake's division. In the absence of a signal the *America* returned to her place in the line, but the *Russell* continued towards the centre and like the *Canada* later engaged the *Ville de Paris*.

During the afternoon de Grasse tried in vain to reform his fleet and from 3.30 pm to 5.45 pm made a succession of signals which were recorded as being 'not executed'.[33] This was not strictly accurate as de Vaudreuil made some attempt to comply with them but de Bougainville ignored them or, as suggested charitably by one source, mistook one such signal as a signal for flight.[34] Fierce fighting took place around de Grasse's flagship, the *Ville de Paris*, which by 5.30 pm was surrounded by nine British ships. At around 6.00 pm Hood's flagship, the *Barfleur*, came up and de Grasse surrendered to her at sunset. However the day might have shown up de Grasse's deficiencies as a fleet commander, there can be no doubt about his personal courage. With rigging, masts and sails all damaged, without a rudder, outgunned, by his own estimation, by 400 cannon to his 100, and his crew not having eaten from dawn to dusk, de Grasse fought the *Ville de Paris* to a standstill. Towards the end, with ammunition nearly exhausted, the guns had to be recharged with gunpowder by the spoonful by candlelight. Finally, unable to continue firing, he surrendered.[35] Shortly afterwards Rodney called off the chase to the dismay and chagrin of Hood, whose views have on the whole been supported by later commentators including Nelson. The command of the French fleet now devolved upon de Vaudreuil who tried to impose a semblance of order on it and continue the withdrawal to the north-west.

During the evening Rodney sent Lord Cranstoun, the supernumerary captain of the *Formidable*, to take possession of the *Ville de Paris* and to receive de Grasse's sword. Later Cranstoun took Rodney's despatch to England where he gave a personal account of the action to Lord George Germain, the former Secretary of State. As reported by Wraxall, presumably at second hand, the *Ville de Paris* presented a terrible sight when Cranstoun boarded her:

> Between the fore-mast and main-mast, at every step he took, he said that he was over his buckles in blood, the carnage having been prodigious; but as numbers of cattle and sheep were stowed between decks, they had suffered not less than the crew and troops, from the effects of the cannon. On the quarter-deck, which remained still covered with dead and wounded, only de Grasse himself, together with two or three other persons, continued standing. The French admiral had received a contusion in the loins, from a splinter, but was otherwise unhurt; a circumstance the more remarkable, he having been, during the whole action, for so many hours, exposed to a destructive fire, which swept away almost all his officers, and repeatedly cleared the quarter-deck. He was a tall, robust, and martial figure; presenting, in that moment, an object of respect, no less than of concern and sympathy. Lord Cranstoun said, that de Grasse could not recover from the astonishment into which he was plunged; the expressions of which he often reiterated, at seeing, in the course of so short a time, his vessel taken, his fleet defeated, and himself a prisoner. He was allowed to pass the night on board his own ship, with every testimony of attention and regard, on the part of the British Commander.[36]

At about 9.30 pm in the evening after the battle the *César*, with a prize crew on board, blew up having caught fire half an hour earlier. Rodney blamed the accident on indiscipline among the French seamen but it is more likely that the fire was started by the ignition of rum by a marine in the prize crew searching for liquor with a lighted candle.[37] During the day her captain, Bernard de Marigny, had been grievously wounded and had been carried to his cot where he was when some of his own men told him that the ship was on fire. He exclaimed, 'So much the better. The English won't have her. Close the door, my friends, and try to save your-selves.'[38] More than 400 French sailors perished together with nearly forty of the British prize crew.[39]

Excluding the members of the prize crew lost in the *César* total British casualties for the engagements of 9 and 12 April were 274 killed and 853 wounded, some of whom later died of their wounds.[40] There are no reliable figures for French losses but three weeks after the battle Rodney estimated that the total of killed, wounded and taken prisoner was 15,000.[41] That figure must represent more than half of those embarked in de Grasse's fleet including soldiers, and sounds excessive, but the casualties in captured ships were certainly very high. Blane estimated that nearly 300 were killed and wounded in the *Ville de Paris* and described the scene in the *Glorieux*, when boarded, as one of complete horror:

> The numbers killed were so great that the surviving, either from want or leisure, or through dismay, had not thrown the bodies of the killed overboard, so that the decks were covered with the blood and mangled limbs of the dead, as well as the wounded and dying, now forlorn and helpless in their sufferings.[42]

The British lost three captains: Captain Bayne of the *Alfred* killed on 9 April, Captain Blair of the *Anson* killed on the 12th and Lord Robert Manners, who died of wounds received on the 12th. The French lost six, all on 12 April. In addition to Bernard de Marigny of the *César*, these were d'Escars of the *Glorieux*, de la Vicomté of the *Hector*, de Sainte-Césaire of the *Northumberland*,* du Pavillon of the *Triomphant* and Chadeau de la Clocheterie of the *Hercule*.

---

* A nephew of de Grasse.

De Grasse came voluntarily aboard the *Formidable* the following morning where he was treated with every consideration. There he renewed his acquaintance with Sir Charles Douglas, who had met him thirty-five years earlier when the *Gloire*, in which de Grasse was an ensign, was captured on 3 May 1747 by the *Centurion* in which Douglas was a midshipman.[43] Douglas introduced him to Gilbert Blane who found him affable and communicative. According to Blane he attributed his misfortune to 'the base desertion of his officers in the other ships'. He said also that the French navy was a hundred years behind the British and noted the 'superior discipline, neatness and order' that prevailed in British ships.[44] Cornwallis, who was also introduced to de Grasse by Douglas, was struck by his apparent equanimity in defeat, relating how while they were talking on the quarterdeck the alarm was given from aft that a shark had been hooked, an event which caused great excitement in an English man-of-war. They went together to the captain's stern gallery to watch and Cornwallis was astonished to see the French Admiral 'enter into the spirit of this shark-catching with all the eagerness of any man or boy in the ship . . . without seeming to recollect or feel, that but a few hours before he was in a French first rate at the head of his fleet'.[45]

In his official despatch Rodney's praise for his subordinate commanders was so fulsome and in such contrast to his criticisms after the Battle of Martinique, that it is worth quoting in full:

> The noble conduct of my second in command, Sir Samuel Hood, who in both actions most conspicuously exerted himself, demands my earnest encomiums. My third in command, Rear Admiral Drake, who with his division led the battle of the 12th, deserves the highest praise; nor can less be given to Commodore Affleck, for his gallant behaviour in leading the centre division.
>
> My own captain, Sir Charles Douglas, merits every thing I can possibly say. His unremitted diligence and activity greatly eased me in the unavoidable fatigue of the day. In short, I want words to express how sensible I am of the meritorious conduct

166

of all the captains, officers, and men who had a share in this glorious victory obtained by their gallant exertions.[46]

His praise was well deserved. The performance of the British fleet on that day was admirable. Whereas its discipline had been found wanting off Martinique, it was beyond reproach at the Saintes. Interestingly too, whereas Rodney had poured scorn on the unfortunate Admiral Rowley for using his initiative two years earlier, the Saintes was replete with examples of personal initiative – Gardner going through a gap in the the French line on his own and Affleck leading Hood's division through another, Hood marshalling his ships to pursue the enemy after the line had been broken, Cornwallis seeking out ships to capture, Saumarez wearing out of the line to regain contact with the enemy. Clearly, something had changed in two years. For a start it was a different fleet. Of the twenty ships of the line which fought off Martinique only five were among the thirty-six present at the Saintes and none of the twenty captains nor any the subordinate commanders were there. Having said that, the available evidence does not suggest that there was anything about the ships or the officers involved which in itself would explain so marked a difference in the spirit pervading the fleet, unless it was that unlike Parker and Rowley in 1780, both Hood and Drake had significant earlier service under Rodney. Furthermore, whereas Rodney had only nineteen days in which to make his ways known before Martinique he had been in command for over two years at the time of the Saintes. That he now had more ships than the French, healthier men and better gunnery could not but improve morale, but the most important influence on morale is the quality of leadership. During the two years that Rodney had been Commander-in-Chief Hood had effectively commanded the fleet for a year and he must share some of the credit for its morale and discipline, particularly as a result of his actions at St Kitts, but ultimately the Commander-in-Chief takes the blame if things go wrong and is therefore entitled to the lion's share of the credit if they go well. However, Rodney's achievement at the Saintes is to some extent marred by criticism of his decision to call off the pursuit at sunset on 12 April.

Should Rodney have pursued the enemy after the battle? Hood and Cornwallis were most emphatic that he should have done so. Hood, who was critical not only of Rodney's signal to bring to at sunset, but also of his having failed to order a general chase in the early afternoon, wrote to Middleton the day after the battle: 'Had I, my dear Sir Charles, had the honour of commanding His Majesty's noble fleet yesterday, I may, without the imputation of vanity, say, the flag of England should at this hour have graced the sterns of upwards of twenty sail of the enemy's ships of the line.'[47] Cornwallis, who had commanded the *Canada* with distinction during the battle, was equally indignant, commenting that he 'could think of nothing for a week after the 12th April but what could be the motive for his [Rodney's] forbearance having such an opportunity thrown in his way – not to have taken advantage of it!' He related also that when the fleet had gone on to Jamaica he became convinced that Rodney had regretted his decision and that during the three months before news was received of reaction at home to his despatches 'he was like a man that did not know whether he was to be rewarded or punished.'[48]

The following note in Rodney's own handwriting, entitled 'Reasons for not pursuing the Enemy after the victory', was found among his papers after his death[49]:

1st. The length of the battle was such as to cripple the greatest part of the van and centre, and some ships of the rear, that to have pursued all night would have been highly improper, as the prisoners on board the prizes could not have been shifted, and those, with the much-crippled ships of the British fleet, might have been exposed to a recapture, as the night was extremely dark, and the enemy going off in a close connected body, might have defeated, by rotation, the ships that had come up with them, and thereby exposed the British fleet, after a victory, to a defeat; more especially as some of the British fleet were dispersed, and at a very considerable distance from each other; and I had reason to conclude that they would have done more damage to each other than to the enemy, during a night action, and considering the very great fatigue they had undergone during the battle of a whole day.

If I had inconsiderately bore away in the night, and left the two ninety-gun ships, the Prince George and Duke, and several others greatly damaged, with the Ville de Paris and the captured ships, without shifting the prisoners, the enemy, who went off in a body of twenty-six ships of the line, might, by ordering two or three of their best-sailing ships or frigates to have shown lights at times, and by changing their course, have induced the British fleet to have followed them, while the main of their fleet, by hiding their lights, might have hauled their wind, and have been far to windward before day-light, and intercepted the captured ships, and the most crippled ships of the English; as likewise have had it in their power, while the British fleet had during the night gone far to leeward, and thereby rendered themselves incapable of gaining their station to windward; to have anchored in their own ports, and from thence have conquered the British islands of Antigua, Barbadoes, and St Lucie, while the British fleet must, from the damages they had received, have repaired to Jamaica, as the condition of all their masts would not have permitted their return to St Lucie; and though Jamaica might have been saved, the Windward Islands might have been lost.

It is not known when this was written and to what extent it might be a rationalization after the event. Gilbert Blane, who was close to Rodney, referred ten days after the battle to the lack of moonlight and the possibility of British ships damaging each other in a night action as one of the reasons for non-pursuit and we may assume therefore that this part, at least, of Rodney's reasoning was in his mind at the time.[50] However, taken as a whole Mahan found his arguments unconvincing. He dismissed Rodney's fears that the French might double back during the night to attack captured ships and even threaten the Windward Islands as 'wildly improbable to a fleet staggering under such a blow as the day had seen, which had changed its commander just as dark came on , and was widely scattered and disordered up to the moment when signals by flags became invisible'. In particular he attacked Rodney's supposition that the French went off 'in a body of twenty-six ships of the line'. De Vaudreuil had only ten ships with him the next morning and was joined by five more on the way to Cap Français where another four awaited him. A further six, bringing the total to twenty-six, did not join him until May, having gone to Curaçao.[51]

In his standard biography of Rodney in 1969 David Spinney endorsed the conventional view that Rodney was old and tired and that in his younger and more vigorous days he would not have hesitated to maintain the pursuit. However, in 1982 in a lecture commemorating the 200th anniversary of the battle, Spinney revealed that he had revised his former opinion mainly as a result of his inspection of the damage returns of the British ships which revealed that only fourteen would have been in a fit state to pursue the French ships still at large. Furthermore, he now believed that Rodney's overriding duty was to ensure the safety of Jamaica and to keep his fleet intact with that in view.[52] Spinney's information on the state of the British fleet is corroborated by Tornquist who recorded that the French counted twenty-two disabled British ships (leaving fourteen fully operational) compared with seventeen disabled ships of their own, but notwithstanding this he argued that Rodney should have pursued because of the general lack of powder in the French fleet.[53] (Given the higher rate of fire by the British fleet it too must presumably have been low on powder.)

On balance, Rodney probably would have continued the pursuit had he been younger and fitter. What he would have achieved by doing so is a matter of speculation. Part of his fleet did, in fact, continue to give chase throughout the night, but to no avail. Because he had not seen Rodney's signal to bring to, Affleck in the *Bedford* continued the pursuit with five other ships until 2.45 am the next morning when he brought to in the hope of seeing the enemy at daylight. Seeing nothing at 5.00 am his ships hauled their wind and stood to the south-east to rejoin the rest of the British fleet, which at 6.00 am was visible from the masthead some 20 miles away.[54]

For much of the time during the five days following the battle the British fleet was becalmed and occupied with refitting. Sails, masts and rigging had been much damaged. On the 17th Rodney detached Hood with ten ships of the line to go ahead to St Domingo in search of the enemy with an injunction to remain in sight ('hull down'), but with discretion to press on if he thought fit. This Hood did and on the 19th he sighted a small French squadron near the western end of Puerto Rico. After ordering a general chase he captured the *Jason* and the *Caton*, the two ships which de Grasse had detached from his fleet before the engagement on 12 April, together with the frigate *Aimable* and the sloop *Cérès*. The frigate *Astrée*, probably with the Marquis de Bouillé aboard, escaped by superior sailing.

Reporting to Rodney, Hood could not conceal his frustration at the lack of earlier and more vigorous pursuit, 'It is a very mortifying circumstance to relate to you, Sir, that the French fleet which you put to flight on the 12th went through the Mona Channel on the 18th, only the day before I was in it.' Mahan found this conjunction of events persuasive evidence that Hood had been right all along, but James was less convinced, arguing that the relative positions of the fleets on the 18th was not necessarily conclusive as to what their relative positions would have been if the chase had been continued.[55]

On 18 April Rodney, with the rest of the fleet and the prizes, followed Hood to St Domingo having first looked into the roads of Basseterre, St Kitts and St Eustatius for any signs of the French. He joined Hood near the south-west end of St Domingo on the 25th and the whole fleet continued westward to Cape Tiburon where Hood, with twenty-five ships of the line, was detached to cruise and Rodney proceeded with the remainder to Jamaica, arriving on 29 April. He remained ashore, once again in ill health, and it was there that he learned on 10 July that, following the fall in March of Lord North's government, one of the early actions of the incoming Whig administration had been to appoint Admiral Hugh Pigot to replace him as Commander-in-Chief in the West Indies. Pigot had been virtually retired for twelve years and never flown his flag at sea. News of Rodney's victory at the Saintes reached the Admiralty on the day that Pigot sailed to take up his appointment and it was too late to recall him.

The French ships captured during the battle and later, apart from the *César* which had blown up after the battle, left Jamaica early in August in a convoy escorted by three ships under the command of Rear Admiral Thomas Graves (*Ramilles*, *Centaur* and *Canada*). Rough weather proved too much for the *Ardent* which soon turned back. Before long, the *Caton* sprang a leak and had to be towed to Halifax. The *Glorieux* and the *Ville de Paris* sank in a violent storm off the coast of Europe on 16 to 17 September, in which the *Centaur* also sank and the *Ramilles* was wrecked, while the *Hector* was abandoned after she had been attacked by two French frigates.[56]

Chapter 10

Aftermath

Rodney, having been raised to the peerage as the first Baron Rodney of Stoke-Rodney, sailed for England in the *Montagu* on 23 July 1782 and arrived in Bristol, after being diverted by adverse winds, on 15 September. At the age of sixty-four he went ashore for the last time.

The decision to award a peerage to Rodney, as recommended by Keppel,* seems to have been taken by the new government in deference to public opinion, rather than out of any enthusiasm on its own part. There was even consideration of awarding him an Irish peerage, but an English barony was decided upon, with the approval of the King, because it would require Rodney to vacate his seat in the House of Commons as a member for Westminster and create a vacancy which might be filled by a supporter of the government. However, when the vote of thanks to Rodney and other officers was debated in the House of Lords on 27 May, and agreed to by all who spoke, some thought that an earldom or viscountcy at least would have been appropriate for Rodney, and an English peerage for Hood.[1]

Rodney's retirement was plagued by ill health and by litigation in connection with his actions at St Eustatius. For reasons which are not clear he and his wife agreed to live apart from about 1784. She went to France, where she lived until the early years of the

* First Lord of the Admiralty.

Revolution, when she returned to England. She died aged ninety in 1829.[2] The wealth that eluded Rodney came the way of his son and heir, George, through his marriage to Anne Harley. Through her the Rodney family acquired Berrington Hall, near Leominster in Herefordshire, which is now owned by the National Trust. It remained in the family until it was sold by George, the seventh Lord Rodney in 1901.[3] Alresford House, which Rodney had made over to George before he went to Jamaica, remained in the family until 1870.[4] Rodney died at George's London house early in the morning on 24 May 1792, aged seventy-three.[5]

Hood went on to become a Lord of the Admiralty from 1788 to 1795 and Commander-in-Chief in the Mediterranean from 1793 to 1794. There he nurtured the career of the up-and-coming Captain Horatio Nelson, who revered him. In August 1793 he captured Toulon with the help of Admiral Don Juan de Lángara, Rodney's opponent in the Moonlight Battle, but was unable to hold on to it and relinquished it four months later. He returned home in 1794 and was dismissed after a disagreement with the new First Lord of the Admiralty, Earl Spencer. In 1796 he was created a Viscount and appointed Governor of Greenwich Hospital, a post which he held until his death at the age of ninety-one in 1816.[6] Drake remained in the West Indies until the peace in 1783, when his active career ended, but he was appointed a junior Lord of the Admiralty shortly before he died in 1789.[7] Of the captains who fought in the Battle of the Saintes, James Saumarez, William Cornwallis and Alan Gardner went on to have distinguished careers.

De Grasse, having arrived in Jamaica in the *Formidable* with Rodney on 29 April 1782, spent three weeks in Spanish Town before embarking in the *Sandwich* for the passage to England. Rodney's old flagship now flew the flag of Vice Admiral Sir Peter Parker, who was under orders to escort a convoy home together with four other warships. The convoy sailed on 25 May and de Grasse arrived in England on 2 August, some six weeks before Rodney. During his brief stay in London he had an audience with the King who returned his sword, and with Lord Shelburne, with whom he discussed the terms of the forthcoming peace. He had declined the offer of accommodation at St James's Palace on the grounds that he did not wish to be separated from his officers, but the King ordered that the expenses of himself and his officers, while he was in England, should be met by the government. He was well received generally in London as a gallant enemy and sat for his portrait. He sailed for France on 12 August and arrived in Paris as a paroled prisoner of war.[8]

The French could have forgiven de Grasse much because of his heroic defence of his flagship during the closing stages of the Battle of the Saintes, but he was not helped by the warmth of his welcome in London.[9] He also did his reputation in France immeasurable harm by attempting to blame the defeat on his officers. He did this first in the official despatch which he wrote while a prisoner in the *Formidable*. He was entitled to do so if the allegations could be substantiated, but he made the fatal error, while in London, of writing various memoranda on the subject and distributing them widely. Because of his standing his allegations were taken seriously and investigated thoroughly in the ports to which the French fleet returned. The results of those investigations were then considered by a Council of senior officers which met in Lorient early in 1784 and amongst whose members were de Guichen and la Motte-Piquet. Several captains had been accused of failing in their duty and the allegations were particularly severe in the case of Mithon de Genouilly and D'Arros d'Argelos, captains respectively of the *Couronne* and the *Languedoc*, the seconds of the *Ville de Paris*, whom de Grasse accused of having deserted his flagship. They had been held in custody since their return to France. The Council delivered its judgment in May 1784. Mithon de Genouilly and d'Arros d'Argelos were cleared of the allegations against them and released from custody. Although de Bougainville was reprimanded for lack of zeal during the afternoon action, the King later expressed his confidence in him.[10] A small number of captains were reprimanded and one was imprisoned.* Taken as a whole the

---

* The Comte de Framond whose ship, the *Caton*, took no part in the action, having been sent to Guadeloupe for repair, but was captured by Hood later in the Mona passage.

findings fell far short of substantiating de Grasse's allegations. He rejected them and asked the King to judge for himself. The King did this in detail and supported the Council. His displeasure at the injustice done to honourable officers was made to clear to de Grasse, who was forbidden to appear before him.[11] He retired to his chateau at Tilly, between Paris and Rouen, the great service he had rendered to the Americans in their fight for independence largely forgotten by his fellow-countrymen. He died on 14 January 1788, having been restored to royal favour some two years earlier.[12] Thereafter his reputation languished until well into the twentieth century. The first statue of him in France, the gift of an American, was erected in Paris in 1931. Construction began in 1938 for the French Navy of an anti-aircraft cruiser named after him which finally joined the fleet after the Second World War, and in 1945 a passenger ship, refloated after war damage, was renamed *de Grasse* and subsequently became the flagship of the French Merchant Navy.[13] He is also commemorated in a small museum in his ancestral town of Grasse.

In the years immediately following the Battle of the Saintes, Rodney enjoyed the esteem of the public for the successful outcome of the action, attributable, it was believed, to his decision to break the enemy's line. The view within the service, apart from criticism of his failure to pursue the enemy after the battle, was summed up by Lord St Vincent who wrote in 1806: 'Lord Rodney passed through the enemy's line by accident, not design, although historians have given him credit for the latter.'[14] St Vincent was commenting on the work of John Clerk, the laird of Eldin, near Edinburgh, an enthusiastic amateur in the field of naval tactics who had devoted much thought and ingenuity to finding a solution to the apparent inability of the Royal Navy to achieve decisive results in fleet actions because of the unwillingness of the French to stay and fight. His recommended manoeuvres to deal with this problem were based on the concept of breaking the enemy's line and he was convinced that it was he who had inspired Rodney's tactics not only at the Saintes but also in the action against de Guichen off Martinique on 17 April 1780. In January 1780, before he had published anything,

176

Clerk had arranged a meeting in London with John Atkinson, whom he understood to be a friend of Rodney and to whom he had given papers and sketches explaining his tactical theories. Atkinson had undertaken to pass these on to Rodney, and Clerk, believing Rodney to be in England at the time, had no reason to suppose that he had not done so. In Rodney's attempt four months later to concentrate his force on part of de Guichen's force, Clerk saw conclusive evidence that Rodney had profited from the material which Atkinson had passed on to him, and regretted the fact that Rodney had apparently neglected to apply his recommended tactics in his subsequent encounters with de Guichen on 15 and 19 May 1780. Clerk's first published work, *An Enquiry into Naval Tactics*, appeared in January 1782, before Rodney returned to the West Indies after his sick leave. This was Part One, dealing with attacks from to windward,* of Clerk's complete work, *An Essay on Naval Tactics*, which was first published in 1790. A second edition of the full work, published in 1804, attracted a favourable notice in the *Edinburgh Review*, which enthusiastically espoused Clerk's entitlement to the credit for Rodney's tactics[15] and it was possibly this which in 1806 prompted the First Lord, Viscount Howick, to seek the views of Lord St Vincent on Clerk's tactical theories. Apart from his assertion that Rodney had broken the French line at the Saintes by accident, St Vincent was politely dismissive of Clerk's theories, as one might expect of a vastly experienced practitioner commenting on the views of an amateur theoretician. Despite this, in response to Howick's enquiry about the possibility of some reward for Clerk, St Vincent commented: 'I do not see, however, that Ministers can withhold some reward to Mr Clark (sic), after what has been lavished by former Administrations.'[16] That his recommendation was not heeded is apparent from a letter signed 'M&D' dated 8 January 1809 in the *Athenaeum Magazine* deploring the lack of official recognition for Clerk's contribution to naval tactics and specifically claiming the credit on his behalf for the breaking of the line at the Saintes.[17] This prompted a reply by

---

* Not stricly applicable to the Saintes where until the breaking of the French line Rodney's fleet was to leeward.

Sir Gilbert Blane in defence of Rodney, in which he demolished one of Clerk's arguments by pointing out that at the time of Clerk's meeting with John Atkinson in January 1780, Rodney had already sailed for the West Indies, and could not therefore have received the papers which Atkinson had undertaken to pass on to him.[18] Thereafter the debate lay dormant for many years, but in 1824 a new element was introduced by Admiral Ekin in his *Naval Battles* in which he suggested that it was Sir Charles Douglas, Rodney's Flag-Captain, who had persuaded his reluctant Admiral to seize the opportunity offered by the gap in the French line.[19] The publication three years later of the third edition of Clerk's *Essay*, with notes by Rodney, ushered in the final and most heated phase of the controversy, conducted by the supporters of the three long-deceased contenders for the credit of breaking the French line, namely Rodney himself, John Clerk of Eldin and Sir Charles Douglas. In 1829 Sir Charles's youngest son, Major General Sir Howard Douglas, issued a *Statement of Some Important Facts . . . relating to the Operation of Breaking the Enemy's Line, as practised for the first time in the celebrated Battle of the 12th April, 1782,* in which he put forward his grounds for believing that the credit for the tactic was his father's. His case rested largely on the testimony, forty-seven years after the event, of Captain (later Admiral) Sir Charles Dashwood who as a seventeen-year-old[20] midshipman had been on the *Formidable*'s quarterdeck at the time. He maintained that not only had Rodney initially rejected Douglas's urgent plea to break the French line, but that Rodney and Douglas had actually given contradictory orders to the helmsman. This provoked an article in the *Quarterly Review*, signed by 'ART', understood to be Sir John Barrow, Secretary of the Admiralty since 1824 and the biographer of Admiral Lord Howe, who strongly defended Rodney.[21] Among other arguments he introduced two practical considerations: firstly, that the time within which a decision could be made was very brief; and secondly, that any conversation that Dashwood might have overheard between Rodney and Douglas would have been against a background of sustained and heavy gunfire. Barrow's contribution was followed by a further statement by Sir Howard Douglas, and

178

by the publication by Rodney's son-in-law, Major General Godfrey Mundy of *The Life and Correspondence of the late Admiral Lord Rodney*, in which he refuted the claims of Douglas. These claims were rejected also by the *Edinburgh Review*, which, as it had done twenty-five years earlier, strongly supported the claims of Clerk of Eldin.[22] Apart from Dashwood, naval officers had thus far not joined this final phase of the debate but Admiral Sir Charles Knowles, who as a young officer had known Rodney, now published a pamphlet entitled *Observations on Naval Tactics*. He reaffirmed the view expressed many years earlier by Lord St Vincent that the breaking of the line was accidental, but argued that, in fact, it was the French who had broken the British line and that 'it was a bad thing' since it allowed the French to escape and robbed Rodney of a more conclusive victory.[23] He also attached to his pamphlet an extract from a letter dated 19 September 1829 to Sir Howard Douglas from Sir James Saumarez, who had commanded the *Russell* during the battle and who expressed his firm conviction that neither Rodney nor Douglas were 'in any manner actuated by having perused Mr Clerk's Essay on Naval Tactics'.[24] Finally, Captain Thomas White, who had been a midshipman in Hood's flagship during the action, dismissed in his *Naval Researches* the claims made on behalf of both Clerk of Eldin and Sir Charles Douglas. In particular he cast doubt on Dashwood's recollection after forty-seven years of the conversation between Rodney and Douglas as being inconsistent with the latter's 'well known suavity of manners and uniform correctness of conduct'. He recorded also that he had heard no mention of the story either at Hood's table, to which he was admitted at least once and often twice a week, or in the cockpit of the second-in-command, 'the usual emporium of all news in the fleet'.[25] Like Knowles, White asserted that the British victory would probably have been more complete if Rodney had managed to remain to leeward of the French.

There is anecdotal evidence that Rodney had some concept of breaking the enemy line before the Battle of the Saintes. Richard Cumberland mentioned in his memoirs that when a dinner guest of Lord George Germain, Rodney held forth on tactics and illustrated with cherry stones how he proposed to break the line.[26] At the end of 1781 Rodney stayed with Captain Paul Ourry, Commissioner at Plymouth dockyard, while awaiting a favourable wind to return to the West Indies after his sick leave in England. Ourry's son recalls Rodney boasting to his father that he would break de Grasse's line.[27] Wraxall wrote of Rodney, while still in London after his appointment in October 1779 as Commander-in-Chief in the Leeward Islands:

> Naturally sanguine and confident, he anticipated in his daily conversation, with a sort of certainty, the future success which he should obtain over the enemy; and he had not only already conceived, but he had delineated, on paper the naval Manoeuvre of breaking, or intersecting the Line, to which he afterwards was indebted in an eminent degree, for his brilliant victory over de Grasse.[28]

All three recollections were committed to paper a long time after the event, but they do, to some extent, corroborate one another. However, they are at odds with the fact that although Rodney would have been aware from 1779 onwards that there was a signal for breaking the enemy line in the signal book in use in Sir Charles Hardy's Channel fleet, he did not adopt it for his own fleet in the West Indies. It may be worth noting that both Sir Charles Douglas and Edmund Affleck, who led Hood's division through the third gap at the Saintes, came to Rodney from the Channel fleet.[29] All things considered, Lord St Vincent's assertion that the breaking of the line at the Saintes was accidental remains the best explanation.

One unresolved question is the extent to which Rodney might have influenced Nelson's plan for Trafalgar. On 10 September 1805, six weeks before the battle, Nelson called on his friend Lord Sidmouth* at White Lodge in Richmond Park. During their meeting Nelson sketched out with his finger on Sidmouth's study table how, if he were fortunate enough to meet them, he proposed to deal with

---

* Formerly Henry Addington, Tory Prime Minister 1801–4.

the combined French and Spanish fleets, saying 'Rodney broke the line in one point; I will break it in two.'[30] This episode, if correctly reported, provides reasonable evidence that Nelson intended to emulate and to improve on Rodney's tactics of a generation earlier; but to which of Rodney's actions was he referring?

Rodney broke the enemy line in two actions while Commander-in-Chief in the Leeward Islands from 1780 to 1782. In his biography of Nelson, Captain Mahan assumed that he was referring to the Saintes but that Nelson had got the details wrong: 'Rodney's fleet actually, though accidentally, broke through de Grasse's order in two (if not three) places.'[31] Mahan's interpretation seems to have prevailed but it is not entirely convincing. Nelson was an assiduous student of naval tactics and the Battle of the Saintes was one of Britain's most celebrated naval actions. Furthermore, from the end of 1782 as captain of the frigate *Albemarle*, he had been attached in the West Indies for a few months to Hood's squadron, which had fought in the battle. That he was conversant with it is evident from a letter he wrote to Cornwallis, who took part in the battle, on 30 December 1804: 'on the score of fighting, I believe, my dear friend, that you have had your full share, and in obtaining the greatest victory, if it had been followed up, that our country ever saw.'[32]

It is possible that Sidmouth misreported Nelson's comments. He did not record the conversation until many years later but, according to his biographer, he was accustomed to relate to his friends 'the interesting particulars' of his last meeting with Nelson[33] and it is likely that these were engraved on his mind. Precisely what Nelson said and what he meant are matters of conjecture, but it is possible that it might not have been the Battle of the Saintes which he had in mind, but Rodney's less successful action against the Comte de Guichen off Martinique on 17 April 1780, in which he did, incidentally, break the French line in one place when his flagship, the *Sandwich*, went through it alone and unsupported. The essence of Nelson's Trafalgar plan was concentration of force. In that respect it had nothing in common with the Battle of the Saintes, which began as a conventional passing action between two fleets in line ahead, and in which breaking the enemy line was not part

181

of Rodney's plan. When a sudden shift in the direction of the wind took part of the French line aback and opened up gaps in it, Rodney and others went through it in three places. Although the name of Rodney was associated thereafter, particularly in the public mind, with the concept of breaking the line, he himself attached little importance to it. In his own mind the earlier action against de Guichen off Martinique on 17 April 1780 was the more important, even though tactically the result was probably a draw.[34] That action, or the intention behind it, had far more in common with Trafalgar than had the Saintes. It too had been planned as a concentration of force. But whereas Rodney had planned to concentrate the whole of his fleet against part of the French line, Nelson achieved a double concentration of force, of his own division and of Collingwood's, against part of the combined French and Spanish fleets. That Nelson succeeded brilliantly where Rodney had failed was due both to Nelson's genius for leadership and to the fact that the standard of discipline and competence in the British fleet had greatly improved over the intervening twenty-five years, an improvement to which Rodney and others had contributed.[35]

Whatever the merits of Rodney's decisions during and immediately after the Battle of the Saintes, the battle itself illustrated the tactical opportunities presented by the mêlée which resulted from the breaking of the line. It came to symbolize the end of the iron grip of tactical rigidity and to be seen as the first of a series of unorthodox British naval victories, including such battles as the Glorious First of June, Camperdown, the Nile and the greatest of them all, Trafalgar. As for Rodney himself, controversial character though he may have been, he had an instinct for battle as acute as that of any of our great admirals and he deserves to be ranked among them.

Appendix 1

Prizes taken by Rodney in HMS *Eagle* in the Western Approaches between May 1746 and June 1747*

Date Taken	Eagle *in company with*	Prize
1746		
24 May		Spanish privateer *Esperance* 16 guns 136 men
8 June	*Nottingham* and *Falcon*	French brigantine *Joseph Louis* (sloop)
14 June		French privateer *Ponte Quarré* 12 guns 138 men
17 July		Spanish privateer *Nuestra Señora del Carmen*
		26 guns 148 men
15 October		Spanish Merchant Ship *Prudent Sarah*
30 October		French privateer *Shoreham* 22 guns 260 men
1747		
2 January		French privateer *Grand Comte* 20 guns 77 men
3 February	*Edinburgh* and *Nottingham*	French privateer *Bellona* 36 guns 310 men

* Based on *Rodney Papers* Vol. 1, D. Syrett (ed.) NRS No. 148, 2005, pp. 15–17.

Date Taken	Eagle *in company with*	Prize
11 April		French privateer *Mary Magdalene* 22 guns 170 men
1 May		French privateer *Marshal de Saxe*
21 June	*Kent, Hampton Court, Lion, Chester, Hector* and fireships *Pluto and Dolphin*	Merchant ships in convoy from St Domingo, *St Malo, Europa, Charlotta, Espérance, Marshal de Saxe, Ste Claire*

Appendix 2

Opposing Fleets at the Battle of Martinique, 17 April 1780

(Based on Chevalier pp. 186–8 and James, pp. 441–2)

THE BRITISH LINE OF BATTLE

VAN

Stirling Castle	64	Robert Carkett
Ajax*	74	S. Uvedale
Elizabeth	74	Hon F. Maitland
Princess Royal	90	Hyde Parker, Rear Admiral of the Red
		H. Harmood
Albion	74	George Bowyer
Terrible	74	John Douglas
Trident	64	A.J.P. Molloy

Frigate: *Greyhound*

CENTRE

Grafton	74	Thomas Collingwood, Commodore
		T. Newnham
Yarmouth	64	N. Bateman
Cornwall	74	Tim. Edwards
Sandwich	90	Sir G.B. Rodney, Admiral of the White
		Walter Young
Suffolk	74	H. Christian

* Ships in bold type fought in the Moonlight Battle.

Boyne	70	Charles Cotton
Vigilant	64	Sir George Hume, Bart.

Repeating ship: *Venus*

Frigates: *Pegasus, Deal Castle*

REAR

Vengeance	74	W. Hotham, Commodore J. Holloway
Medway	60	William Affleck
Montagu	74	J. Houlton
Conqueror	74	Joshua Rowley, Rear Admiral of the Red
		Thomas Watson
Intrepid	64	Hon Henry St John
Magnificent	74	John Elphinstone
Centurion*	50	R. Braithwaite

Frigate: *Andromeda*

THE FRENCH LINE OF BATTLE (in reverse order)

VAN

Destin	74	Du Maitz de Goimpy Feuquieres
Vengeur	64	De Retz
Saint-Michel	60	D'Aymar
Pluton	74	De La Martonie
Triomphant	80	Comte de Sade, *chef d'escadre*
		De Gras-Préville
Souverain	74	De Glandevez
Solitaire	64	De Cicé -Champion

CENTRE

Citoyen	74	De Nieuil
Caton	64	De Framond
Victoire	74	D'Albert Saint-Hippolyte
Fendant	74	De Vaudreuil, *chef d'escadre*
Couronne	80	Comte de Guichen, *lieut-général* Buor
		de la Charoulière
Palmier	74	De Monteil, *chef d'escadre*

* To assist the Rear in case of need.

186

| *Indien* | 64 | De Balleroy |
| *Actionnaire* | 64 | De Larchantel |

REAR

Intrépide	74	Du Plessis Parscau
Triton	64	Brun de Boades
Magnifique	74	De Brach
Robuste	64	Comte de Grasse, *chef d'escadre*
Sphinx	64	De Soulanges
Artésien	74	De Peynier
Hercule	74	D'Amblimont

Frigates: *Résolue Iphigenie, Courageuse, Médée, Gentile*
(*Dauphin Royal* (70) (Mithon de Genouilly), joined after the action on the 17th)

Appendix 3

Battle of Martinique, 17 April 1780 – Signals by Rodney's Flagship*

Time	To	Signal	Comment
5.45 am	General	Form line of battle ahead at two cables length asunder; fleet on starboard tack.	
6.45 am	General	Admiral's intention to attack enemy's rear.	
7.00 am	General	Line of battle ahead at one cable's length asunder. Starboard tack.	
8.30 am	General	Line of bearing NbyW, SbyE of each other; 2 cables; wind then on starboard beam.	
9.00 am	General	Line of battle ahead at 2 cables; haul to the wind on larboard (port) tack.	
9.42 am	General	Repeated line of battle ahead at 2 cables, on larboard (port) tack.	
10.10 am	General	Wear and bring to the wind on the starboard tack.	
10.18 am	General	Repeated do.	

* Based on the evidence given at the court martial of Captain Bateman of the *Yarmouth* in October 1780 by Captain Francis Pender who did duty as signal officer in the flagship in April 1780. See Laughton, Sir John Knox (ed.), *Letters & Papers of Charles, Lord Barham 1758–1813*, Vol I, 1906, Appendix A, pp. 390–1.

Time	To	Signal	Comment
10.19 am	*Stirling Castle*	Wear.	She being the sternmost ship.
10.36 am	General	Line of battle ahead at 2 cables, on starboard tack.	
11.00 am	General	Prepare for battle.	
11.00 am	General	Alter course to port.	
11.28 am	Rear Division	To close the centre.	
11.50 am	General	For every ship to steer for her opposite in the enemy's line, agreeable to the 21st Article of the Additional Fighting Instructions.	
11.55 am	General	Engage.	
11.55 am+	General	Come to closer engagement.	
1.25 pm	General	Repeated do.	
1.45 pm	*Yarmouth*	Make more sail.	She then lying to windward of the line with her main & mizzen topsails aback.
2.40 pm	*Yarmouth* and *Cornwall*	Come to closer action.	They being both on the weather bow.
2.40 pm*	General	Hauled down the union jack from the mizzen peak.	
3.25 pm	Ships to windward	Bear down into the admiral's wake.	
3.26 pm	*Yarmouth*	Bear down into the admiral's wake.	
4.00 pm			Action ceased

* Immediately after or at about the same time as the preceeding signal.

189

Appendix 4

Opposing Fleets at the Battle of the Saintes, 12 April 1782

(Based on Chevalier, pp. 293–4 and James, pp. 448–50)

THE BRITISH LINE OF BATTLE (in reverse order)

VAN

	Marlborough	74	T. Penny
	Arrogant	74	S. Cornish
Frigates:	*Alcide*	74	C. Thomson
Triton	*Nonsuch*	64	W. Truscott
Eurydice	*Conqueror*	74	G. Balfour
	Princessa	70	F.S. Drake, Rear Admiral of the Blue
			C. Knatchbull
	Prince George	90	J. Williams
	Torbay	74	J.L. Gidoin
	Anson	64	W. Blair
	Fame	74	R. Barbor
	Russell	74	James Saumarez

CENTRE

	America	64	S. Thomson
Frigates:	*Hercules*	74	H. Savage
Flora	*Prothee*	64	C. Buckner
Alert	*Resolution*	74	Lord Robert Manners
Sybil	*Agamemnon*	64	B. Caldwell
Andromache	*Duke*	90	Alan Gardner

Endymion	Formidable	90	Sir G.B. Rodney, Admiral of the White
			Sir C. Douglas
			J. Symons
			Lord Cranstoun
	Namur	90	R. Fanshawe
	St Albans	64	C. Inglis
	Canada	74	Hon W. Cornwallis
	Repulse	64	T. Dumaresq
	Ajax	74	N. Charrington
	Bedford	74	Ed. Affleck, Commodore
			T. Graves

REAR

	Prince William	64	G. Wilkinson
	Magnificent	74	R. Linzee
Frigates:	Centaur	74	J. Inglefield
Lizard	Belliqueux	64	A. Sutherland
Nymphe	Warrior	74	Sir J. Wallace
Champion	Monarch	74	F. Reynolds
Zebra	Barfleur	90	Sir Samuel Hood, Rear Admiral of the Blue
			J. Knight
	Valiant	74	G.S. Goodall
	Yarmouth	64	A. Parrey
	Montagu	74	G. Bowen
	Alfred	74	W. Bayne
	Royal Oak	74	T. Burnett

THE FRENCH LINE OF BATTLE (in reverse order)

THIRD (BLUE) SQUADRON

Hercule	74	Chadeau de la Clocheterie
Souverain	74	De Glandevez
Palmier	74	De Martelly-Chautard
Northumberland	74	De Sainte-Césaire
Neptune	74	Renaud d'Aleins
Auguste	80	De Bougainville, *chef d'escadre*
		De Castellan
Ardent	64	De Gouzillon
Scipion	74	De Chavel

Brave	74	D'Amblimont
Citoyen	74	D'Ethy

FIRST (WHITE) SQUADRON

Hector	74	De la Vicomte
César	74	De Marigny
Dauphin-Royal	70	De Roquefeuil-Montperoux
Languedoc	80	D'Arros d'Argelos
Ville de Paris	104	Comte de Grasse, *lieut-général*
		De Lavilleon
		De Vaugirauld, *major d'escadre*
Couronne	80	Mithon de Genouilly
Eveillé	64	Le Gardeur de Tilly
Sceptre	74	De Vaudreuil
Glorieux	74	D'Escars

SECOND (BLUE AND WHITE) SQUADRON

Diadème	74	De Monteclerc
Destin	74	Dumaitz de Goimpy
Magnanime	74	Le Bègue
Réfléchi	64	De Medine
Conquerant	74	De la Grandière
Magnifique	74	Macarthy Macteigne
Triomphant	80	De Vaudreuil, *chef d'escadre*
		Du Pavillon
Bourgogne	74	De Charitte
Duc-de-Bourgogne	80	Coriolis d'Espinouse, *chef d'escadre*
		De Champmartin
Marseillais	74	De Castellane Majastre
Pluton	74	D'Albert de Rions

Appendix 5

Battle of the Saintes, 12 April 1782 – Signals by de Grasse's Flagship*

Time	To	Signal	Comment
12.45 am	General	Wear together.	
(02.45 am)	(by *Zélé*)	Request for tow.	Following collision at 0215 between *Zélé* and *Ville de Paris*.
5.00 am	General	Recognition Signal.	French fleet seen to windward of the flagship and the *Zélé* to leeward under tow by a frigate (*l'Astrée*) which signalled the approach of the enemy.
5.45 am	General	Line of battle on port tack in reverse order.	
A little later	General	The same repeated.	
6.15 am	General	Make more sail.	
7.30 am	General	Prepare for action.	
8.00 am	General	Alter course to SSW.	(Literally bear away together to SSW. The purpose of the signal was to bring the van closer to the British line and away from the calms off Dominica).

* Based on an extract of the signals log included in *Mémoire du Comte de Grasse sur le Combat Naval du 12 Avril 1782*, pp. 24–6, and certified by the Chevalier de Vaugirauld, *major d'escadre* (chief-of-staff).

Time	To	Signal	Comment
8.15 am	General	Wear together.	Not executed.
8.45 am	General	Haul to the wind together on the port tack.	
A little later	General	Wear in succession.	Not executed
10.45 am	Frigates	Come closer to repeat signals.	Executed by *Richmond* only.
11.00 am	Frigates	Take *Glorieux* under tow.	Executed by *Richmond* only.
1.15 pm	General	Close up.	Not executed by third squadron (de Bougainville).
1.15 pm	General	Form line of battle on the port tack in reverse order.	
A little later	Second squadron (Vaudreuil)	Haul to the wind together.	
1.35 pm	*Sceptre*	Shorten sail.	Executed (*Sceptre* was the 2nd ship of the first squadron).
2.00 pm	General	Form line of battle on the port tack in reverse order.	
2.45 pm	Second squadron	Shorten sail.	
3.07 pm	Second squadron	The same repeated.	Executed.
3.30 pm	General	Haul to the wind together on the starboard tack.	Not executed.
4.00 pm	General	Form line of battle on the starboard tack in normal order (*l'ordre naturel*).	Not executed.
4.15 pm	General	Haul to the wind together on the starboard tack.	Not executed.

Time	To	Signal	Comment
5.45 pm	General	Form the line.	Not executed.
A little later	General	Haul to the wind together on the starboard tack.	Not executed.

Appendix 6

Battle of the Saintes, 12 April 1782 – Principal Signals by Rodney's Flagship*

Time	To	Signal	Comment
4.54 am	General	All cruisers.	Requiring all frigates and repeating ships to close up for instructions.
5.02 am	General	Close up.	
5.12 am	General	Order of sailing.	
5.25 am	Drake's Division	Haul the wind on the port tack.	
5.45 am	Drake's Division	Make more sail.	
5.50 am	General	Line ahead at 2 cables apart.	
5.56 am	Hood's Division	Chase to the north.	
5.57 am	Drake's Division	Take the lead.	
6.15 am	General	Line of bearing NNE to SSW.	The effect of this signal was for the fleet to come on to the starboard tack in succession, Drake's division leading.
6.33 am	General	Line of battle at 2 cables apart.	
7.00 am	General	All cruisers.	
7.10 am	General	Line of battle at one cable apart.	

* Based on Sir Samuel Hood's journal.

Time	To	Signal
7.45 am	General	Close up.
7.59 am	General	Action.
8.05 am	General	Close Action.
8.08 am	Leading ships	Alter course one point to starboard.
11.00 am	General	Signal for line of battle hauled down.
11.15 am	Drake's Division	Headmost & weathermost ships to tack.
11.33 am	Drake's Division	The same repeated.
12.30 pm	Drake's Division	Van to close up on the centre.
1.00 pm	General	Close Action.
1.32 pm	General	The same hauled down.
3.45 pm	General	Ships to windward to bear down into flagship's wake.
4.00 pm	General	The same hauled down.
4.00 pm	General	Wear.
4.10 pm	General	The same hauled down.
6.45 pm	General	Bring to on the port tack.

Appendix 7

Rodney's Dispositions in August 1781*

Of the twenty-four ships under Rodney's command following the arrival on the Leeward Islands station of Sir Samuel Hood in January 1781, three had gone home with convoys (*Suffolk*, *Vengeance* and *Vigilant*) from January to May, leaving twenty-one on the station in August as follows:

Russell
> Under repair in Antigua, following damage in the action of 29 April.

Triumph, Panther
> Escorted convoy home in August. Both in need of refit and coppering. (The *Panther* was an old-fashioned 60-gun ship).

Gibraltar
> Took Rodney home in August. In need of some repair and said to have too deep a draught to go over the bar at Sandy Hook, thus restricting her usefulness on the North America station.

Sandwich
> Urgently in need of refit. To Jamaica with convoy and refitting there.

Torbay, Prince William
> To Jamaica with convoy and then to proceed to America (both these ships were detained on the Jamaica station by Sir Peter Parker apparently without good reason and reached America too late to take part in the Battle of the Chesapeake).

Barfleur, Ajax, Alcide, Alfred, Centaur, Invincible, Monarch, Montagu, Resolution, Shrewsbury, Terrible, Princessa, Belliqueux, Intrepid

* Based on the table in *Sandwich Papers* iv 126–7.

to America with Hood, fourteen in number, all of which were present at the Battle of the Chesapeake together with five ships of Admiral Graves's squadron *(London, Bedford, Royal Oak, America* and *Europe).*

During the Battle of the Chesapeake on 5 September 1781 the British fleet, nineteen ships in all, was deployed in reverse order as follows:

Van
> *Shrewsbury, Intrepid, Alcide, Princessa* (Drake), *Ajax, Terrible*

Centre
> *Europe, Montagu, Royal Oak, London* (Graves), *Bedford, Resolution, America*

Rear
> *Centaur, Monarch, Barfleur* (Hood), *Invincible, Belliqueux, Alfred*

Appendix 8

Advice from Lord Rodney to his son, Captain John Rodney, on the Duties of a Captain*

Instructions from Sir George B. Rodney, then on board the *Montagu* of 74 guns at Sea, on the voyage from Jamaica to England, August 1782, to his son Captain John Rodney, commanding the *Anson* of 64 guns, then in company.

MEMORANDUM

The first consideration of a captain of a man of war is to be particularly attentive in perusing and studying the Sailing and Fighting Instructions he may receive from the Admiralty, or from any admiral under whose command he may be put; nothing indicates such gross neglect and inattention, as being at a loss and not instantly obeying any signal that may be made by his admiral; or more exposes an officer in the eyes of the fleet.

2

When a signal is made for a line of battle, you are not to execute it slowly and deliberately, but to set every sail you can crowd till you get into the station allotted to you; though other officers may neglect to do so, notwithstanding the First Article of the Additional Fighting Instructions expressly commands them to hasten to their stations with every sail they can crowd.

3

Whenever your ship is ordered on a cruise, or sails in company with a fleet, take particular care that no chests or lumber of any kind be suffered to be between decks; and that most of the cables be unbent, unless near a coast, that your ship may be always ready at a moment's warning for battle, and when in chase,

---

* PRO 30/20/22/10 ff. 95–8.

(whether of a 1st rate or a small sloop), have your men at their quarters and the guns ready to fire, and be not induced by any officer whatever to deviate from this practice, who may impertinently presume to give his opinion by saying ''tis only a small vessel; a Dane; a Swede, a neutral vessel, or an English ship' – Reprimand that officer who presumes to give his opinion in this case unasked; trust no colours; keep your men at their quarters, and be ready to fire till you are thoroughly ascertained and have spoke to the chase.

4

When your ship's company are at their quarters and your ship near coming to action, order your carpenters to their stations below, lay all the gun deck hatches, and if likely to be hard pressed, bar them down, particularly in the night, that no cowardly men may desert their quarters, and by that means intimidate others – such men there are in all fleets; when they know there is no place to skulk they must fight or perish. This is an old maxim which I have known often put into execution; it can do no harm; it may do great good – Follow it.

5

When your ship is cleared for battle, lay the scuttle of the hatchway leading down to the powder room, and keep it shut during the whole action; let four scuttles be cut in the angles of the fore hatchways grating in order to hand up the powder – under the said grating have four tubs filled with water, to receive the loose powder – have thrummed mats on the platforms on the orlop deck, leading to the boatswain's and carpenter's store rooms, and the entrance to the magazine; take care they are all well wetted and the cisterns leading to the magazine filled with water. Let all your decks be well wetted and sanded, frequently renewing it during the action; let your chains be filled with water; the lanyards of your shrouds and rigging well wetted and, if it can be done, all your sails, particularly such staysails as may be in nettings, viz. main topmast staysail, middle staysail, mizzen staysail, fore topmast staysail, etc. Should the action be of any duration frequently renew the wetting (of) your ship's sides, etc., etc.

6

Should you have the misfortune of being overpowered in battle, let no inducement whatever prevail upon you to strike the colours or submit, while there is a possibility of defending H.M. Ship; or some of her masts carried away, which may prevent her escape; and should any officer dare to give you intimidating counsel, put him instantly in arrest and on no account pardon him.

7

Whatever squadron or fleet you may serve in be strictly obedient to the orders you may receive from your admiral or superior officer; he is responsible for the orders he gives, your duty is to obey them. Be attentive to all signals that may be made, and obey them with briskness and alacrity. Never attempt to deviate from the orders you may receive, unless on very particular occasions and where you can answer, as an officer, for the deviation.

8

Keep your ship's company in strict and good discipline, a good natured, not an ill natured discipline. Treat all your officers with good manners, politeness and civility – 'tis your duty so to do; and take care that they perform their duty. If they are gentlemen, they will do so; if they are not, treat them as they deserve and fear them not.

Be attentive, follow the foregoing maxims, and you cannot fail of having the approbation of your King and Country, and being an honour to your family.

Notes

ABBREVIATIONS

DNB   *Oxford Dictionary of National Biography*, 2004.
PRO   Public Record Office (National Archives), Kew (references prefixed ADM,
      CO, PRO and T relate to documents in the PRO).

NOTE ON MONEY, MEASUREMENTS AND TERMINOLOGY

1 Spinney, D., *Rodney*, 1969, p.288n.
2 *How Many? A Dictionary of Units of Measurement*, Russ Rowlett and the
  University of North Carolina at Chapel Hill (website), 2005.

INTRODUCTION

1 *Concise Dictionary of First Names.*
2 David Syrett (ed.), *The Rodney Papers*, Vol. 1 (1742–1763) NRS Vol. 148,
  Oxford University Press 2005.
3 Lloyd Christopher, 'Sir George Rodney: Lucky Admiral' in *George
  Washington's Generals and Opponents*, Billias, G.A. (ed) 1994, p. 327.
4 P. Mackesy, *The War in America 1775–1783*, 1964, pp. 321–2.
5 Lacour-Gayet, G., *La Marine Militaire de la France sous la Règne de Louis
  XVI*, 1905, p. 314.
6 *Barham Papers,* i xl.
7 Hamilton, Adm. Sir R. Vesey, 'Rodney' in *From Howard to Nelson*, J.K.
  Laughton (ed.), 1900, p. 317.
8 Wraxall, *Historical Memoirs of My Own Time* (1772–1784), One Vol.,
  Reprint, Kegan Paul, Trench, Trubner & Co., 1904 (Or. 2 vols, 1815),
  pp. 190–2.
9 Mundy, G.B., *The Life and Correspondence of the late Admiral Lord Rodney*,
  Reprint, Gregg Press Boston, 1972 (Or. 1830), i 162–3.

10 Rodger, N.A.M., *The Wooden World,* p. 323.
11 Spinney, D., *Rodney,* 1969, pp. 86 and 89.
12 Spinney, p. 209.
13 For a full account of the Northampton Election see Spinney, Chapter 13.
14 Spinney, pp. 238–45; PRO 30/20/22/10 ff. 129–32.
15 Rodger, pp. 273–94.
16 Syrett, D. 'Admiral Rodney, Patronage and the Leeward Islands Squadron, 1780–2' in *The Mariner's Mirror* Vol. 85 No. 4, November 1999, pp. 411–20.
17 Rodger, p. 326.
18 Syrett, D., *The Royal Navy in European Waters during the American Revolutionary War,* 1998, p. 92.
19 *Sandwich Papers,* iii 160.
20 PRO 30/20/22/10 ff. 95–98.
21 Rodney to Sandwich, 16 Feb 1780, in *Sandwich Papers,* iii 200–2; Rodney to Carkett, 30 July 1780, PRO 30/20/20/11.
22 PRO 30/20/22/10 ff. 95–98.
23 Rodger, p. 162.
24 Spinney, p.126–7.
25 PRO 30/20/22/10 ff. 95–98.
26 PRO 30/20/10 Letter Book (i).
27 Nelson to his wife, 12 September 1794, Nicolas i 483.

CHAPTER 1
 1 According to David Spinney Rodney spelt his second name Bridges.
 2 Mundy i 1–37; Hannay, David, *Rodney,* 1969, pp. 1–6; Spinney, pp. 17–28.
 3 Main sources for period 1732–45, Spinney Chaps. 2–5 and *Rodney Papers* i 4–15.
 4 Mackay, R.F., *Admiral Hawke,* London, 1965, pp. 53–54; Rodger, N.A.M., 'George, Lord Anson' in *Precursors of Nelson* (eds Le Fevre & Harding) London, 2000, pp. 182–4.
 5 See Appendix 10.
 6 Rodney to Corbett, 5 Feb 1747, and Rodney and de Saumarez to Corbett, 7 Apr 1747, both in *Rodney Papers* i 109–111.
 7 Fox to Corbett, 20 June 1747, ADM 1/1782, Captain's Journal *Kent* ADM 51/501, Spinney, pp. 75–80.
 8 Corbett to Rodney, 13 July 1747, in *Rodney Papers* i 116.
 9 Main source for the 2nd Battle of Finisterre, Mackay, pp. 69–88.
10 Minutes of court martial of Captain Thomas Fox ADM 1/5291.
11 Spinney, pp. 86 and 89.
12 Sandwich to Rodney, 7 June 1749 in Mundy i 46–8.
13 Rodney to Clevland, 26 Mar 1752 and reply 27 Mar 1747 in *Rodney Papers* i 167–8.

14 Spinney, 102–3.
15 *Rodney Papers* i 131.
16 Erskine D. (ed.), *Augustus Hervey's Journal 1746–1759*, 1954, pp. 238, 240.
17 Spinney, p. 112.
18 Mackay, p. 168.
19 Corbett, J.S. *England in the Seven Years' War*, 1907, i 315.
20 Rodney to Clevland, 29 and 31 March 1758 in *Rodney Papers* i 251–2 and commentary p. 133.

CHAPTER 2

1 Corbett, ii 24n.
2 Admiralty to Rodney, 8 June 1759 in *Rodney Papers* i 280.
3 Rodney to Clevland, 18 Jun 1759 in *Rodney Papers* i 284.
4 Admiralty to Rodney, 26 June 1759 in *Rodney Papers* i 287.
5 Ireland, B., *Naval Warfare in the Age of Sail*, 2000, p. 118.
6 Rodney to Clevland, 30 June 1759 in *Rodney Papers* i 290.
7 Rodney to Clevland, 4 July 1759 in *Rodney Papers* i 291–2.
8 Spinney, p. 156.
9 Rodney to Clevland, 6 July 1759 in *Rodney Papers* i 292–3.
10 Quoted by Spinney, p.157n.
11 Rodney to Clevland, 30 Aug 1759 in *Rodney Papers* i 303–4.
12 Rodney to Clevland, 11 Sept 1759 in *Rodney Papers* i 308–9.
13 Rodney to James West, 27 Feb 1761 in *Rodney Papers* i 417–8.
14 *Rodney Papers*, i 266–7.
15 Rules to be observed by that part of His Majesty's Fleet under the command of Rear Admiral Rodney in Landing and Re-embarking the Troops, PRO 30/20/19; Spinney, p. 175.
16 *Rodney Papers*, i 422–8.
17 Spinney, Appendix 5.
18 *Dublin* (74), *Culloden* (74), *Temple* (70), *Raisonable* (64), *Belliqueux* (64), *Bienfaisant* (64) and *Montagu* (60).
19 *Marlborough* (68), *Foudroyant* (80), *Dragon* (74) *Vanguard* (70), *Modeste* (64), *Nottingham* (60), and bombs *Thunder* and *Granado*.
20 From Dominica with Lord Rollo's troops the *Stirling Castle* (64), from Belle Isle the *Téméraire* (74) and from New York the *Devonshire* (64) and *Alcide* (64).
21 Spinney, p.181.
22 Rodney to Clevland, 19 Jan 1762 in *Rodney Papers* i 433–4.
23 *Rodney Papers*, i 269.
24 Quoted in Mundy i 74.
25 Rodney to Clevland, 24 Mar and 10 Apr 1762 in *Rodney Papers* i 444 & 448–9.
26 Lyttleton to Rodney, 24 Jan 1762 and Forrest to Rodney, 27 Jan 1762 in D.

Syrett (ed.), *The Siege and Capture of Havana 1762*, NRS Vol. 114, 1970, pp. 63 and 67–8.

27 Rodney to Clevland, 26 Mar 1762 in *Rodney Papers* i 445–7.
28 Corbett, ii 240.
29 Admiralty to Rodney, 5 February 1762 in *Rodney Papers* i 435–7.
30 Egremont to Monckton, 5 February 1762 in Syrett, *Havana* pp. 26–28.
31 Rodney to Clevland, 26 May 1762 in *Rodney Papers* i 452–4.
32 Corbett ii 241–2; 244–5.
33 Syrett, *Havana* p. xvii.
34 Ibid. p. xxxv.
35 Rodney to Clevland, 3 Nov 1762 in *Rodney Papers* i 468–70.
36 Rodney to Brigadier Rufanes 19 June 1762 in *Rodney Papers* i 460–1.
37 Rodney to Duff, 3 Jun 1762 and Duff to Rodney, 4 Jun 1762 in *Rodney Papers* i 457–60.
38 Spinney, p. 209.
39 Ibid. p. 219.
40 Mundy i 102–3.
41 Spinney, p. 236.
42 Sandwich to Rodney, 27 Nov 1771 in *Sandwich Papers* i 379–80.
43 Sandwich to Rodney, 30 Dec 1771 in *Sandwich Papers* i 381–2.
44 Spinney, p. 255.
45 Sandwich to Rodney, 20 Apr 1772 in *Sandwich Papers* i 383–4.
46 Davies, J.A., 'An Enquiry into Faction among British Naval Officers During the War of the American Revolution', MA thesis, University of Liverpool, May 1964, pp. 155 and 163.
47 Watson, J. Steven, *The Reign of George III*, 1960, pp. 154–5.
48 Rodney to Sandwich, 28 Jun 1774 in Mundy i 140–1.
49 Spinney, pp. 273–4.
50 Rodney to Germain, 12 Nov 1775 in *Stopford-Sackville Papers*, HMC Document No. 49, Vol. II, p. 19.
51 Willcox, William B., 'Admiral Rodney Warns of Invasion 1776–1777' in *The American Neptune*, Vol. IV No. 3, July 1944, pp. 193–8.
52 Sandwich to Lady Rodney, 1 Oct 1776, quoted by Spinney, pp. 275–6.
53 Rodney to Lord – for Germain 13 Mar 1778 in *Stopford-Sackville Papers*, HMC Document No. 49, Vol. II, pp. 100–1.
54 Rodney to his wife, 6 May 1778 in Mundy i 180–2.

CHAPTER 3
 1 Mackesy, 1993 (Or. 1964), pp. 183–4.
 2 King to Sandwich, 13 Sept 1779 in *Sandwich Papers* iii 163.
 3 Tuchman, Barbara, *The First Salute*, London, 2000 (or. 1989), p. 56; Jameson, J. Franklin, 'St Eustatius in the American Revolution' in *The American Historical Review* Vol. 8, July 1903, p. 686.

4 Mundy i 194–202.
5 PRO 30/20/26/5 f.21 (Sandwich) and PRO 30/20/21/11 (Germain), 10 Mar 1779.
6 Tunstall, Brian, *Flights of Naval Genius*, 1930, pp. 47–8.
7 Spinney, p. 287.
8 Ibid. p. 291.
9 Mundy i 185. Macintyre, Capt. Donald, *Admiral Rodney*, 1962, p. 72. Henry Drummond was a brother-in-law of Rodney's first wife.
10 *Sandwich Papers* iv 298.
11 Fortescue, Sir J. (ed.), *The Correspondence of King George the Third from 1760 to December 1783*, 6 vols, Macmillan and Co., 1927–1928.
12 *DNB* (Laughton, J.K. rev. Jamieson, A.G.).
13 Spinney, p. 297.
14 *Barham Papers* i xli–xliii, 50n and 52n.
15 Beatson, Robert, *Naval and Military Memoirs of Great Britain from 1727 to 1783*, 6 vols, 1804, v 101.
16 Spinney, p. 436 (App 6).
17 Rodney's Despatch, 9 Jan 1780 in Mundy i 218–19; Beatson 105–6, Mahan, Capt. A.T. *The Major Operations in the War of American Independence*, 1913, p. 122.
18 Mahan, p. 123.
19 Duro, C.F., *Armada Espanola* vii 256–7.
20 De Lángara's Despatch of 21 Jan 1780 in *Armada Espanola* vii 258–9; Chevalier, Capt. E., *Histoire de la Marine Française pendant la Guerre de l'Indépendance Américaine*, 1877, p. 181.
21 Rodney's Despatch of 27 Jan 1780 in Mundy i 220–25; Syrett, D., *The Royal Navy in European Waters during the American Revolutionary War*, 1998, pp. 86–9.
22 Rodney to Sandwich, 27 Jan 1780, *Sandwich Papers* iii 193–5.
23 Rodney to Sandwich, 7 Feb 1780, *Sandwich Papers* iii 198–200.
24 Macbride to de Lángara, 17 Jan 1780, *Sandwich Papers* iii 198.
25 Rodney to Sandwich, 27 Jan 1780, *Sandwich Papers* iii 193–5.
26 Rodney to Sandwich, 16 Feb 1780, *Sandwich Papers* iii 200–2.
27 Rodney to Sandwich, 16 Feb 1780, *Sandwich Papers* iii 200–2.
28 *Barham Papers* i 64–6.
29 Rodney to Sandwich, 4 Feb 1780, *Sandwich Papers* iii 195–6.
30 Sandwich to Rodney, 8 Mar 1780, *Sandwich Papers* iii 205–7.
31 Sandwich to Rodney, 17 Mar 1780, *Sandwich Papers* iii 209–11.
32 De Lángara's Despatch of 21 Jan 1780 in *Armada Espanola* vii 261.

CHAPTER 4

1 Lacour-Gayet, G., p. 335.
2 *DNB* (Laughton, J.K., rev. Jamieson, A.G.); Spinney, p. 434; Macintyre, pp. 109–10.
3 Rodney's Despatch of 26 April 1780, quoted in Mundy i 283–9.
4 Lacour-Gayet, p. 334 and James, Capt. W.M., *The British Navy in Adversity*, 1926, p. 198.
5 For details of signals made by Rodney to his fleet on this day see Appendix 3.
6 Sir Gilbert Blane (Scrutator), letter dated 19 Feb 1809 to the editor of the *Athenaeum* (April 1809), p. 303.
7 Creswell, Capt J., *British Admirals of the Eighteenth Century*, 1972, p. 146.
8 James, p. 199; Castex R., *Les Idées Militaires de la Marine du XVIIIme Siècle*, 1911, pp. 83–4, quoting from the log of de Guichen's Chief of Staff, Buor de la Charoulière.
9 Rodney's Despatch of 26 April 1780.
10 Mahan, pp. 137–8.
11 Rodney's Despatch of 26 April 1780.
12 Tunstall P. and Tracy N., *Naval Warfare in the Age of Sail*, 1990, p. 165. According to Creswell, p. 146, the distance was 5 or 6 miles.
13 Creswell, p. 148.
14 Master's journal *Grafton* quoted in *Sandwich Papers* iii 159n.
15 Rodney to Sandwich, 31 May 1780, *Sandwich Papers* iii 217.
16 Young to Middleton, 28 Apr 1780 *Barham Papers* i 54.
17 Maitland to Middleton, 5 Jul 1780 *Barham Papers* i 102.
18 Spinney, p. 328; Master's Journal, *Ajax* ADM 52/1543.
19 Castex, p. 85.
20 Young to Middleton, 28 Apr 1780 *Barham Papers* i 55.
21 Castex, p. 87–8.
22 Young to Middleton, 28 Apr 1780 *Barham Papers* i 55.
23 James, pp. 201–3.
24 Damage returns attached to Rodney's Despatch of 26 Apr1780, ADM 1/311.
25 Minutes of the *Montagu* Court Martial, *Barham Papers* i Appendix A pp. 371–82.
26 Master's Journal *Conqueror* ADM 52/1667; Mahan, p. 136; Spinney, pp. 327–8.
27 Mundy i 293–4n
28 Rowley to Rodney, 20 Apr 1781 attached to Rodney's Despatch of 26 Apr 1781, ADM 1/311.
29 *Sandwich Papers* iii 160.
30 Mahan, p. 140.
31 Rodney to Sandwich, 26 Apr 1780, *Sandwich Papers* iii 212.
32 Rodney to his wife, 30 Jul 1780; Mundy i 359.

NOTES

33 Sir Gilbert Blane (Scrutator), letter dated 19 Feb 1809 to the editor of the *Athenaeum* (April 1809), p. 305.
34 Sir Gilbert Blane (Scrutator), letter dated 19 Feb 1809 to the editor of the *Athenaeum* (April 1809), p. 303.
35 Robison, Rear Adm. S.S. & Mary L., *A History of Naval Tactics*, 1942, p. 315.
36 Article 21 of Rodney's *Instructions and Signals by Day*, commonly referred to as *Additional Fighting Instructions*, quoted in *Barham Papers* i 376.
37 Cresswell, p.149; Robison, p. 315.
38 Letters of Lord Barham i 54.
39 Rodney's Despatch of 26 Apr 1780, ADM 1/311.
40 *DNB* (Laughton, J.K. rev. Tracy, N.); Corbett, i 259.
41 Rodney to Carkett, 30 July 1780 PRO 30/20/20/11.
42 *DNB*.(Laughton, J.K. rev. Tracy, N.)
43 Rodney to Sandwich, 26 April 1780, *Sandwich Papers* iii 211.
44 Rodney to Sandwich, 31 May 1780, *Sandwich Papers* iii 216.
45 Ibid. p. 217.
46 Ibid. p. 218.
47 Charnock, J., *Biographia Navalis* vi 160–2.
48 Minutes of the *Montagu* Court Martial, *Barham Papers* i Appendix A pp. 371–82.
49 *Barham Papers* i xlviii.
50 Minutes of the *Yarmouth* Court Martial, *Barham Papers* i Appendix A pp. 382–98.
51 Rodney to Jackson, 12 Nov 1780 PRO 30/20/10.
52 Young to Middleton, 3 Jun 1780, *Barham Papers* i 56.
53 Rodney's Despatch of 26 April 1780.
54 Young to Middleton, 3 Jun 1780, *Barham Papers* i 56; Rodney's Despatch of 31 May 1780.
55 Mackesy, p. 332.
56 Rodney's Despatch of 31 May 1780.
57 Rodney to his wife, 27 May 1780; Mundy i 295.
58 Rodney's Despatch of 31 May 1780.
59 Castex, pp. 94–7.
60 Mahan, p. 144.
61 Rodney's Despatch of 31 May 1780.
62 Young to Middleton, 24 Jun1780, *Barham Papers* i 62.
63 Hotham to Sandwich, 6 July 1780, *Sandwich Papers* iii 219.
64 Sandwich to Rodney, 25 September 1780, *Sandwich Papers* iii 232.
65 Chevalier, p. 191.
66 Castex, pp. 82–3, 85.
67 Ibid. p. 89.
68 Quoted by Chevalier, p. 192 and James, p. 213.

69 James, p. 217.
70 Rodney's despatches of 31 Jul and 15 Sep 1780.

CHAPTER 5
1 Lewis, C.L., *Admiral de Grasse and American Independence*, 1945, p. 10.
2 For biographical details of de Grasse see Lacour-Gayet, pp. 389–90; Lewis, Antier, J-J, *L'Amiral de Grasse*, 1965.
3 Mundy i 348n.
4 PRO 30/20/26/11 ff. 39–40.
5 Rodger, N.A.M., *The Insatiable Earl*, 1994, pp. 284–7, which contains an account of this episode sympathetic to Arbuthnot and critical of Rodney. See also Mackesy, pp. 351–2.
6 Sandwich to Rodney, 25 Sept 1780, quoted in Mundy i 402.
7 Sandwich to Rodney, 7 Jul 1781, *Sandwich Papers* iv 164–5.
8 Willcox, W.B., *Portrait of a General*, 1964, pp. 337–40, 349.
9 *DNB* (Baugh, D.A. and Duffy, M.).
10 Nelson to his wife, 12 Sept 1794.
11 *DNB* (Breen, K.); Spinney, p. 435; *Sandwich Papers* iii 240n.
12 Sandwich to Rodney, 25 Sept 1780 in *Sandwich Papers* iii 231–3.
13 Rodney to the Navy Board, 12 Dec 1780, *Rodney Letters & Order Book* i 97–9; Mahan, p. 160; James, p. 253.
14 Rodney to Vaughan, 17 Dec 1780, *Rodney Letters & Order Book* i 101; Rodney's Despatch of 22 Dec 1780 in Mundy i 466 seq.; Rodney to Sandwich, 25 Dec 1780, *Sandwich Papers* iv 145; Young to Middleton, 26 Dec 1780, *Barham Papers* i 89–91; Spinney, p. 358.
15 Lacour-Gayet, pp. 320–3, 389–91; Mahan, p. 158; Lewis, pp. 95–7.
16 Hood to Jackson, 21 May 1781, *Hood Letters*, p. 16.
17 Rodney's Despatch of 12 Feb 1781 in Mundy ii 22–4.
18 Rodney's Despatch of 6 Mar 1781 in Mundy ii 43.
19 Rodney to Hood, 15 Mar 1781, in Mundy ii 63–7 (letter incorrectly dated 25 Mar); *Sandwich Papers* iv 129.
20 Ibid.
21 Hood to Rodney, 1 Apr 1781, *Hood Letters*, p. 17.
22 Beatson vi 264–5 Note 216.
23 Chevalier, p. 228 Note 1.
24 Hood to Jackson, 21 May 1781, *Hood Letters*, p. 16.
25 Main sources for encounter of 28 to 30 April 1781 are Hood to Rodney, 4 May 1781, in *Barham Papers* i 109–116; Mahan, pp. 163–7; James, pp. 258–60.
26 Chevalier, p. 229; James p. 261.
27 Rodney's Despatch, 29 June 1781, Mundy ii 120–37; Hood to Jackson, 24 June 1781, *Hood Letters*, p. 20; James, pp. 261–3.

NOTES

CHAPTER 6

1 Jameson, J. Franklin, 'St Eustatius in the American Revolution', *The American Historical Review*, Vol. 8, July 1903, p. 686; *Hood Letters* p. xxviii.
2 Rodney's Despatch, 12 Aug 1780, Mundy i 371–4.
3 Jameson, p. 691.
4 *Sandwich Papers* iii 167.
5 *DNB* (Thomas, Peter D.G.); Hurst, R. *The Golden Rock*, pp. 26–31; Willcox, *Portrait of a General*, pp. 187–9; Mackesy, p. 329.
6 Rodney's Despatch, 4 Feb 1781.
7 Barck, Dorothy C. (ed.), *Rodney Letter-Books and Order-Book. Lord Rodney, Admiral of the White Squadron, 1780–1782*, 2 vols, 1932 i 192–3.
8 Rodney's Despatch, 5 Mar 1781.
9 Rodney's Despatch, 4 Feb 1781; Rodney to his wife, 7 Feb 1781, Mundy ii 19; Rodney to Sandwich, 7 Feb 1781, *Sandwich Papers* iv 148–9; Breen, K. *Sir George Rodney and St Eustatius*, in *Mariner's Mirror* 84(2), 1998, p. 197; Jameson, p. 700.
10 Rodney to his wife, 7 Feb 1781.
11 Hamilton, Adm. Sir R. Vesey, p. 303.
12 Fortescue No. 2782.
13 Hood to Jackson, 21 May 1781, *Hood Letters* pp. 15–16.
14 Rodney to Hood, 15 Mar 1781 in Mundy ii 63–7 (letter incorrectly dated 25 Mar); *Sandwich Papers* iv 129.
15 Hood to Jackson, 24 June 1781, *Hood Letters* pp. 18–24.
16 Vaughan to Germain, 7 Feb 1781, CO 5/238 pp. 293–4.
17 Hood to Rodney, 1, 9 and 28 Apr 1781, PRO 30/20/22/2 ff. 135–54.
18 Ibid.; Hurst pp. 130–2, 153–5; Spinney p. 369.
19 Rodney's Despatch of 6 Mar 1781 quoted in *Letters to His Majesty's Ministers*, pp. 28–9; Rodney to Laforey, 27 Feb 1781, PRO 30/20/9.
20 Spinney, p. 365.
21 Macintyre, p. 163.
22 See Breen, p. 197 *seq.*
23 Jameson, pp. 703–4.
24 Breen, pp. 198–9.
25 Hurst, p. 134.
26 Rodney to Parker, 16 Apr 1781 in *Letters to His Majesty's Ministers*, pp. 67–9.
27 Hurst, pp. 139–40.
28 Young to Middleton, 13 Feb 1781, *Barham Papers* i 95.
29 Rodney to Hood, 24 Mar 1781 in Mundy ii 69.
30 Jameson, p. 700.
31 *Letters to His Majesty's Ministers*, p. 9.
32 Mundy ii 79–80.

33 See page 100.
34 *Hood Letters*, p. 12.
35 Mundy ii 13.
36 PRO 30/20/22/10 f. 81–4.
37 Details in Mundy i 360n.
38 Rodney to his wife, 23 Apr 1781, Mundy ii 98, and 30 Jun 1781, Mundy ii 140.
39 Hood to Rodney in *Barfleur* off C. Tiberon, 5 Feb 1783, PRO 30/20/22/2 ff. 155–8.
40 Mundy ii 13.
41 Rodney to Cunningham, 17 Feb 1781 in Mundy ii 29.
42 Rodney to Parker, 16 Apr 1781, Mundy ii 91.
43 Rodney to Laforey, 14 Apr 1781 in Mundy ii 88–9.
44 Rodney to Robinson, 1 May 1780, T 1/558/90–91 (PRO).
45 Twenty-four out of thirty merchant ships were captured according to Chevalier (p. 268), and eighteen according to Lacour-Gayet (p. 372), who states the realized value of the prizes as 4,717,195 livres (£236,000).

CHAPTER 7

1 Lewis, p. 117.
2 Tornquist, 1942, p. 53.
3 Lewis, pp. 117–36; Chevalier, p. 245.
4 Mahan, p. 178.
5 J.G. Shea (ed.), *The Operations of the French Fleet under the Count de Grasse*, 1864, p. 152.
6 Tornquist, p. 53–5.
7 Shea, p. 64; Willcox, *Portrait of a General*, p. 445.
8 Ibid. p. 66.
9 Lewis, p. 145.
10 Rankin, H.F. 'Charles Lord Cornwallis – Study in Frustration' in Billias (ed.), p. 223.
11 Rankin, pp. 215–6.
12 Larrabee, H.A., *Decision at the Chesapeake*, 1964, p. 120; Shea, p. 66.
13 Harvey, R., *A Few Bloody Noses*, 2001, pp. 398–401; Syrett, D., *The Royal Navy in American Waters* 1775–1783, 1989, pp. 187–9.
14 Mahan, p. 179.
15 Memorandum in Middleton's writing, *Barham Papers* i 97.
16 Hood to Jackson, 24 June 1781, *Hood Letters*, p. 18.
17 Rodney to Parker, July 1781, part quoted by eds in *Sandwich Papers* iv pp. 134–5.
18 Hunt to Middleton, 29 Aug 1781, *Barham Papers* i 123.
19 *Sandwich Papers* iv 136.

20 *Graves Papers* pp. 46–9.

21 Hood's Despatch, 30 Aug 1781; Spinney, p. 378.

22 Hood's Despatch, 30 Aug 1781.

23 *DNB* (Breen, K.C.).

24 Hood to Middleton, 11 Dec 1781, Barham *Papers* i 130; Tilley, J.A., *The British Navy and the American Revolution*, 1987, p. 250.

25 *Graves Papers* lxvii–lxviii; Syrett, pp. 190–1.

26 Graves to Sandwich, 14 Sept 1781, enclosing extract of *London*'s log, *Sandwich Papers* iv 183–6; Cresswell, pp. 155–7.

27 *Graves Papers,* lxix–lxx.

28 Shea, p. 69.

29 *London*'s log in *Sandwich Papers* iv 183–6.

30 Graves' Despatch, 14 Sept 1781 in *Graves Papers,* p. 62.

31 *London*'s log in *Sandwich Papers* iv 183–6.

32 White, Capt. Thomas, *Naval Researches*, 1830, p. 42.

33 'Graves and Hood at the Chesapeake', K.C. Breen, in *Mariner's Mirror* Vol. 66(1), 1980, p. 61.

34 Tunstall and Tracy, pp. 173–4; Corbett, J.S., *Signals & Instructions 1776–1794*, NRS Vol. 35, 1909, pp. 53–6.

35 *London*'s log in *Sandwich Papers* iv 183–6; Tunstall & Tracy, pp. 174–5.

36 White, pp. 44–5.

37 Hamilton, Adm. Sir R. Vesey, p. 377; Larrabee, p. 177.

38 Graves' Despatch, 14 Sept 1781; *London*'s log in *Sandwich Papers* iv 183–6; Tunstall & Tracy, pp. 174–5.

39 *Graves Papers* lxxi; Enclosure A to Graves' Despatch, 14 Sept 1781.

40 Graves' Despatch, 14 Sept 1781 and enclosures, *Graves Papers,* pp. 61–84; *Graves Papers* lxxi; *Sandwich Papers* iv 183–6; Hood to Jackson, 16 Sept 1781 and Enclosure 2, 10 Sept 1781, *Hood Letters* 28–34.

41 Resolution of a Council of War, 13 Sept 1781, *Graves Papers,* pp. 83–4.

42 Graves' Despatches, 26 Sept, 16, 19 and 29 Oct 1781 in *Graves Papers,* pp. 94, 119, 131 and 137 respectively; *Sandwich Papers* iv 144.

43 Hood to Jackson, 16 Sept 1781, Enclosure 1 dated 6 Sept 1781 in *Hood Letters,* pp. 31–3.

44 *Barham Papers* i 127 (Memo wrongly dated 6 Nov 1781); Corbett, J.S., *Signals & Instructions* pp. 260–1.

45 Corbett, *Fighting Instructions 1530–1816*, NRS Vol. 29, 1905, p. 225; Breen, *Graves and Hood at the Chesapeake,* p. 62.

46 See Breen, K., 'Graves and Hood at the Chesapeake', pp. 53–65; Sulivan, J.A., 'Graves and Hood' in *Mariner's Mirror* Vol. 69(2), 1983, pp. 175–94.

47 Graves to Sandwich, 14 Sept 1781, *Sandwich Papers* iv 182.

48 Rodney to Jackson, 19 Oct 1781, *Hood Letters,* pp. 44–7.

49 Cobbett, William (ed.), *The Parliamentary History of England*, xxii Col. 781.

50 Ibid. xxii Col. 647.
51 *Sandwich Papers*, pp. 132–3.
52 Jamieson, A.G., 'The War in the Leeward Islands 1775–1783', Oxford D.Phil. Thesis, 1987, pp. 256–8.
53 Breen, K.C., 'A Reinforcement Reduced? Rodney's Flawed Appraisal of French Plans, West Indies 1781', *Ninth Naval History Symposium*, 1989.
54 Syrett, *The Royal Navy in American Waters*, pp. 185–6, 218.
55 Sandwich Memorandum, 18 Feb 1782, *Sandwich Papers* iv 345.
56 Hood to Middleton, 30 Sep 1781, *Barham Papers* i 125.
57 *Two Letters from W. Graves, Esq. Respecting the Conduct of Rear Admiral Thomas Graves in North America during his Accidental Command there for Four Months in 1781*, 1783.
58 Graves, *Two Letters*, pp. 5–11.
59 Quoted in Breen, 'Graves and Hood at the Chesapeake', p. 59.
60 Tilley 248–9; Graves' Despatch 20 Aug 1781, *Graves Papers* p. 32–3.
61 *Graves Papers*, p. 39.
62 *Graves Papers*, pp. 59–60.
63 *Graves Papers*, p. 50.
64 Graves' Despatch of 14 September 1781, on which Rodney commented in his letter to Jackson of 19 October, reported the delayed arrival on 8 September of the *Pegasus*.
65 Rodney to Jackson, 19 Oct 1781, *Hood Letters*, p. 46.
66 Rodney to Hood, 24 Jul 1781, *Graves Papers*, pp. 47–9.
67 Willcox, *Portrait of a General*, p. 411 n.7.
68 *Graves Papers*, p. 61; Willcox, p. 409 n.3; Larrabee p. 153.
69 Breen, 'A Reinforcement Reduced?', p. 168; ADM/1/313.
70 Sulivan, p. 183; White, p. 75n.

CHAPTER 8
1 Lewis, pp. 196–9.
2 Lacour-Gayet, p. 413.
3 Tornquist, pp. 42, 62; Lewis, p. 159.
4 Lacour-Gayet, pp. 413, 419–20; Chevalier, pp. 262–3; *Letters to Ministers*, p. 84; *Sandwich Papers* iv 215.
5 Hood's Despatches of 10 and 12 Dec 1781 in *Hood Letters*, pp. 48–57; Sandwich Papers iv 215.
6 Mahan, pp. 195–6; James, pp. 312–5.
7 Lacour-Gayet, p. 420.
8 Lewis, pp. 208–9.
9 Chevalier, p. 282.
10 Mahan, p. 204.
11 Tornquist, p. 86.

12 *Hood Letters*, pp. 59–64; *Barham Letters*, pp. 133–47; White, pp. 75–92; Mahan, pp. 195–205; James, pp. 320–8; *Sandwich Papers* iv 232–43.

13 Lord Robert Manners to the Duke of Rutland, 8 Feb 1782 in *Hood Letters*, p. 79.

14 Manners to Rutland, 22 Feb 1782 in *Hood Letters*, pp. 82–3.

15 Rodney's marginal comments on copies of Hood's Despatches of 7 and 22 February 1781, PRO 30/20/22/10 ff. 35–42.

16 Mahan, p. 202.

17 Mahan, Capt. A.T., *The Influence of Sea Power upon History 1660–1783*, 1890, pp. 476 and 479.

18 Mundy ii 156; Spinney, p. 381.

19 Jameson, p. 701.

20 Middleton to Hood, 14 Jan 1782 in *Barham Letters* i 134.

21 Spinney, p. 381.

22 Rodney to Sandwich, 4 Nov 1781 in *Sandwich Papers* iv 225.

23 Lewis, p. 205.

24 Rodney to Sandwich, 4 Nov 1781 in *Sandwich Papers* iv 225.

25 Spinney, p. 384: ADM 1/314 Rodney to Admiralty, 20, 24, 28 Nov and 5, 6, 7 Dec 1781.

26 Cobbett, xxii Col. 646–7 (Shelburne), 770–8 (Burke).

27 Cobbett, xxii Col. 778–85.

28 Lloyd, p. 343.

29 Blane, Sir Gilbert, *Select Dissertations on Medical Science*, 1833, p. 126; Mundy ii 169.

30 Rodney to his wife, 1 Jan 1782 in Mundy ii 178–80; Rodney to Sandwich, 6 Jan 1782 in *Sandwich Papers* iv 229–31.

31 Sandwich to Rodney, 2 Jan 1782 in Mundy ii 182.

32 Spinney, pp. 387–8 and Captain's Log *Formidable* ADM 51/365.

33 Rodney's Despatch, 15 Mar 1782 in *Rodney Letters & Order Book* i 295.

34 Lewis, p. 226; *Rodney Letters & Order Book* i 295, 302–3.

35 Chevalier, p. 287.

36 Mundy ii 227n.

37 Lewis, p. 228.

38 Brigadier General Archibald Campbell to Major General Edward Mathew, 8 Mar 1780, *Rodney Letters & Order Book* i 269.

39 Rodney to Dalling, 5 Mar 1782; Rodney to Parker, 5 Mar 1782, *Rodney Letters & Orders* i 262–5.

40 James, pp. 330–2; Lacour-Gayet, pp. 425–6; Rodney to Hood, 22 Mar 1782 and Hood to Jackson, 31 Mar 1782, *Hood Letters*, pp. 95–101; Rodney's Despatch of 14 April 1782.

41 Creswell, pp. 175–7.

42 After the Battle of the Saintes an officer stationed on the middle deck of the *Formidable* reported that he never fired less than two, sometimes three, broad-

sides at each passing Frenchman before such Frenchman could bring a gun to bear on him – Douglas to Middleton 28 April 1782, *Barham Papers* i 284.

43 Tunstall and Tracy, pp. 182–3; Creswell, pp. 86, 93; *Barham Papers* i 268–84.

44 Caruana, A., *The History of English Sea Ordnance 1523–1875*, 1997 ii 174–5.

45 Chevalier, pp. 309–10.

46 Syrett, *The Royal Navy in European Waters*, p. 92.

47 Lloyd, C. (ed.), *The Health of Seamen*, NRS Vol. 107, 1965, p. 132.

48 Ibid. pp. 154–5.

49 Ibid. p. 142.

50 Ibid. pp. 140, 145–6.

51 Ibid. pp. 167–71.

52 Ibid. p. 167.

53 Ibid. p. 146.

54 Ibid. p. 148.

55 Ibid. p. 149.

CHAPTER 9

1 James, p. 332.

2 Lacour-Gayet, p. 427.

3 Cornwallis-West, G., *The Life and Letters of Admiral Cornwallis*, 1927, pp. 118–19.

4 Master's logs *Endymion* (ADM 52/ 1715) and *Andromache* (ADM 52/2136).

5 Marshall, John, *Royal Naval Biography*, 1823, Vol. 1.

6 *Rodney Letters & Orders* i 360; *Sandwich Papers* iv 219, White, pp. 95–6.

7 White, pp. 96–7; Chevalier, p. 289.

8 *Biographie Universelle* (Michaud) and James Appendices VI, VIII and XV.

9 Chevalier, p. 290 n.1.

10 Times of engagements from Mahan, p. 210, quoting Hood's log.

11 Captured narrative, 22 Apr 1782, *Barham Papers*, p. 171.

12 Lacour-Gayet, p. 428.

13 *Hood Letters*, pp. 109–11.

14 Macintyre, p. 219.

15 Chevalier, p. 291; Mahan, p. 212.

16 Tornquist, p. 91n.

17 Laughton, J.K. (ed.), *Naval Miscellany* Vol. 1, NRS Vol. 20, 1902, p. 235.

18 Chevalier, p. 291–2 n. 2.

19 Ibid. p. 321 ; Mahan, p. 212; White, p. 103.

20 Creswell, p. 167.

21 Ibid. p. 169.

22 Lewis, p. 237; Chevalier, pp. 303–4; Tornquist, pp. 92–4.

23 White, p. 106.

24 Spinney, pp. 399–400.

25 Blane, pp. 127–8; Cornwallis-West, p. 122.
26 Mahan, p. 217; Douglas to Middleton, 28 Apr 1782, *Barham Papers* i 279–80; Spinney, D., 'Rodney and the Saintes: A Reassessment', *Mariner's Mirror* Vol. 68, 1982, p. 384.
27 Cresswell, p. 173.
28 Mahan, pp. 218–19.
29 Chevalier, p. 297.
30 White, pp. 111–15; Hood's journal in *Hood Letters* pp. 121–3.
31 *Hood Letters*, p. 103; Mahan, pp. 220–1.
32 See Appendix 6.
33 See Appendix 5.
34 Laughton, 1902, i p. 234.
35 Chevalier, p. 306.
36 Wraxall, p. 463.
37 Blane to Lord Dalrymple, 22 April 1782 quoted in Mundy ii 244: *Hood Letters*, p. 177; Tornquist, pp. 97–8.
38 Lacour-Gayet, p. 433.
39 *Rodney Letters & Order Book* i 355, 382.
40 Ibid. i 353–5.
41 Ibid. i 380–3 (Rodney's Despatch from Jamaica, 3 May 1782).
42 Blane to Lord Dalrymple, 22 April 1782, quoted in Mundy ii 234–7.
43 *Barham Papers* i 278.
44 Blane to Lord Dalrymple, 22 April 1782, quoted in Mundy ii 234–47.
45 Cornwallis-West, G. pp. 124–5.
46 Rodney's Despatch, 14 Apr 1782.
47 Hood to Middleton, 13 Apr 1782, *Barham Papers* i 161–2.
48 Cornwallis-West, p. 126.
49 Mundy ii 248–150; PRO 30/20/26/7.
50 Blane to Lord Dalrymple, 22 April 1782, quoted in Mundy ii 234–47.
51 Mahan, pp. 222–4.
52 David Spinney, 'Rodney and the Saintes: A Reassessment' in *Mariner's Mirror* Vol. 68, 1982, pp. 377–89.
53 Tornquist, pp. 99, 103.
54 Affleck to Sandwich, 25 April 1782, *Sandwich Papers* iv 265–6; Master's Log HMS *Anson* ADM 52/2142; White, p. 117.
55 *Sandwich Papers* iv 258–64; Mahan, pp. 224–5; James, pp. 347–8.
56 Lacour-Gayet, p. 434n; Mundy ii 319n; James, p. 356.

CHAPTER 10
1 Fortescue, vi 3761, 3768, 3773 and 3779.
2 Spinney, pp. 418, 427.

3 The National Trust Guide to Berrington Hall, 2003, p. 5.
4 Pemberton, Vincent 'Alresford House, Old Alresford' in *Alresford Displayed*, No. 8, 1983, p. 16.
5 Spinney, p. 424.
6 *DNB* (Baugh, D.A. and Duffy, M.); Duffy, M. 'Samuel Hood', *First Viscount Hood* in *Precursors of Nelson*, P. le Fevre and R. Harding (eds), 2000.
7 *DNB* (Breen. K.).
8 Lewis, pp. 265–7, 275; 'Account of the Life and Military Services of the Count de Grasse' in *The European Magazine and London Review*, August 1782, pp. 85–6.
9 Lacour-Gayet, pp. 432–3.
10 Troude, O., *Batailles Navales de la France*, Paris, 1867, ii 163–4.
11 Chevalier, pp. 311–23.
12 Lewis, pp. 300, 302.
13 Antier, pp. 456–9.
14 Tucker, J.S., *Memoirs of the Earl of St Vincent*, 1844, ii 281–3, quoted by Cresswell, p. 194.
15 *Edinburgh Review*, 1805, pp. 301–13.
16 Quoted by Cresswell, p. 194.
17 *Athenaeum Magazine*, February 1809 (Vol. 5), Letter to the Editor signed 'M&D' dated 8 January 1809, pp. 123–4.
18 *Athenaeum Magazine*, April 1809 (Vol. 5), Letter to the Editor from Dr Gilbert Blane signed 'Scrutator' dated 19 February 1809, pp. 302–6.
19 Ekin, Rear Adm. Charles, *Naval Battles, from 1744 to the Peace in 1814*, 1824, p. 145 and preface p. xv.
20 O'Byrne, William R., *A Naval Biographical Dictionary*, J.B. Hayward & Son, Polstead, Suffolk, 1990, Reprint (Or. 1849) and Passing Certificate for the Rank of Lieutenant (PRO) (some accounts wrongly state his age at the Battle of the Saintes as thirteen).
21 *Quarterly Review*, January 1830, pp. 50–79.
22 *Edinburgh Review*, April 1830 No. CI.
23 Knowles, Adm. Sir C.H., *Observations on Naval Tactics and on the Claims of Mr Clerk, of Eldin, &c*, 1830, pp. 5–14.
24 Knowles, p. 36.
25 White, pp. 108–9.
26 *Memoirs of Richard Cumberland* 2 vols, 1807, i 407–8.
27 Spinney, p. 387.
28 Wraxall, p. 192.
29 Corbett, NRS 35, pp. 121–3.
30 Pellew, G. *The Life and Correspondence of the Rt. Hon. Henry Addington, First Viscount Sidmouth*, 3 vols, 1847 ii 380–4.
31 Mahan, Capt. A.T., *The Life of Nelson – The Embodiment of the Sea Power of Great Britain*, 2nd Ed., 1899, p. 704 and footnote 2.

32 Cornwallis-West, p. 130.
33 Pellew ii 381.
34 Sir Gilbert, Blane (Scrutator), letter dated 19 Feb 1809 to the editor of the
    Athenaeum, April 1809, p. 305.
35 Macintyre, p. 113.

BIBLIOGRAPHY

ABBREVIATIONS

HMSO – Her Majesty's Stationery Office
NRS – Navy Records Society
Or. – First published in (date)
PB – Paperback

FB – Full biography of Rodney
SB – Includes a short biography of Rodney

'Account of the Life and Military Services of the Count de Grasse' in *The European Magazine and London Review*, August 1782.
Guide to Berrington Hall, The National Trust, 2003.
How Many? A Dictionary of Units of Measurement, Russ Rowlett and the University of North Carolina at Chapel Hill (website), 2005.
Inflation: The Value of the Pound in 1750–2001, House of Commons Library Research Paper 02/44 11 Jul 2002.
Letters from Sir George Brydges, now Lord Rodney, to His Majesty's Ministers relative to the Capture of St Eustatius, 1789.

Antier, J-J, *L'Admiral de Grasse – Héros de l'indépendence américaine*, Plon, France, 1965.
Barck, Dorothy C. (ed.), *Letter-Books and Order-Book of George, Lord*

Rodney, Admiral of the White Squadron, 1780–1782, 2 vols, New York Historical Society, New York, 1932.

Barnes, G.R. & Owen, J.H. (eds), *The Private Papers of John Earl of Sandwich, First Lord of the Admiralty 1771–1782,* 4 vols, NRS Vols 69, 71, 75 and 78, 1932-8.

Beatson, R., *Naval and Military Memoirs of Great Britain from 1727 to 1783,* 6 vols, various publishers, 1804.

Billias, G.A., *George Washington's Generals and Opponents,* Da Capo Press, New York, 1994, **SB.**

Blane, Sir Gilbert, *Select Dissertations on Several Subjects of Medical Science,* 2 vols, Baldwin & Cradock, 1833.

Breen, K.C., 'Graves and Hood at the Chesapeake', *Mariner's Mirror* Vol. 66(1), 1980.

——, 'A Reinforcement Reduced? Rodney's Flawed Appraisal of French Plans, West Indies 1781', *Ninth Naval History Symposium,* 1989.

——, 'Sir George Rodney and St Eustatius', *Mariner's Mirror* Vol. 84(2), 1998.

——, 'George Bridges, Lord Rodney, 1718?–1792', *Precursors of Nelson,* Le Fevre, P. & Harding, R. (eds), 2000.

Campbell, Dr John, *Lives of the British Admirals,* 8 vols, J. Harris, 1817–1818, **SB.**

Caruana, A., *The History of English Sea Ordnance 1523–1875: Vol. 2: 1715–1715: The Age of the System,* Rotherfield Jean Boudriot, 1997.

Castex, R., *Les Idées militaires de la Marine du XVIIIme Siècle,* L. Fournier, Paris, 1911.

Chadwick, Rear Adm. F.E., *The Graves Papers and Other Documents relating to the Naval Operations of the Yorktown Campaign, July to October 1781,* Reprint, Arno Press, New York, 1968 (Or. 1916).

Charnock, J., *Biographia Navalis – Impartial Memoirs of the Lives and Characters of Officers of the Navy from the year 1660 to the present time,* 6 vols, 1798.

Chevalier, E., *Histoire de la marine francaise pendant la guerre de l'indépendence américaine,* Libraire Hachette et cie, Paris, 1877.

Clerk, John of Eldin, the Elder, *An Inquiry into Naval Tactics,* Edinburgh, 1782.

——, *An Essay on Naval Tactics, Systematical and Historical,* 2 vols, T. Cadell, 1790.

——, *An Essay on Naval Tactics, Systematical and Historical,* 2nd Edition, A. Constable & Co., Edinburgh, 1804.

——, *An Essay on Naval Tactics, Systematical and Historical, with Notes by Lord Rodney, and an Introduction by a Naval Officer,* 3rd Edition, Adam Black, Edinburgh, 1827.

Cobbett, William (ed.), *The parliamentary history of England from the earliest period to the year 1803,* 36 vols, various publishers, 1806–1820.

Corbett, J.S., *Fighting Instructions 1530–1816,* NRS Vol. 29, 1905.

——, *Signals and Instructions, 1776–1794,* NRS Vol. 35, 1909.

——, *England in the Seven Years' War,* 2 vols, Reprint, Greenhill Books, 1992 (Or. 1907).

Cornwallis-West, G., *The Life and Letters of Admiral Cornwallis,* Robert Holden & Co, 1927.

Creswell, Capt. J., *British Admirals of the Eighteenth Century – Tactics in Battle,* George Allen & Unwin, 1972.

Cumberland, Richard, *Memoirs of Richard Cumberland,* 2 vols, Lackington Allen & Co, 1807.

Davies, J.A., 'An Enquiry into Faction among British Naval Officers During the War of the American Revolution', MA Thesis, University of Liverpool, May 1964.

Duffy, M., 'Samuel Hood, First Viscount Hood, 1724–1816', *Precursors of Nelson,* P. le Fevre and R. Harding (eds), 2000.

Duro, Cesáreo Fernandez, *Armada Espanola desde la unión de los Reinos de Castilla y de Aragón,* 9 vols, Sucesores de Rivadeneyra, Madrid, 1895–1903.

Ekin, Rear Adm. Charles, *Naval Battles, from 1744 to the Peace in 1814,* 2nd Edition, Baldwin & Cradock, 1828.

Erskine, D. (ed.), *Augustus Hervey's Journal,* William Kimber, 1954.

Fortescue, Sir J. (ed.), *The Correspondence of King George the Third from 1760 to December 1783,* 6 vols, Macmillan and Co., 1927–1928.

Graves, W., *Two Letters from W. Graves, Esq. Respecting the Conduct of Rear Admiral Thomas Graves in North America during his Accidental Command there for Four Months in 1781,* 1782.

Hamilton, Adm. Sir R. Vesey, 'Rodney' in *From Howard to Nelson,* J.K. Laughton (ed.), 1900.

Hannay, D., *Rodney,* Macmillan, 1891, **FB**.

——, *Letters of Sir Samuel Hood,* NRS Vol. 3, 1895.

Hart, F. Russell, *Admirals of the Caribbean,* Houghton Mifflin Company, Boston and New York, 1922, **SB**.

Harvey, R., *A Few Bloody Noses,* John Murray, 2001.

Historical Manuscripts Commission, *Report on the Manuscripts of Mrs*

Stopford-Sackville of Drayton House, Northamptonshire, 2 vols constituting HMC Document No. 49, HMSO Vol I Cd. 1892, 1904; Vol II Cd. 5038, 1910.

Hurst, R., *The Golden Rock – An Episode of the American War of Independence 1775–1783,* Leo Cooper, 1996.

Ireland, B., *Naval Warfare in the Age of Sail – War at Sea 1756–1815,* Harper-Collins, 2000.

James, Capt. W.M., *The British Navy in Adversity – A Study of the War of American Independence,* Reprint, Russell & Russell, New York, 1970 (Or. 1926).

Jameson, J. Franklin, 'St Eustatius in the American Revolution', *The American Historical Review,* Vol. 8, July 1903.

Jamieson, A.G., 'The War in the Leeward Islands 1775–1783, Oxford D.Phil. Thesis, 1987.

Knowles, Adm. Sir C.H., *Observations on Naval Tactics and on the Claims of Mr Clerk, of Eldin, &c. To which are added, Extracts of Letters from Sir J. Saumarez in refutation of Mr Clerk's Tactics being known to Admiral Lord Rodney in 1782,* R. Fenn, 1830.

Lacour-Gayet, G., *La Marine Militaire de la France sous las Règne de Louis XVI,* Librairie Spéciale pour L'Histoire de la France, Paris, 1905.

Larrabee, H.A., *Decision at the Chesapeake,* William Kimber, 1965 (Or. 1964).

Laughton, J. Knox (ed.), *From Howard to Nelson – Twelve Sailors,* William Heinemann, 1900, **SB**.

——, *The Naval Miscellany,* Vol. 1, NRS Vol. 20, 1902.

——, *Letters and Papers of Charles, Lord Barham, 1758–1813,* Vol. 1, NRS Vol. 32, 1907.

Le Fevre, P. & Harding, R. (eds), *Precursors of Nelson,* Chatham Publishing, 2000, **SB**.

Lewis, C.L., *Admiral de Grasse and American Independence,* United States Naval Institute, Annapolis, MD, 1945.

Lloyd, C., 'Sir George Rodney: Lucky Admiral', *George Washington's Generals and Opponents,* Billias, G.A. (ed.), 1994.

——, (ed.), *The Health of Seamen,* NRS Vol. 107, 1965.

Macintyre, Captain D., *Admiral Rodney,* Peter Davies, 1962, **FB**.

Mackay, R.F., *Admiral Hawke,* Oxford University Press, Oxford, 1965.

Mackesy, P., *The War for America, 1775–1783,* PB, University of Nebraska Press, Lincoln, NE, 1993 (Or. 1964).

Mahan, Capt A.T., *The Influence of Sea Power upon History 1660–1783,* PB, Methuen & Co, 1965 (Or. 1890).

——, *Types of Naval Officers, drawn from the History of the British Navy*, Reprint, Books for Libraries Press, Freeport, NY, 1969 (Or. 1901), **SB**.

——, *The Life of Nelson – The Embodiment of the Sea Power of Great Britain*, 2nd Edition, Sampson, Low, Marston, 1899.

——, *The Major Operations of the Navies in the War of American Independence*, Sampson, Low, Marston, 1913.

Marshall, John, *Royal Naval Biography*, 12 vols, Longman, Hurst, Rees, Orme and Brown, 1823–1830.

Michaud, J.F. & L.G. and Desplaces, E.E., *Biographie Universelle (Michaud) Ancienne et Moderne*, 45 vols, Desplaces and Michaud, Paris, 1854–1865.

Mundy, G.B., *The Life and Correspondence of the Late Admiral Lord Rodney*, Reprint, Gregg Press Boston, 1972 (Or. 1830), **FB**.

Nicolas, Sir N.H., *The Dispatches and Letters of Vice Admiral Lord Viscount Nelson*, 7 vols, PB, Chatham Publishing, 1997–1998 (Or. 1884–1886).

O'Byrne, William R., *A Naval Biographical Dictionary*, J.B. Hayward & son, Polstead, Suffolk, 1990, Reprint (Or. 1849) 1849.

Pellew, G., *The Life and Correspondence of the Rt Hon Henry Addington, First Viscount Sidmouth*, 3 vols, John Murray, 1847.

Pemberton, Vincent, 'Alresford House, Old Alresford', *Alresford Displayed*, No. 8, 1983.

Ralfe, J., *The Naval Biography of Great Britain: consisting of historical memoirs of those officers of the British Navy who distinguished themselves during the reign of His Majesty George III*, Whitmore & Fenn, 1828, **SB**.

Rankin, H.F., 'Charles Lord Cornwallis: Study in Frustration', *George Washington's Generals and Opponents*, Billias, G.A. (ed.), 1994.

Robison, Rear Adm. S.S. & Mary. L., *A History of Naval Tactics from 1530 to 1930 – The Evolution of Tactical Maxims*, The United States Naval Institute, Annapolis, MD, 1942.

Rodger, N.A.M., *The Wooden World – An Anatomy of the Georgian Navy*, PB, W.W. Norton & Company, New York, 1996 (Or. 1986).

——, 'George, Lord Anson, 1697–1762', *Precursors of Nelson*, Le Fevre, P. & Harding, R. (eds), 2000.

——, *The Insatiable Earl – A Life of John Montagu, Fourth Earl of Sandwich 1718–1792*, W.W. Norton & Company, New York, 1994.

Shea, J.G. (ed.), *The Operations of the French Fleet under the Count de Grasse,* Reprint, Da Capo Press, New York, 1971 (Or. 1864).

Spinney, D., *Rodney,* George, Allen and Unwin, 1969, **FB**.

——, 'Rodney and the Saints: A Reassessment', *Mariner's Mirror* Vol. 68, 1982.

Sulivan, J.A., 'Graves and Hood', *Mariner's Mirror* Vol. 69(2), 1983.

Syrett, D. *The Royal Navy in American Waters 1775–1783,* Scolar Press, Aldershot, 1989.

——, *The Royal Navy in European Waters during the American Revolutionary War,* University of South Carolina, Columbia, SC, 1998.

——, 'Admiral Rodney, Patronage and the Leeward Islands Squadron, 1780–2', *Mariner's Mirror* Vol. 85 No. 4, November 1999.

Syrett, D. (ed.), *A Siege and Capture of Havana 1762,* NRS Vol. 114, 1970.

——, *The Rodney Papers – Selections from the Correspondence of Admiral Lord Rodney,* Vol. 1 (1742–1763), NRS Vol. 148, 2005.

Tilley, J.A., *The British Navy and the American Revolution,* University of South Carolina, Columbia SC, 1987.

Tornquist, K., *The Naval Campaigns of Count de Grasse during the American Revolution 1781–1783* (translated by Amandus Johnson), Swedish Colonial Society, Philadelphia, PA, 1942.

Troude, O., *Batailles Navales de la France,* 4 vols, Vol 2 – 1778–1795, Libraire Commissionaire pour la Marine, les Colonies et l'Orient, Paris, 1867.

Tuchman, Barbara W., *The First Salute – A View of the American Revolution,* PB, Phoenix Press, 2000 (Or. 1988).

Tucker, J.S., *Memoirs of the Earl of St Vincent,* 2 vols, Richard Bentley, 1844.

Tunstall, B., *Flights of Naval Genius,* Philip Allan & Co., 1930, **SB**.

——, & Tracy, N., *Naval Warfare in the Age of Sail: The Evolution of Fighting Tactics,* Conway Maritime Press, 1990.

Watson, J. Steven, *The Reign of King George III – 1760–1815,* Oxford University Press, 1960.

White, Capt. Thomas, *Naval Researches: Or a Candid Inquiry into the Conduct of Admirals Byron, Graves, Hood and Rodney, in the Actions off Grenada, Chesapeak, St Christophers, and of the Ninth and Twelfth of April, 1782,* Reprint, Gregg Press, Boston, MA, 1972 (Or. 1830).

Willcox, William B., 'Admiral Rodney Warns of Invasion 1776–1777', *The American Neptune,* Vol. IV No. 3, July 1944.
——, *Portrait of a General – Sir Henry Clinton in the War of Independence,* Alfred A. Knopf, New York, 1964.
Wraxall, N.W., *Historical Memoirs of My Own Time (1772–1784),* One vol., Reprint, Kegan Paul, Trench, Trubner & Co., 1904 (Or. 2 vols, 1815).

Index